NEW DIRECTIONS IN GERMAN STUDIES

Vol. 11

Series Editor:

Imke Meyer

Editorial Board:

Katherine Arens, Roswitha Burwick, Richard Eldridge,
Erika Fischer-Lichte, Catriona MacLeod, Stephan
Schindler, Heidi Schlipphacke, Ulrich Schönherr, James
A. Schultz, Silke-Maria Weineck, David Wellbery, Sabine
Wilke, John Zilcosky.

Volumes in the series:

Vol. 1. *Improvisation as Art: Conceptual Challenges, Historical Perspectives*
by Edgar Landgraf

Vol. 2. *The German Pícaro and Modernity: Between Underdog and Shape-Shifter*
by Bernhard Malkmus

Vol. 3. *Citation and Precedent: Conjunctions and Disjunctions of German Law and Literature*
by Thomas O. Beebee

Vol. 4. *Beyond Discontent: 'Sublimation' from Goethe to Lacan*
by Eckart Goebel

Vol. 5. *From Kafka to Sebald: Modernism and Narrative Form*
edited by Sabine Wilke

Vol. 6. *Image in Outline: Reading Lou Andreas-Salomé*
by Gisela Brinker-Gabler

Vol. 7. *Out of Place: German Realism, Displacement, and Modernity*
by John B. Lyon

Vol. 8. *Thomas Mann in English: A Study in Literary Translation*
by David Horton

Vol. 9. *The Tragedy of Fatherhood: King Laius and the Politics of Paternity in the West*
by Silke-Maria Weineck

Vol. 10. *The Poet as Phenomenologist: Rilke and the* New Poems
by Luke Fischer

Vienna's Dreams of Europe: Culture and Identity beyond the Nation-State
by Katherine Arens (forthcoming)

The Laughter of the Thracian Woman

A Protohistory of Theory

Hans Blumenberg

Translated, with annotations and an afterword, by Spencer Hawkins

BLOOMSBURY ACADEMIC
NEW YORK · LONDON · OXFORD · NEW DELHI · SYDNEY

Bloomsbury Academic
An imprint of Bloomsbury Publishing Inc

1385 Broadway, New York, NY 10018, USA
50 Bedford Square, London, WC1B 3DP, UK
29 Earlsfort Terrace, Dublin 2, Ireland

www.bloomsbury.com

BLOOMSBURY and the Diana logo are trademarks of Bloomsbury Publishing Plc

Originally published as "Das Lachen der Thrakerin. Eine Urgeschichte der Theorie"
© 1987 Suhrkamp Verlag Frankfurt am Main 1987
All rights reservered by Suhrkamp Verlag Berlin
This English language translation © Bloomsbury Academic 2015

Translation © Spencer Hawkins, 2015

All rights reserved. No part of this publication may be reproduced or transmitted in any form or by any means, electronic or mechanical, including photocopying, recording, or any information storage or retrieval system, without prior permission in writing from the publishers.

No responsibility for loss caused to any individual or organization acting on or refraining from action as a result of the material in this publication can be accepted by Bloomsbury or the author.

Library of Congress Cataloging-in-Publication Data
Blumenberg, Hans.
[Lachen der Thrakerin. English]
The laughter of the Thracian woman : a protohistory of theory / Hans Blumenberg ; translated, with annotations and an afterword by Spencer Hawkins.
pages cm. -- (New directions in German studies ; Vol. 11)
Includes bibliographical references and index.
ISBN 978-1-62356-230-4 (pbk.) -- ISBN 978-1-62356-461-2 (hardback) 1. Theory (Philosophy)--History. I. Title.
B105.T52B5813 2015
190--dc23
2014043348

ISBN: HB: 978-1-6235-6461-2
PB: 978-1-6235-6230-4
ePub: 978-1-6235-6853-5
ePDF: 978-1-6235-6336-3

Series: New Directions in German Studies

Typeset by Fakenham Prepress Solutions, Fakenham, Norfolk NR21 8NN

Contents

	About this Book	vii
1	Theory as Exotic Behavior	1
2	Socrates is Transferred into Protohistory	5
3	Knowledge about Heaven and Competence on Earth	14
4	The Theorist between Comedy and Tragedy	22
5	Reoccupations	29
6	Astrological Predominance	46
7	Applause and Reproach from the Moralists	54
8	In the Grip of Historical Criticism	67
9	From Cursing Sinners to Reproaching Creation	78
10	Tycho Brahe's Coachman and the Earthquake in Lisbon	86
11	Absentmindednesses	92
12	Where Thales had Failed, According to Nietzsche	103
13	How to Recognize what Matters	118
14	Interdisciplinarity as Repetition of Protohistory	130
	Afterword: Reading into the Distance	133
	Note on Translation and Annotations	173
	Acknowledgments	175
	Notes	176
	Bibliography	194
	Index	204

About this Book

We will have to continue to do without the protohistory of theory because we cannot know anything about it. There was no desire on the part of theory to leave a record of it. *A* protohistory of theory cannot replace *the* protohistory of theory.[i] It can only recall what has eluded us.

Given that this is only *a* protohistory, there could also have been a different one. But not easily would another one have claimed the vacant position with a better fit—and thus claimed it so obstinately. This obstinacy against fading, against merely lasting without value,[ii] indicates the "quality"[iii] of the moment that followed thinking itself and does not cease to go after it. It is a story that has stood the test of history (*Es ist eine Geschichte, die sich in der Geschichte bewährt hat*). Instead of offering to tell what no one can know, this story can at least offer an account of what sustains the strangeness that something like "theory" exists at all—an account of how theory lacks self-evidence.

At some point, an "attitude"[iv] develops, a purpose that pervades many particular activities, and from this attitude emerges a stream of claims and teachings, collections of teachings and schools, along with all manner of rivalry against theory as a whole—all together this comprises a movement of history that perpetually releases products. This movement continually harkens back to the attitude of the *theoros*, the spectator of world and things, as it was originally branded. It is he, not his product, that protohistory exhibits: the alienating, nocturnal world-spectator who clashed with reality, reflected in the laughter of the spectator's spectator. The fact that all theorists up to the present day could still recognize themselves in this story (though neither do they all, nor must they) constitutes the underhanded test to which theory's strangeness can be subjected in every "realistic"[v] world.

That it happens to be a story about the putative first philosopher, Thales of Miletus, is only an accident of history, but this accident yields the benefit of knowing the two propositions between which logic allows a space for the origin of theory: "everything is full of gods," reads one. "Everything is from and on the water," reads the other.

That everything is full of gods could just as well be a declaration of satisfaction as of burnout. Were it of satisfaction, then there would be no need for the other proposition. Its existence betrays that the world's divine saturation was experienced as an excess that no longer explained anything. Propositions of another type than those with divine names in them had to arise, and one model was the general thesis of water. In the port city of Miletus, opening one's eyes was enough—and during the day at that—to come upon the new proposition.

What "happened" between the two propositions is the business of protohistory: the philosopher does not look at the water during the day; he falls into it at night because he renders even the starry sky the concern of the world-observer. That is not coincidental. The one looking at the sky, after all, had also achieved theory's very first "success" by dispelling, in a new way, his fellow citizens' fear of a natural event: he had managed to predict a solar eclipse. That theory works well against fear would remain valid across the millennia up through to the discoveries of Halley's comet, Pasteur's microbes, Röntgen's rays, and one day even Hahn's uranium fission. But the Thracian woman's distrust of theoretical machinations, her laughter at theory's backfire against its practitioner—transferring her exoticism to his, this basic relationship would still find its martyr in Socrates. It will not disappear from this world, even if one day the number of theorists should grow to a majority. They will always find their Thracian women where they had not expected them.

The modern creators of the product "theory" are much more comedic indeed than their ancient ancestor, and they become more so to the degree that the means of pursuing their "attitude" become more abstract. Watching the spectators of a sporting event, if we do not know its conventions or rules, can provoke laughter, and only a culture of respect prevents us from perceiving the zeal among adherents of an unfamiliar religion as a comedy of the absurd. The domesticated theory in the midst of our world usually offers us nothing to watch, because it occurs within enclosures that resemble our bureaucratic ones closely enough to be mistaken for them. As to theory's non-concealable forms of behavior, professional seriousness marks them as an integral part of a reality whose existence relies on so many unknown conditions that our wisdom and way of life include the preference not to laugh at what is peculiar.

Ihr müßt mehr Brunnen bauen!

—Heinrich Lübke[vi]

One Theory as Exotic Behavior

Theory is something that no one sees. While the behavior that constitutes theory does consist of actions that follow intentional rules and lead to complex systems of statements in regulated contexts, these actions are visible as "procedures" only on their surface. To someone uninitiated in their intentionality, who perhaps does not even suspect that they fall under the category of "theory," these actions must remain puzzling; indeed, they can appear objectionable or even laughable.[vii] It does not even take the bewildering toil that drives the institutional apparatus of highly specialized scholarship to give that impression. Since the Enlightenment, with its thought experiments about inhabitants of alien worlds who come to visit Earth—as an imaginative step beyond the fictional travel narratives by exotic travelers arriving at the European metropoles—we have become used to imagining the appearance of those procedures that characterize the "modernity" of our life as seen by visitors from other stars. In fact, the more improbable such visits have become, the more some of our contemporaries have decided that they can barely wait for them—so intensely have we imagined them. If extraterrestrials did observe earth, theory—as organized and conducted in masses—might appear as the least intelligible of the rituals that follow the law of our unknown deity.

To those who live in the scientific world and age, the exoticism of the phenomena presented by science has simply become everyday; or concealed. Within scientific institutions, everyone is credited *a limine* with pursuing meaningful activity, even when others' high-level specialization makes their work inaccessible: by providing a sphere where everyone is familiar with everyone else's rules of action, scientists have constructed enclosures that prevent the seemingly ritualized foreignness of their procedures from clashing with the outside world. The figure of the scatterbrained professor has functioned at best to promote tolerance towards theorists, as it presents the fossil of their type to an environment that smiles respectfully, even forgivingly, at them; theorists could largely remove themselves from the public and remain, in every sense, bound[viii] to their instrumentaria. Even if they produce no "theory" as aggregates of propositions, the transitive sense of the Greek *theoria*[ix] authorizes us to think of them as constantly at work on theory.

Another process accompanies this. The more a scientific discipline approaches the "ideal" of exact empiricism, the more exclusively it operates on specimens and measured data that make it independent from the haphazardness of its objects' appearance. Under the pathologist's microscope, the sick patient is not to be seen. Our imagination projects the astronomer nightly into his fortress of instruments while he is quietly sleeping and allows the illuminated plate to wake up by itself—when he does not even sit at the display terminal of an overflowing data stream, not even in the next step. No one would perceive the frenzy of arcane and disconcerting activity in him; he can perform his work during normal office hours, while instruments, parabolic antennae, or orbiting satellites deliver him what was once called a "star" but no longer bears any resemblance to the classical "object" of study, because it cannot be grasped by sensory means and can no longer be located from the surface of the earth. As many a mathematician no longer calculates, many an astronomer can no longer point out the old constellations. For him the object has positional data, which are fed into the controlling computer of the instrument: whatever the instrument reports back is then the object.

With the separation of instrument and observer, the outward appearance of "theory" as a procedure becomes more normal, and this trend increases the more science intentionally withdraws from the field of what the average person is willing and able to comprehend. Most importantly, this also means that the everyman can no longer empathize with what it is about those "objects" that can absorb a working life. To counteract this divergence from people's familiar experiences, growing swarms of publicists try to keep theory and theorists "interesting" to a paying public. Meanwhile—how could it be otherwise?—professional theorists are most readily accepted when they approach the phenotype of the now universally familiar bureaucrat and thereby lay claim to the seriousness that mainly comes with dealing in large amounts of money.

None of this lends support to apocalyptic sentiments about science's finalisms.[x] Science may wither from disinterest, vanish by completing its task, or continue on and on, operating under its normal conditions—all that matters here is the view that science offers of the world- and time-spanning distance from its beginning's *imago*, about which Heidegger, in his unhappiest hour, said that "the beginning of this greatness remains what is greatest."[1, xi]

---

1   Heidegger, "The Self-Assertion of the German University," 8. A speech held at

To put it more simply, this beginning has less formative (*prägende*) than memorable (*einprägsame*) force through the *imago* that it offered or, more correctly, drew towards itself. The interaction between the protophilosopher and the Thracian maidservant *was* not, but rather *became* the most enduring prefiguration (*Vorprägung*) of all the tensions and misunderstandings between the lifeworld[xii] and theory, tensions which would determine both realms' inexorable histories.

There are no beginnings in history; they are "assigned" as such. When Thales of Miletus turned into the protophilosopher, he might have recommended himself for the position, by marking myth's finale with the proposition that now "everything is full of gods."[xiii] This was not pulled out of thin air in Miletus, for a city with the renowned oracle of Didyma nearby could afford many gods; at the May procession, honor was rendered continuously to the divine statues mounted alongside the "Sacred Street" between Miletus and Didyma for no fewer than sixteen kilometers. So Thales knew what he was talking about and what he meant by "full."[xiv] His transition from myth to philosophy was by no means executed inconsiderately; his "new solution" to the riddle of the world—that everything emerged from the water and is therefore still on top of it—was well attested on Homer's authority. In the *Iliad*, the river god Oceanus is the "sire of the gods," just as he is the "origin of us all."[xv] Annexing the world that comes from water and rests on it to the world of the gods hardly constituted the first bold move of reason. If we knew more about how Thales had done it, we would perhaps be reminded more of the exegesis of a canonical text than of the founding of a philosophical system.

What became more important for the future and for the reputation of the protophilosopher was that he had presented theory's first spectacular success to the Greeks—though he may have hailed from Phoenician stock—by announcing a solar eclipse before the fact. No matter which facts and methods may be attributed to the prognosis (above all, how he determined the eclipse's site of visibility)—once the position of protagonist fell to him he simply had to attract significances of all sorts. Reception would thus smile on him, but also leave him exposed. In this regard, it can remain open what was primary and what was secondary material in equipping this inaugural figure. In any case, Thales the astronomer had become important for appraising what a philosophical implementation of theory could mean;

---

the official assumption of rectorship at the University of Freiburg im Breisgau on May 27, 1933. "The beginning still is. It does not lie behind us, as something that was long ago, but stands before us … The beginning has invaded our future. There it stands as the distant command to us to catch up with its greatness."

theory's "achievement" could be identified as lessening human anxiety. Precisely for that end, there needed to be a successful beginning.

We can determine what the astronomer had to see, in order to provide progress for his science; what he actually saw in order to be shackled to his *theoria*, we do not know. We can only think abstractly about this beginning or idealize it; how it is intertwined with the world's divine saturation remains inaccessible to us. For the Thracian maid, who sees the Milesian wandering around at night in the most inadvisable posture, it would be obvious to assume that she had spied him caught up in the cult of his gods. Then, he fell down justly, since his gods were the wrong ones. That unintelligible behavior could be a symptom of seeing a god—and even had to be if the degree of bizarreness escalated to the point of madness—was common knowledge not only among the Greeks, who were reminded repeatedly by Homer that a god can become visible to just one person and no one else, as when Athena restrains Achilles from drawing his sword against Agamemnon. Everyone else resists the exclusivity of the relationship of an individual to his or her special vision, the modern public just like the Thracian maid. In the direction of the starry heavens, where Thales had fixed his gaze, there were no gods that she knew from home. They were down there, where the Greek would now tumble. On those grounds, her *Schadenfreude* was allowed.

Two Socrates is Transferred into Protohistory

"Theory" already had a history—just a short two centuries—when it came across an activity beloved again and again over the course of this history: returning to its origins, or at least re-examining them. It had just begun to be worthwhile to measure contemporary luminaries by their archaic prototypes when Plato confronted the fate of his teacher Socrates by comparing him to the figure of the protophilosopher. In the corpus of Aesopic fables, which were familiar to every Greek from childhood, and which the condemned Socrates had still grabbed after from within his cell before death, a pertinent morsel appears concerning an astronomer who meets his downfall through the self-forgetting entailed by his theoretical activity:

> An astronomer (*astrologos*) was in the habit of going out regularly in the evening to observe (*episkopēsai*) the stars. Once as he was strolling through the outskirts of the town with his attention (*ton noūn holon*) completely fixed on the heavens, he fell into a well before he knew what was happening to him. While he was howling and shouting, a passer-by who heard his pitiful tones came up and, as soon as he found out what had happened, remarked, "My good fellow, while you're trying to watch things in the heavens, you don't even see things on the earth."[1]

In the *Theaetetus* dialogue, Plato lets his Socrates transfer this story to Thales of Miletus. The formerly unnamed astronomer turns into the founder of philosophy; the equally anonymous witness of his fall becomes the Thracian woman in the status of domestic slave

---

1   Aesop, *Aesop without Morals*, 110. The *epimythium* runs: this story (*logos*) can be applied to the sort of people who make themselves conspicuous through unusual behavior, but bring nothing of common utility to humanity.

for Milesian citizens. The figures of the confrontation have gained concreteness and background:

> The story is that Thales, while occupied in studying the heavens above and looking up, fell into a well. A good-looking and whimsical maid from Thrace laughed at him and told him that while he might passionately want to know all things in the universe, the things in front of his very nose and feet were unseen by him.[2]

As befits the structure of the fable, to which Plato unmistakably refers, he lets himself immediately supply the moral of the story: "The jest also fits all those who become involved in philosophy." This *epimythium* cannot have been the fable's original one; the wisdoms tacked on after fables are generally not of the same origin (*gleichurspünglich*) as the fables.[xvi] There is no basis for reading anything into Plato's version about humanity in general, but only about the philosopher's bizarreness on its way to becoming tragic.

Of course, it is not Thales who is the reference point in the Platonic context, but Socrates. When the dialogue was written, the philosopher's unbearability had already reached its limit among Socrates' contemporaries, and the polis had punished him with death. What had been announced in the laughter of the maid reached its conclusion in hatred. At this point, the Socrates of the dialogue cannot be identical with the historical figure whom the reader and author have in mind; as a literary figure, he still has his end ahead of him and does not even imagine it when he makes fun of himself and philosophy's particular form of "realism" through the image of the Milesian philosopher. For Plato and his public, theory is introduced as fate; fate binds theory's prototype to the figure of its culmination, who had become unsurpassable in understanding the world and the human. From Plato's perspective, in that comedy at the well's edge, as in the tragedy at the civil court, a similar clash of worlds is at stake: a clash between concepts of reality,[xvii] whose unintelligibility to one another can manifest as the emergence of laughter or the effect of deadliness. In the dialogue, Socrates still accepts the ridicule alongside his prefiguration, as he would accept the cup of poison in jail and reject offers of escape.

By projecting the servant's ridicule onto Thales, Socrates only indirectly hears it directed at himself. At the end of the *Protagoras*, when ironic cluelessness turns out to be the result of all dialectic, Socrates hears the ridicule of Failure personified: "The recent outcome of our speeches is, like a human being, accusing and ridiculing us; and should it attain

---

2 Plato, *Theaetetus* 174A–B. Translation by Martin Heidegger, *What Is a Thing*, 3.

a voice, it would say: 'You two are strange, Socrates and Protagoras.'"xviii The futility of the philosopher's primary occupation, however, is not the only image of ridiculousness that he displays, but his practical behavior in its entirety appears ridiculous as a consequence of philosophical eccentricity. In the *Gorgias*, Socrates tells Polus, not without satisfaction, about the time when the lot had appointed his *demos* to count the votes in the public assembly, and when he found no way to deal with the task, he drew general ridicule to himself. It is no accidental bad luck; ridicule follows him, even confirms to him that he has long abandoned the position of the everyman. In Kierkegaard's dissertation on the concept of irony,[3] he argued that Aristophanes approached the truth in making Socrates a figure in the comedy *The Clouds*.

Aristophanes had ridiculed Socrates in the comedy, at a time when the latter was still pursuing natural philosophy in Thales' tradition and investigating the celestial phenomena with Anaxagoras as his model:

> Socrates, who otherwise did not visit the theater often, partook eagerly this time. He said to those who sat near him that it seemed to him as if he were attending a funny dinner party, where one was making an artful joke out of him. As even some strangers wanted to know just who this Socrates was, he stood up and let his original be seen against his copy, which was presented on the stage.[4]

Plato's Socrates recounts his turn away from natural philosophy and his flight to the "logoi" in the *Phaedo*. The stargazer, whom Aristophanes still mocks in the comedy, can no longer be detected in the narrator of the Thales anecdote, although the young Socrates in *The Clouds* is indeed much more similar to the Milesian. But Socrates does not lay claim to the fable as an heir to Thales' natural philosophy. His claim concerns the theorist's eccentricity, no matter what the object, although it was the choice of philosophy as his object that cost Socrates all sanction and endangered his life. This all bespeaks an immanent logic: in the two centuries since Thales, it had become more evident what was actually laughable about theory. The anecdote must be read with the knowledge that Socrates had turned away from the interest in nature, which prevailed during his youth, in favor of probing human life and behavior. Then it becomes clear that the spatial distance

---

3   "Aristophanes has come very close to the truth in his depiction of Socrates." Kierkegaard, *The Concept of Irony*, 6.
4   Fénélon, *Abrégé des vies des anciens Philosophes* (quoted from a German translation: J. F. Fleischer: *Kurze Lebensbeschreibungen und Lehrsätze der alten Weltweisen*. Frankfurt: 1762, 204) (my translation).

and inaccessibility of the objects in the starry sky—in comparison to the nearness of practical existence's pitfalls—did not *constitute* the theorist's exoticism, but only *represented* it.

What Socrates had discovered, after abandoning natural philosophy, was the sphere of *conceptuality* for things human, but even from this perspective the reality of the obvious (*des Nächstliegenden*) was missed and therefore turned into a pitfall. For the theory of practice is no less theory than the theory of the stars. That is apparent in the philosopher himself—not as he was represented in the anecdote, but as the Platonic Socrates portrays the philosopher—the figure whose theoretical peculiarity unmistakably marked him as a being captivated by the "essences" (*von den Wesen erfaßten "Wesen"*): "For really such a man pays no attention to his next door neighbor; he is not only ignorant of what he is doing, but he hardly knows whether he is a human being or some other kind of creature."[xix] Here the Thracian maid's reproach is decoupled from the Milesian astronomer's object, which is noble (*erhaben*), but ultimately arbitrary; no further information is necessary about his nocturnal machinations to position him as eccentric. The "Socratic turn"—which was supposed to have fetched philosophy down from the sky and given it over to the most obvious of all interests, investigating "what a human being is and what is proper for such a nature to do or bear different from any other"—had not changed theoretical behavior by a hair. It had only removed its object from everyday familiarity and thrust it into the distance, so that the everyday would appear as bewildering as the stars.

What ultimately made the difference was thus not his change in object, but theory's changing demand on its practitioner: the Socratic type of philosopher does not recognize a human being (*menschliches Wesen*) in his neighbor, while—and because—he is preoccupied with studying the essence of the human (*Wesen des Menschen*). Everyone else's laughter, represented by the Thracian maid's, has become the indicator for a philosopher's successful concentration on thematizing his object. Awkwardness while performing any practice that mimics theory at all advances to the status of proof of having attained unprecedented access to the matter in question.

What had played out at the cistern[xx] of Miletus occurred on the scale of a private misunderstanding. Between Thales' time and Plato's writing came the polis, which showed suspicion towards the philosopher's machinations in the market. Theoretical success becomes an offense within the state's reality:

> The leaders [among philosophers], in the first place, from their youth, remain ignorant of the way to the agora, do not even know where the court-room is, or the senate-house, or any other public place of assembly; as for laws and decrees, they neither hear the

debates upon them nor see them when they are published; and the strivings of political clubs after public offices, and meetings, and banquets, and revelings with chorus girls—it never occurs to them even in their dreams to indulge in such things.[xxi]

A deficiency sticks to Socrates and to his self-description as philosophy's shaping force; the avant-garde of practical philosophy appears not to have really tested their leading man's commitment to the cause: for his deficiency is in his socialization. In this depiction (*Zeichnung*)—perhaps a distortion (*Verzeichnung*) or caricature (*Überzeichnung*)—the Platonic Socrates prefigures the separateness (*chorismos*) of forms conceived by his greatest pupil, not yet as a doctrine, but still as a way of life. For only in his corporality does Socrates belong to the community, and he even yielded that up to them as his kind of tax payment. The timelessness of philosophical objects has not yet been declared as their exceptional quality since the philosopher had already made timelessness into his own quality. "Well, Socrates, we have plenty of leisure (*skholê*), have we not?"[xxii] asks his interlocutor Theodorus. Socrates agrees, after a little delay.

No criterion for differentiating between theory and "realism" will prove more precise than their dispositions towards time as infinite or finite, respectively.[xxiii] Only later will the theorist trade leisure for industry, when everyone must demonstrate how little time he or she has. In Plato's time, the sophists were already coached and coaching others to watch the water-timer during a court trial; rhetoric generally meant standing under time pressure—the temporality of slaves.

One last thing must still be withheld from the philosopher, if he has not already lost everything in the abyss of his broken relationship to the polis: "And all of these things the philosopher does not even know that he does not know ..."[xxiv] He does know, as Socrates says, *that* he knows nothing; but in the knowledge of *what* he does not know he is badly informed. Otherwise he would not be so fundamentally deficient in life's realism. Astronomy, which Thales supposedly brought to the Greeks, was now nothing but an exceptional case where engaging with fundamental problems looked bizarre; it was nothing but a metaphor for bizarreness when he went "studying the stars, and investigating the universal nature of every thing that is, each in its entirety ..."[xxv] The accusation of the Thracian maid, about which we know neither how the philosopher answered nor whether he really felt touched by it, is now accepted as a professional stigma: "never lowering [his mind] to anything close at hand."[5] This is the context in the dialogue where Socrates introduces the Thales anecdote.

---

5   Plato, *Theaetetus*, 173C–175D, 121.

It remains disputed whether Plato was the first to name the figures in the fable from Aesop's corpus and to link the piece with Thales, in order for Socrates to shine forth by outdoing Aesop. Alternately, Plato could have found Thales' name already there in his *Aesopica* and had his Socrates faithfully cite what he had read. The anonymization would only have come about later: in other words, the anecdote could have fallen victim to the fable genre's obligatory typification.

The case for this objection rests on two premises: both Thales and Aesop belong to the same century, and both come from Miletus. Behind the anecdote stands the real situation of the astronomer observing the stars—although the fable account of this promotes the misunderstanding that this only happens at night and that his stay in the cistern could only be considered an accident, while in fact astronomers also had to determine the position of stars during the day in order to calculate the calendar cycle, and the optics at the bottom of a well served that end best.[xxvi]

And yet both sides of the argument do not fit together properly. Aesop is not established as a historical figure; even if one thinks of him as an on-site observer of Thales, or even just as a collector of local gossip about him, it remains unconvincing that Aesop should have violated the rules he gave the fable genre, which he had imprinted if not invented. But that would be the case if the piece were equipped by Aesop himself with the name of the unlucky hero. Then again, Plato could have encountered a story regarding Thales of Miletus elsewhere, such as among the treasury of anecdotes about the Seven Wise Men. In that case, his Socrates would only be imitating the fable form ironically—and the whole argument about Aesop's possible relationship to Thales would become unnecessary. This possibility cannot be entirely excluded; but it is unlikely because Plato characterizes Socrates as so intimate with Aesop's fables that he reaches into his memory bank from prison and—acting as an author for the first time and the last— puts Aesop's fables into verse. Through the report on his imminent death in the *Phaedo*, a connection between Socrates and Aesop was established for Plato's public; we then receive an inverted view of Socrates' reworking Aesop when Socrates applies the stargazer fable indirectly in the *Theatetus*. Between the two pieces, we witness the skill and desire to compose. Only a literary stylist like Plato was up to the task of changing the fable for his purposes, and these changes involved more than just naming the anonymous astronomer-type, who is foreign on his home planet.

Plato's sources matter if we want to determine how the configuration would have been available to be placed in Socrates' mouth. In the historical background of two centuries, a misunderstanding may have caused astronomical protocol from the depth of a well to look like the result of an accident, and that may have influenced the invention of the little piece—without the sky watcher's tumble, the story would not have its premise. The view of the man in the cistern must have come after the perception of strange behavior, so that its consequence would draw taunts and lessons to him; or the man crying for help from the depths would have needed to announce the sequence of events to the passerby who had rushed over, so that the latter could render the wisdom of the extant fable. In comparison to the story we consider Aesopic, Plato made a masterpiece of liveliness by staging the immediate perception of the event. As he hurried from out of nowhere towards the cries for help, the passerby in the fable, who could not have been a spectator, could have concluded from the pitiful situation that the inattentiveness of an air-gazer had prompted it; but he could hardly have suspected the intensity of an astronomical theorist. In that form, the story was a general warning against the danger of nocturnal accidents, since such threats could just as well befall lovers sneaking around. It may not then be overlooked that the passerby in the extant fable announces himself to the fall victim after the fact (*mathōn ta symbebēkota*). The fallen astronomer verbally delivers the information required for the reprimand imparted to him.

Even without considering the invention of the female figure, it is now clear how much the fable would still be lacking if it were supposed to depict the confrontation between theory and lifeworld. Taking the tale as a reference to Thales of Miletus would not be enough. The path was not one from fact to type, from namedness to anonymity, from anecdote to fable, but rather the reverse. Plato was interested in the identity of the astronomer and the protophilosopher, in order to let Socrates project his identity onto that of the protophilosopher, while the poet of the fable could not utilize the stargazer's identity to make his point. Anyone was acceptable for him; and because everything in the fable rushes towards the epigrammatic ending, he even misses the chance to make the bearer of wisdom into a witness of the event. For that effect as well, the Thracian woman will be much more suitable.

The public that ridiculed Plato's hero could no longer be called barbarians; the Sophistic Enlightenment, which was blossoming in Athens, had mastered the art of exposing weakness and rendering it contemptible. In order to speak in a pre-figurative way about Socrates' fate from Socrates' own mouth, long before the cup of hemlock, the focus must be on martyrdom for the cause of pure ideality. The blood of the witness to truth is not yet spilt; it rises to a blush in his face, whenever he is supposed to speak in court or anywhere else about the things "at his feet and before his eyes[.] He is a laughing-stock not only to Thracian girls but to the multitude in general."[xxvii]

12 The Laughter of the Thracian Woman

The one-time tumble down the well puts no end to the problem. Socrates masters rhetorical augmentation at the very point when he speaks about philosophers' rhetorical incapacity; he grasps onto the plural of wells and tumbles, so that his philosopher—and thereby he himself—"falls into pits and all sorts of perplexities ..." His public is merciless, for it is educated. That is the change in conditions which Plato expressly establishes through Socrates: "... he stammers and becomes ridiculous, not in the eyes of Thracian girls or other uneducated persons, for they have no perception of it, but in those of all men who have been brought up as free men, not as slaves."[xxviii] In order to complete this viciously sharpened paradigm, in which the opposite of a slave's upbringing is made into the precondition of the philosopher's imminently fatal situation and thereby of Socrates' fate, the nameless-unspecified passerby from the fable—who do not need to be anything more than that before—must now become a slave.

Not necessarily a female slave and by no means necessarily a Thracian one. But a Thracian slave woman could do more than provide a mocking joke to contrast with the theorist's gravity; she also had the background—which Plato evokes again elsewhere—of a world of alien gods, feminine, nocturnal, subterranean. The thought that she would be silently thinking of these gods when she sees the philosopher plummet into the earth should be thoroughly permitted to the reader. Plato by no means needs to tell the Athenians to which goddess Socrates has just prayed at the opening of the *Republic*, when he is making the return trip from the Piraeus; there the first festival for the Thracian goddess Bendis was celebrated—which would have allowed Plato's contemporaries to date the dialogue's events. And Socrates remarks about how particularly impressed he was by the ceremonial procession of the Thracians, who had built a strong merchant community at the Athenian city's harbor. Wilamowitz-Moellendorff recalls this context to his father-in-law Mommsen, who was interested in the peoples of the late Roman Empire, by emphasizing the Thracians' role in greater Athens: "And the race was good. Thucydides, Aristotle, Antisthenes have Thracian blood. This nation, which was not destroyed until the assaults of the Byzantine Period, particularly from the Bulgarians, certainly deserves an epitaph."[6]

This means that the Athenians did know something about what may have passed through that Thracian woman's mind two centuries earlier. She was certainly not the one who let the protophilosopher fall, yet she was in league with those who had staunchly expressed

---

6   Ulrich von Wilamowitz-Moellendorff to Theodor Mommsen, November 9, 1884. Mommsen and Wilamowitz-Moellendorff, *Mommsen und Wilamowitz*, 205.

disapproval of anyone who interrupts nocturnality and worships the heavenly. For them, during the night's silence, even the city gods of Miletus lost some of their standing and authority. And once again that reveals a subterranean link between the anecdote and Socrates' case. The recipients of Plato's text would have noticed this link if we impute to them any rudimentary form of "hermeneutics." For they would know the following: the Attic polis always considers the gods of their civic cult, or at least acts that way. The polis thus cannot find a philosophy harmless that first says virtue is knowledge and then teaches them to know that they know nothing. Plato invented that laughter as a response to the sight of the Milesian philosopher, in order to associate it with Socrates' death sentence. And it would have been no stretch for Plato's public to see the tragic aspect of the comic figure, even long after Socrates' execution and even without the author's insinuation. The Socrates of the dialogue lets the gods fade into the background; in their place the conflict between concepts of reality, the hopelessness of their ever reaching consensus, rises to the fore as the crisis of which the laughter then, and the death sentence now, were just the symptoms. Over the anecdote's reception history, it has retained an ambiguous position between comedy and tragedy; the equivalence that Plato evokes, between a case of state violence and a fall down a well, has lost its significance.

Three Knowledge about Heaven and Competence on Earth[xxix]

The figure of Socrates does not exhaust its polysemy in Socrates' departure from natural philosophy and his turn to the question of the human and of human virtuousness. Socrates, or Plato through him, laid a trap right at this turn by determining virtue through knowledge. Cicero's formula has since become imprinted on Socrates' historical image: "Socrates was the first who brought philosophy down (*devocavit*) from the heavens, placed (*conlucavit*) it in cities, introduced (*introduxit*) it into families, and obliged it to examine life and morals, and good and evil."[1] This, in turn, has become a common expression through the formula: what is "over our heads" has nothing to do with us.[2]

Yet precisely this change, philosophy's transition to the thesis of virtue as knowledge, drove philosophy back out of human houses and turned its sights to a different sky, one still higher and farther than that of the stars: the heaven of forms (*Himmel der Ideen*). In the forms lay the explanation for why the norms of virtuous behavior are binding. The first step down the path shows up in the Platonic dialogues as the qualification that not *all* virtues can rely on knowledge, for instance, not that of courage. Yet the question of how knowledge is possible at all remains, and it raises greater difficulties than ever, now that virtue is expected to be founded on it. The generality of the problem once again drives the philosopher back from the human things whose proximity he had sought when he turned away from natural phenomena. The question of knowledge cannot be posed differently for morality and for physics if knowledge is to be captured within the brevity of this heading. But at the same time the theory of forms restores universality

---

1 Cicero, *Tusculan Disputations*, V 10, 166 (translation modified).
2 Lactantius, *Divine Institutes*, III 20 10, 208. "[Socrates] held the following proverb in high esteem: 'what is above us is irrelevant to us.'" ("*Celebre hoc proverbium Socrates habuit: quod supra nos, nihil ad nos.*")

to the interest in the world, within which the human appears only among other things, as an answer to the question of the possibility of knowledge. In that context, the Thales anecdote also illustrates how objects' nearness or farness—the criterion that gives the Thracian maid something to taunt—cannot be a disjunction that matters for the philosopher's work.

Calling philosophy down from the sky to settle among humans had proven to be Socrates' too simple dream, and it remained his student Plato's dream in the early dialogues about the virtues. Not so easily could he extract himself from comedy, from being made a mockery by Aristophanes. Again and again, philosophers want to pass collectively as "practical" people, when theory has alienated its appearance too much. This too reflects the anecdotal placement of the protophilosopher. There is no challenge in imagining Thales, standing in the reverberation of the Thracian maid's laughter, as someone who believed that his reputation in the city of Miletus derived from a solid piece of "realism." In keeping with Miletus' character as a port and trade city, this could only be evidence that knowledge about celestial phenomena could enable someone not only to cast off the fear of solar eclipses, but also to be more successful than others in business.

It is extremely telling, particularly of the difference in the profiles of the two philosophers, that Aristotle transmits a counter-anecdote to Plato's:

> He was reproached for his poverty, which was supposed to show that philosophy was of no use. According to the story, he knew by his skill in the stars while it was yet winter that there would be a great harvest of olives in the coming year; so, having a little money, he gave deposits for the use of all the olive-presses in Chios and Miletus, which he hired at a low price because no one bid against him. When the harvest-time came, and many were wanted all at once and of a sudden, he let them out at any rate which he pleased, and made a quantity of money. Thus he showed the world that philosophers can easily be rich if they like, but that their ambition is of another sort.[3]

We must note how far away we have already come from Socrates, who would not have said that philosophers could easily be rich if they only wanted to, but do not try to be. In this respect, Aristotle has already integrated sophism into philosophy: the philosopher can too, but he just does not want to. Thales could not have been as strict as Socrates because Thales was not in the position to say he knew that he

---

3 Aristotle, *Politics*, Part A, Book XI 1259 a9–18, 111.

knew nothing. He knew something and exploited it. "What does this story mean to teach?" asks a recent philosopher, who then asks, "the capitalist relationship of exploitation in bourgeois science? It is not that; for Thales gave away the wealth he made ..."[4] Thus the protohistory of theory obtains a turn to morality, which seems to have become indispensible upon its first transfer to Democritus. Pliny had put a sanction on restituting the costs of verification in his *Natural History*: theory should prove itself, not pay for itself. Far be it from the ancients, indeed, to exclude star-interpretation from the star-knowledge that led to the protophilosopher's weather prognosis; when, however, Jakob Brucker brings the anecdote into the modern historiography of philosophy, he presumes that the demonstration by the Milesian "was thought up by idle people to strengthen the value of the good-for-nothing star-interpreting-art."[xxx] In that case, abstaining from profit would have been considered respectable only within a later, superfluous confabulation, which meant to justify the previously confabulated evidence of theory's competence. The story, of course, would still be told with relief from that point on; Socrates would not be the first to remove any suspicions about philosophers' moneymaking practices, since philosophy's first exemplar had already proven his generosity.

Pure theory's right to exist stands in question here as it will again and again; drawing no material advantage from it helps it to prove its immaculate "purity." Thales needed to be unambiguously protected by the explanation that he conducted this drastic type of speculation in order to prove the achievement of newly burgeoning theory: the motive is pure, the result is pure, and only what lies between them unfortunately had to occur because others would not be convinced otherwise.

As for Aristotle, did he know the Thales anecdote? The mere detectability of a counter-anecdote does not speak to that. And students do not always read what their teachers have written, so Aristotle was not necessarily required to read Plato's *Theaetetus*, since his knowledge of the theory of forms could derive just as well from other sources than the dialogues. The required evidence is lacking that he knew the fable or the anecdote. Just one passage in the *Nicomachean Ethics*, where the name Thales has just occurred, continues by exalting practical insight (*phronēsis*) and disdaining the representatives of natural philosophy, who may have been wise (*sophoi*) but not insightful (*phronimoi*). They apparently do not recognize what benefits them; they only recognize what is extraordinary, amazing, hard to understand, and divine (*daimonia*),

---

4   Hermann Lübbe, "Thales im Brunnen." First printed in: *Deutsche Zeitung*, November 7, 1975. Reprinted in "Unbehagen an der Wissenschaft," in Lübbe, *Endstation Terror*, 184f. (1978).

what is useless indeed for living life, because they fail to investigate what is good for humans.[5] This accusation sounds completely Socratic and, for that very reason, it carries an even sharper case against natural philosophy, because Aristotle's distinction would be a logical consequence of questioning humanity's privileged position within nature and thus would thus call into question the anthropocentric tendency to relate all insight into nature immediately back around human concerns. Aristotle's case does not support the claim that politics and ethics are the highest forms of knowledge; it is precisely because human beings do not rank highest that they must be concerned with themselves and their needs. The stars, which humanity has expressly privileged as divine beings, need no "praxis" and no intelligibility. Therefore, they and their circular motions are already objects of "pure" theory, which the human can only afford in moderation—unless theory itself could make the theorist as free from needs as a god. Therein lies the deeper reason for what looks like "unsuccessfulness."

Had Aristotle been contemplating the anecdote in its Platonic variant, then Thales would have done just the right thing as a theorist by striving for the most noble objects. However, he would still have failed blatantly to conduct himself with the right moderation, since he forgot his frailty (*Hinfälligkeit*), literally, and the consequentially necessary caution. The counter-anecdote about oil-press speculation portrays Thales as right to pursue his theory, but Aristotle's anecdote is insufficient to validate the claim that even the act of theorizing requires ethical moderation or that theory must be moderate in touting its objects' supremacy.

The biographer of the Greek philosophers, Diogenes Laertius, asserts that Thales not only evinced his usefulness through weather predictions—as the Greek word for "conducting astronomy" can also mean "seeing past the clouds"—but also accomplished exceptional services for the city of Miletus with his political foresight and counsel. To claim that Thales' theory was useful is to take the step that Aristotle, who separated wisdom and insight, was not yet ready to make.[6] Secretly, philosophy always yearned for such competence in the polis, for the reliability of being "realistic." The Socratic line of thinking, as portrayed by Plato, ended up by failing to convince. Ludwig Börne would bring that to its pithiest formulation: "Socrates has been cherished because he took philosophy down from the sky, and thus he

---

5   Aristotle, *Aristotle's Nicomachean Ethics* VI 7 1141 b3–10.
6   Diogenes Laertius, *Lives of Eminent Philosophers*, Vol. 1 I, 25, 27. See also "De Republica" Part I 7 and 9 in Cicero, *The Republic and The Laws*.

became a teacher to humanity. If we want to please him, we have to drag politics earthward from the sky."[7]

After Socrates and Plato, there is an unmistakable effort to return a certain degree of realism to the philosopher; that could no longer permit the anecdote to retain its most pointed form. It is tempting to understand Aristotle's allusion to Thales as a hesitation to let Plato's story emerge yet another time. The theorist's eccentric position became indelibly marked from Plato's theory of forms and was retraced again by Aristotle's critique of it.

Plato's *Theatetus* dialogue does not mention a single word about the theory of forms; the astronomer's bizarreness, which inspired the Thales anecdote and prefigured Socrates, remains completely reliant on the nocturnal undertaking of the sky observer who could *see* what he wanted to *know*. The critic of the theory of forms did not need to resent, though he does mention, that astronomy suffices least for the requirement of a science of experience if it needed to settle for "saving the phenomena."[xxxi] In Aristotle's overview of the whole course of the Platonic theory of forms including its ascent to transcendence, its sharpening of the *chorismus*, and the resulting epistemology of a higher intuition than the empirical one, what made the astronomer suitable for allegorization must be modified in order to typify the philosopher.

In the anecdote, the stargazer's ridiculous appearance to the Thracian maid consisted in the fact that his ridiculousness allowed him to fall over the lower realities in front of his feet, while he was oriented towards unreachably distant objects, which he could simply never have for himself. In the Platonic context, falling down distinguishes the philosopher as the one in possession of truths that matter, even though they transpose him into a position of ridiculed foreignness in the world. This inversion accompanies theoretical success as an apparently unavoidable side effect, as its symptom, not its essence. That appearance is precisely what changes, as an unavoidable consequence of the theory of forms, which may not produce an astronomy of the invisible, but does postulate one. For historical hindsight, this duplication of the sky is reflected in the constellation of the Milesian astronomer and the Thracian maid, in that her laughter must now target the vain expectation of recognizing something through optical experience that can only be reached through an intuition (*Anschauung*) and whose attainment thus requires neither wandering nocturnally nor tumbling into cisterns. What the astronomer aims to accomplish by relinquishing his bodily wellbeing has become worthless not only from the standpoint of lifeworldly ignorance about astronomy: its

---

7   Börne, "Ankündigung der Zeitschwingen," *Gesammelte Schriften von Ludwig Börne*, 37–8 (1819).

empirical objects can no longer compete with the ideality of a "true" astronomy. Moreover, Thales had given a hint of such a science when he announced something that everyone would see without knowing its contexts, before anyone could see it: a solar eclipse.

In the seventh book of the *Republic*, Plato has his Socrates argue with Glaucon about whether astronomy shall belong to the contents of an education within their recently outlined regime. Glaucon affirms that agronomy, sea navigation, and military leadership demand a background in astronomy. Socrates answers with a sentence which could derive from any education reform discussion: "I can't help being amused ... by your apparent fear that people will see no practical value in the subjects you are putting in your curriculum."[xxxii] At that, Glaucon gives in; he wants an astronomy precisely of Socrates' type. Its advantage must lie in the fact that the soul needs to look upwards, away from any objects here and over to the ones beyond.

That would still be the case for the astronomer from the Thales anecdote, with whom the Socrates from *Theatetus* had compared himself. Here Socrates decisively contradicts that comparison; when astronomy is conducted by those who want it to lead to philosophy, it brings about the exact opposite of astronomy: steering the gaze downwards. The perceivable direction of the empirical astronomers' gaze is not that of reason, for only the invisible can be an object of understanding. In retrospect, doubt and derision from the Thracian maid do not so much prove her shortcoming by the astronomer's theoretical standard, but rather that she grasped his shortcoming although she could not have had a clue about it.

The true reality does not lie this side of astronomical objects—in proximity to things over and into which one can fall—rather just beyond everything still graspable by the senses, beyond even the light-spots given in the starry sky. Plato presages Hegel's disparaging assessment of the view towards heaven: the visible cannot be the reasonable.[xxxiii]

This situation unexpectedly recalls the laughable Socrates-figure in Aristophanes' *Clouds* once again. Anyone initiated into the Platonic transcendence of forms would perceive a ridiculousness in this figure, which they may not have noticed before; Aristophanes portrays Socrates lying in a hammock and gaping open-mouthed, resembling a swimmer lying on his back. For a Platonist, any putative "theory" conducted by observation has nothing to do with science. As Glaucon says, "Anyone trying to learn about objects of perception by gaping up at the sky or frowning down at his feet can never learn anything, I would say—since no object of perception admits of knowledge. His soul is looking down, not up, even if he makes his observations lying on his back—whether on land or floating in the sea."[xxxiv] The confrontation has reached a new stage, where the lifeworldly realism of the Thracian maid has lost its role. The anecdote is still memorable, but has lost any function in the revolt against the hypertrophy of "pure" thought.

Who can still be laughing at what now? As the *Republic* approaches the climax of the cave analogy, the philosopher returns from the sight of the forms, at which point he surrenders to the laughter of his one-time fellow prisoners, who amuse themselves over his inability and their experiential advantage in anticipating shadows, at his helplessness in the competition for supremacy in "realism," with the deadly subtext that always relates to Socrates' fate. But shortly afterwards, it is Socrates himself who switches roles and mocks the lower form of theory that Glaucon would like to introduce into the curriculum.[8]

Admittedly, nothing justifies Socrates' laughter. The "real astronomy"[xxxv] that he postulates and whose possibility Glaucon concedes and sees in front of himself as if through a magic spell—we never learn any of it. The viewers of the ideal, the owners of the actual, have constantly found it easier to deride others who wanted to see with their own eyes than to show them what they could gain if they ceased to want only what is available physically. Indeed, an astronomer who no longer looked up—that is more than just Plato's last answer to the derision of the Thracian maid and to that of Aristophanes; it is a type with a future.

Proposing a new system did not require Copernicus to make any observations of his own. What's more, all of the empirical data that could contribute to the founding of the solar system were known since antiquity. First, Tycho Brahe will be the great observer, who achieves the precisions of empiricism in spite of a false system, which would lead to Kepler's laws and, with those in mind, to Newton's physics of the sky. Of course, all of this happens under the precondition of the Copernican interpretation of the observations. Copernicus himself, certainly not without humanistic remorse, declared his reform to be the completion of a warning directed at the astronomer not to forget the earth in front of his feet for the stars high in heaven. In an ironic way, the Thracian maid should once more be right to indict the philosopher if she means: to the extent that he aims to fathom the farthest phenomena, what is nearest (*das Nächste*) remains hidden from him. Copernicus accuses the traditional geocentric system precisely of that: the earth evades that system with its gaze on the heavenly bodies insofar as the earth too is a heavenly body. Above all else, the behavior (*habitudo*) of the earth towards the starry sky must be observed because it is our standpoint for observation (*nobis a terra spectantibus*) and from that follows everything that optics has shown about perspectivistic conditions (*ut*

---

8   Plato, *Republic* VII 517A; 527D–530C.

in Opticis est demonstratum). Because optics itself allows the determinants of rest and movement to alternate between the observer and his object for phenomena of movement, the traditional conclusion about the stationary earth and the heavenly bodies' movements must have prerequisites besides empirical ones. It is the supposed nobility of the stellar objects (*excelsissima*), which distracts us from what lies nearby (*nobis proxima*) and leads to the error of ascribing movement to heavenly bodies when that movement is actually a property of the earth: "not ... to attribute to the celestial bodies what belongs to the Earth."[9]

The theoretical breakthrough, here for the first time as so often afterwards in the history of science, is a shift in the direction of attention: drawing notice to the unnoticed. Here for the first time an element of reflection is exposed in the moralizing words of the anonymous passerby in the Aesopian fable as in the derisive speech of the Thracian maid: not only preferring what lies nearby to the farthest and noblest, but making the nearby into the essential condition for distant objects to appear as they do.

There is no trace of this thought in Plato's appropriation of the fable through his Socrates. Socrates had taken the Thracian woman as a paragon of misunderstanding with regard to the astronomer's right to theoretical purity and, as Socrates transferred that right onto himself, found philosophy's peculiarity reflected in Thales' notion that nothing in the environment mattered. By then Socrates had long turned his gaze from the sky and directed it towards human things. This shift of attention, towards concepts (*Begriffe*) and finally towards the ideas (*Ideen*) that determine human behavior, could alter nothing about the transcendence of the norms that were found in that beyond: the philosopher remained the man with his gaze set on too distant objects, who now more than ever tumbled from one well into another, from one embarrassment into another, and, instead of having just one Thracian woman, had the laughter of the whole crowd against him.

Copernicus' procedure could imply a model of reflection completely different from the one that prevailed during the epoch he introduced: the phenomena of heaven mimic the center of complex movements whose "actual" reality belongs to the terrestrial globe. Right with Copernicus, the triumph of the Thracian woman may have been completed; for she had called attention to the Earth's reality with the hidden sense that the real gods are right here.

---

9   Copernicus, *On The Revolutions of Heavenly Spheres*, 12 ("*nec ... quae telluris sint, attribuamus caelestibus,*" *De revolutionibus* I 4).

Four The Theorist between Comedy and Tragedy

The connection founded by Plato, between the Milesian's tumble down the well and the Athenians' killing of Socrates, did not survive after his dialogue's subtle art. Later quotations, references, and variations reduce the story to its kernel. Insights emerge from the contexts, the avowals, and the changes. New implications are conceived for the story from within and without: from outside, when its function is no longer understood or is organized into other intentions; from inside, when situations and figures are brought into an ostensibly or actually more precise compatibility. Fables, like their adaptation by Plato, think neither in characters nor in motives; therefore the image stands open to such "refinements," such as when Luther gives the Aesopian fable of wolf and lamb the heading "Hate"—an emotional valence completely out of place in the authentic genre.

Was the Thracian maid really *emmeles kai chariessa*, in Schleiermacher's translation: "crafty and witty" ("*artig und witzig*")?[xxxvi] That unnamed man in the Aesopian fable, as Plato could have found it, has friendlier traits, despite his indefiniteness; he hurries over to the cries for help and the whimpers from the cistern, and then only moralizes—still meaning to help though?—upon learning the circumstances of the accident from none other than the unfortunate man.[xxxvii] If he only pursues the audible, he could not know how things had come to the point where someone needed help from the depth. Indirectly, we are also led to understood that the fallen astronomer is still capable of returning to land. From Plato we learn nothing more about Thales' fate, and that tells us enough. Between the maid and the Milesian, no contact occurs; that prompts the reader to assume something vile: she could have disparaged him all by herself and for her own sake, without concerning herself with his predicament any further. Nowhere does the text let us assume that it was Thales' own maid. More likely it was just some stranger; otherwise she would hardly have been surprised at the bizarreness of what had happened.

To the question of *why* Plato transformed the unnamed man of the fable into the Thracian woman of his anecdote, only conjecture can answer. A conjecture would be useful, however, because the reception overwhelmingly either observes this moment without showing interest or accepts the result without understanding where that leaves things standing. Plato loved the figure, which first became a type through Tertullian's "idiota" and will be made into the functionary of the "docta ignorantia" by Nicolaus of Cusa; the slave boy in *Meno* exemplifies it, as does the figure of the Pamphylian Er in the final myth of *The Republic*.[xxxviii]

The Thracian woman betrays more than a knowing kind of ignorance (*verständiger Unverständigkeit*). From Thrace come two known figures of the Hellenic world: the god Dionysus with his epithet *Chthonius*, the Subterranean, and Aesop the slave, who brought over the fable—a Phrygian, according to other sources. More importantly for the Greek consciousness, the Thracians had a great deal of what Jacob Burckhardt ascribes to the Greeks as their own: pessimism—but in a hardened version, of which Schopenhauer had found an example that disconcerted even him: "It was a Thracian custom to receive people at their birth with mourning and lamentation."[1] Thence had come the god of the Bacchae, the Zeus of women, as it was said, and a lot could be projected onto the Thracian woman as enemy of theory, as unproclaimed, prototypical antagonist to Socrates.

Just some maid-stupidity, that would be too low profile for Plato; the enjoyer of *Schadenfreude* should simultaneously be the wronged party for Plato's public, and, in her hasty misjudgment, she had already exposed herself for all eyes over the course of the century—just as Plato wanted to display the Attic republic in its decline through the wronged Socrates, in that he drafted a republic, which could only have received wellbeing from a Socrates. Not only for us is theory a completely Greek matter, only accessible to us through them; Plato himself also insisted on this exclusivity, and once the character of the unnamed man from the fable is specified, it indeed tends towards the uncanny trait of animosity towards the first theorist's embrace of the world. Even if the fable had been invented by Aesop in a way that stigmatized the stargazer sitting at the depth of the well for having fallen, Aesop would already need to have given up on transmitting the content with the fable; to impute such a misunderstanding to the fable's author would misestimate this genre's artistry.[2]

---

1   Böckh and (Crotoniensis), *Philolaos des Pythagoreers Lehren nebst den Bruchstücken seines Werkes*, 181. Note found in Schopenhauer's copy of this book, taken from Schopenhauer's handwritten unpublished writings, ed. A. Hübscher, III 57.
2   Landmann and Fleckenstein, "Tagesbeobachtungen Von Sternen Im

24 The Laughter of the Thracian Woman

In the anecdote's reception history, these connotations lose their meaning to the degree that the onset of Hellenism dilutes the opposition between Hellenes and barbarians, Olympians and Subterraneans, and that the apostrophe to Socrates brings an end to the laughter. That is so, even if the seriousness that spreads over the scene does not yet demand that theory's victim (*Opfer der Theorie*) sacrifice his life for theory (*Opfer für die Theorie*) in order to help theory blend in with the monumental concepts of humanity and of history. Offering such sacrifices requires neither polis nor public—they are only supposed to receive sacrifices.

In this reception, the depth of the earth also goes lost on occasion: the well or cistern (*phrear*) becomes the unspecific dip of a hole (*bothros*) for Diogenes Laertius or of a ditch (*barathron*) for Stobaeus. The cute young maid turns into the old hag, worry grasps at her, even concern for her own salvation; the abyss turns into the pit of sin (*Sündenpfuhl*), and above all the theory of the stars into mere means of exploring astrological curiosity about the future.

And the most important artistic device becomes the role reversal. Among the philosophical schools of the Hellenistic period, that of the Cynics is most disposed to put itself in the derisive maid's position and, from there, to make the theorists of all other denominations contemptible. In the first half of the third century before Christ, Bion of Borysthenes put "philosophy in a clown suit," as Nietzsche will say,[3, xxxix] by ridiculing philosophers for wanting to maintain the seriousness of their subject matter. But Bion himself differed only in his rhetoric from those who indulged in writing catalogues of contradictions (*isostheneia*) between schools and sects, in order to elevate nothing but theory's self-denial to the epitome of theory.[xl] Philosophy has entered its skeptical phase. Not only in the Academic and Pyrrhonian schools, which expressly define themselves thus, also in the Stoic *ataraxia*, especially in Epicurus' general dictum that all theoretical thinking winds up in the same place, namely, having nothing to do with human wellbeing.[xli] Nothing paradoxical then, if that laughter now becomes professionalized within philosophy itself. The counterpoint at its beginning has become the conclusion at its (first) end.

It fits Bion's image well that he himself had been a slave and only [left the Academy][xlii] when his master's inheritance put the notorious

---

Altertum. Eine Philosophisch-astronomiegeschichtliche Rekonstruktion Der Thalesanekdote. Plato Theatet. 174 A," 98–112. Michael Landmann wrote to me (January 13, 1977) with his case against my thesis that Plato was the first to refer the anonymous fable to Thales of Miletus (as found in *Poetik und Hermeneutik VII.* München 1976, 11–24). I hope that I have portrayed his argument fairly.

3   "Ueber die Cyniker und ihre Bedeutung für die Literatur" in Nietzsche, *Gesammelte Werke*, V 471.

school switcher in good enough stead to associate with "cynicism."[xliii] It was not his theoretical curiosity that had let him traverse all schools, but rather his stylized expression of low esteem for them in contrast to life experience. As founder of the hedonistic branch of the Cynics, he emphasized the cheerful calm that comes from letting ourselves rely on opportunities and nature to provide our necessities and letting truths rely on themselves—the theory of a gatherer's existence. A variant of the Thracian maid's statement from the mouth of this philosopher is no longer surprising by this point: "Bion said, 'the most ridiculous are the astronomers, who do not see the fish on the beaches in front of their feet, but claim to recognize them in heaven.'"[4] Modified theory contrasts with observing heaven, represented through the constellation of the fishes, Pisces; the Cynical way of life is registered in their attention towards how to subsist on what nature has put within human reach and made attainable without strain. The punch consists in choosing a food with a likeness in heaven. The epigram's form was known since Aesop.

Another little detail about Bion deserves mention: the Cynical effort to establish the Thracian woman's reproach within philosophy itself and to make theory's departure ridiculous instead of its beginning—which had the right to demonstrable failures—no longer evokes the image of foreignness between the free man and the slave woman; very much, though, he shoves the heckler, who "transcended" philosophy through philosophy, into the role of the pimp of philosophy, over which he pulled the "floral-patterned fabric" (*anthina*), the harlot's robe, as Theophrastes and Eratosthanes would describe it.[5] What Thales of Miletus had demonstrated in all seriousness to his fellow citizens is now shoved onto the stage of comedy, in that the Cynic who maligned philosophy showed that he could still live off of it.

A half-millennium later, the anecdote is withdrawn from relevance to any discussion about the philosopher's place in the world by a biographer in the third century after Christ, Diogenes Laertius. It is not while he is walking around and watching the stars that Thales fell

---

4   Stobaeus, *Ioannis Stobaei Florilegium*, LXXX 3. Even the head Cynic Diogenes of Sinope applies the "formula" of the astronomy fable; he scorns grammarians, mathematicians, musicians, rhetoricians for the discrepancy between their technical educations (*Kunstfertigkeiten*) and their self-betterment (*Selbstbildung*): "That mathematicians should gaze at the sun and the moon, but overlook matters close at hand." Diogenes Laertius, *Lives of Eminent Philosophers*, Vol. 2, VI, 28, 30–1. For the grammarians, the analogy is temporal: Odysseus' foible they discover; their own remains hidden from them.
5   See Niehues-Pröbsting, "Der Kynismus des Diogenes und der Begriff des Zynismus," 184f. on the Aristophanic background of the Cynic diatribe and its *spoudogeloion*.

into a well; he falls into a ditch right when he leaves the house to go watch the stars. An old woman, with no further characteristics, accompanies him and calls to the crying one: "How can you expect to know all about the heavens, Thales, when you cannot even see what is just before your feet?"[xliv] His accompaniment, who evidently comes with him from the house, does not have the freedom to laugh; that much is understandable. But to what end must Thales *be* accompanied on the astronomical trip? The question is so obvious, and yet, as far as I can see, it has not yet been posed.

Information comes from an epigram, which Diogenes had posited as his own, as is his custom, in his biography of Thales. He thanks god for the philosopher's death because god lifted him closer to the objects that *he could no longer have seen* from the earth. Here it becomes clear: this constellation evokes no head-lifting initiator of heavenly theory, but rather a blind man. Driven by his urge for theory he only finds the pity, hardly the reproach, of a woman, whose age indicates nothing other than the decrepitude (*Hinfälligkeit*) of the philosopher himself, who has still not at all reached the place where he can just recollect his observational acts—and who thus still cannot let himself be distracted from his objects of study and notice what lies before him.[6]

Now we have the anecdote in yet another version by Diogenes Laertius. It occurs in the apocryphal correspondence between Pythagoras and Anaximenes, which includes a short biography of Thales.[7] In this testament of the Milesian school's piety towards its founder, the anecdote turns into the legend of Thales' death. The old man is still solely pursuing his lifelong habit and leaving home with his maid at night in order to observe the stars. Sunken into the act of observing heaven, he falls down a slope. Connecting the last effort towards theory with the deadly tumble serves to reinforce Thales' bequeathal through his consecrating death. It justifies the letter's admonition that every collective investigation should begin with Thales. In the meantime, the city of Miletus had fallen into the hands of the Persian king Cyrus, with relatively mild consequences—mild precisely because the citizens had followed Thales' advice to dispatch

---

6   Diogenes Laertius, *Lives of Eminent Philosophers*, Vol. 1 I, 34, 35.—When laughter is no longer possible, it becomes clearer what had been laughed at and that the maid must have been young. The protophilosopher is a neurotic; otherwise, what he set in motion could not approach paranoid madness as the highest form of the "system," as Freud could not have denied seeing it. The astronomer's "reality" is an exclusive world (*Sonderwelt*), like that of the neurotic. And why does the maid ridicule him? Because she recognizes the nocturnal wanderer's neurosis in the fact that he is not sleeping with her at that hour.

7   Ibid., Vol. 1 II, 4, 133–5.

an offer of annexation to the Lydian king Croesus. The astronomer's foresight maintains its force throughout his life.

The city has lost its freedom. This enables Anaximenes, in his second letter, to recall that freedom is a precondition for any theory of heaven, the free man's domain. For his school, Thales, the lifelong star observer, at once becomes a monument to the lost conditions for inaugurating theory: "How then can Anaximenes any longer think of studying the heavens when threatened with destruction and slavery?"[xlv] The Thracian maid has disappeared from the scene; opposing her unfreedom to the free Milesian citizen's theory has lost its transparency. In this altered condition, the clash between her lifeworldly concept of reality and the philosopher's understanding of the world now only finds its reflection in the political fate of the city—whose servitude has rendered it impossible to continue and fulfill the theory founded by Thales. In 494, the city at the mouth of the Meander River is destroyed by the Persians, the inhabitants pronounced slaves. With that, the inaccessibility of theoretical behavior for the female Thracian observer turns into the impediment against everyone's chance at a theoretical existence.

Going blind and falling to his death, impotence of the eye and finitude of the drive to knowledge—it is Faust's end that is announced in Thales' fate.[xlvi] And not by accident. To posit theory is to posit the possibility of its tragedy: in the physical organ's failure to endure this previously unexperienced strain on the senses, and more cuttingly in the world's supremacy over any life lived within space and time. Although the Greeks had combined theory and *eudaimonia* so tightly that Christianity still had to determine its concept of otherworldly happiness as theory of God in a literal sense,[xlvii] the Greeks have a static concept of theory and a stationary concept of the theorist, as someone who does not leave behind directions and assignments, but rather writes down his teaching and hands it over to a school, which must foster and cultivate it. The static and doctrinaire state of theory appears to suit the finitude of the human lifetime; at the same time, however, that state is sensitive to the rise of new schools and their growing inventory of contradicting positions (*isostheneia*).

Yet the conflict of theories does not turn into one between theory and *eudaimonia*. The latter retains the superior rank and defines indifference as the outcome of the first theoretical epoch: if uncertainty is sufficient for living and acting, then virtue is not knowledge. In a *cosmos*, if there even was one, every theory yielded the same result for humans; it informed their hopes as little as their fears. While Eudoxus of Cnidus had said that he only needed to look precisely at the sun one time in order to gauge its size and shape, Heraclitus transmits the paradox that the size of the sun is the breadth of his foot. Indeed, after the direction that theories had headed, no one could still call that a disregard for objectivity any more. Epicurus' methodical attitude varies only the impediment of theory's primacy, in that he would prove—regarding all of the familiar theories about nature and the size of the sun—that they came out the same for humanity: we remain spectators of the world. Given the path that Greek theory took, Protagoras' proposition, that the human being is the measure of all things, reveals the deeper commonality in the Greeks' conception of theory.

Greek theory is also a culture of haughty indifference towards circumstances, from Heraclitus to the Stoic *ataraxia* to the Skeptical *epoché*[xlviii] to Epicurus' sage, whose prototype (*Urbild*) was the gods, who were not imagined as laughing only because they did not look at the worlds for assurance of their insouciance and happiness. The same Thales of Miletus, who tumbled into the well and ended up being mythologized as the man who died by conducting theory, did not prefigure the Epicurean sage, but rather the laughing maid. She most closely resembles the spectator-type as Epicurus conceived it and Lucretius put into an image: he stands on the precipice of the shore and looks indifferently at the shipwreck in the raging sea of the world; he does not laugh, but he enjoys his uninvolvement.

After all of the Epicurean cultural criticism, the spectator can only see one thing in the shipwreck in front of his eyes: the end result of the undertakings and industries, whose extravagance appears to him as the epitome of risks that expose human beings so that the world can impact and injure them. Had not Glaucon said in Plato's *Republic* that astronomy must be conducted for its value to navigation? In such a line of justifications for theory, the shipwreck necessarily stands as counterevidence. Theory leads people to become unnecessarily vulnerable to the world, to lower their guards, as Thales had done. Whoever tumbles made himself too heavy. The Epicurean knows how to exclude whatever does not concern humans by reducing theory to *joie de vivre*. This *theoros* on the high shore does not tumble into the depths, and, above all, he enjoys the fact that he does not fall.[8]

---

8   Blumenberg, *Shipwreck with Spectator*, 26–8, "3. Aesthetics and Ethics of the Spectator" (On the Proemium of Lucretius Book II).

Five Reoccupations[xlix]

We would not expect the Fathers of the advancing Christian epoch to record the Thales anecdote in order to have the sky observer's plummet remind him that what lies at his feet is more urgent than heaven. That would have implicitly settled the competition between the heavenly and the earthly abruptly to the advantage of the lower affairs. On the contrary, the theorist of the stars must now appear as someone who proceeds too much in the foreground and stops too early in the direction in which he set out. Instead of giving oneself over to the being of beings (*Seiendseindem*) behind the appearances of heaven, as Plato had already demanded in the form of a second astronomy of invisible heavenly bodies, the theorist declines what is still visible as long as it remains visible to him. The blinded Thales is no longer a figure for the tragedy of theory as a finite one due to the decay of the organ, but rather for the tragedy of mistaking visibility for the medium of knowledge acquisition in the first place. When Cicero, philosophy's representative so quickly canonized by Latin Christendom, recalls Democritus' self-blinding, the self-purported Platonist is evoking the representative of atomism so assiduously persecuted by Plato and then revived by Epicurus. Epicurus did not balk at the claim that the sharpness of the spirit would only hinder the eyes from seeing. And there is doubtless a recollection of the Thales anecdote and of the maid's mocking words: "While others often could not even see what was before their feet, he travelled through all infinity."[1] Although this infinity only refers to the negatively determined space of atomism, it is still available to aid in constructing a concept, which can surpass the

---

1   Cicero, *Tusculan Disputations*, V114, 204. Democritus "was of the opinion that the intense application of the mind was taken off by the objects that presented themselves to the eye; and while others often could not even see what was before their feet, he travelled through all infinity."—Suddenly, we realize how close Democritus stands to the late Plato, if only based on both parties. This proximity yields an exemplary case of "narcissism of the smallest difference."

finite universe of the astronomical theorist, in order to create space for new realities where salvation matters, realities for which the Earth in the middle of the world would no longer be the preferred arena.

If the Latin Patristic still accepts Ovid's account that humanity was bound to an upright gait with lifted head in order to observe the sky, then it becomes a metaphor: upon setting out toward the edge of the world, coming from what is familiar (*naheliegend*), the observer of heaven is on the right path to transcend that edge.[1] His plummet would represent the downfall of someone who had not wanted to go high enough, who grew weary already at the pagan foreground of the cosmic inner surface, and therefore failed to attain transcendence. He was not someone who failed to understand the importance of the massiveness of the earthly that lay in front of his feet, but rather one who failed to understand the importance of caring about the kernel of all cares, his eternal salvation. Here the metaphorics of the distant correspond to those of the nearby, which no longer has any external reality; it has become the internal horizon of the truth seeker, who must now worry about himself.

And yet the observer of heaven has not come under suspicion of wanting to exalt himself as the incarnation of his purposes in the way that the mysticism of sight (*Anschauung*) allows the delighted observer of divine objects to become similar to them. Too little distance from the earthly corresponds to too much autonomy in reaching for the object: theory has become only the precursor stage to being ready to hear and accept a revelation about what extrapolation from the limits of theory can reveal to be the unknown. In contrast to such readiness, the sky observer receives the traits of libidinal obsession and of intemperance in his pure desire for knowledge; he plummets because he seems to attain access unrightfully to the sphere of his yearning while disregarding divine rights to set limits and, *a fortiori*, disregarding the greater urgency of salvation (*Heilsvordringlichkeiten*). The suspicion, under which he is now placed, can thus be put ungenerously: instead of going the way of grace, he conducts transposition magic.

This suspicion, that theory could be contaminated with magic—a justified suspicion—allows the intermediary between Judaism and Hellenism, Philo of Alexandria, to warn everyone, who has partaken in astronomy or wishes to do so, to come back down from the sky.[2] Augustine would find the rhetorical expression for the danger lurking in the back of theory and would transmit it with his authority into the Middle Ages. He imputes to astronomers, as the demand inherent to their discipline, that they claim to have already achieved with their own means what can in fact only be won through the newly emerged

---

2   Philo of Alexandria, *De migratione Abrahami*,185.

salvation procedure: so great a pride is thus begotten "that one would think they dwelt in the very heavens about which they argue."[3] The accusation of conducting transposition magic prefigures the notion that the human standpoint in the cosmos could no longer incontrovertibly be the privileged one—it can already no longer be so if we take seriously the future implications (*Vorläufigkeit*) of all the truth that entailed as much. An epoch later, with dwindling prospects of attaining transcendent truth, there will be nothing contrary to human nature or to the world itself (*an sich*) about procuring another systematically articulated central point for the orderly movements. The imaginary center becomes the constructive means for astronomy to pierce through its perspectivistic illusions before it takes the further step of criticizing its own presuppositions, and thus of foreclosing every apparent center of the cosmic movements.

For the Enlightenment, it will be a pretense for the study of the human world to alienate the gaze on the earthly as if one possessed none of the rules of the game that work there—and that then again the Thracian maid, now as traveler from the orient, as indigenous Huron or as astronaut of the Canicula. In the introduction to the *Traité de Métaphysique*, Voltaire will demand that thinkers leave their sphere of interests and prejudices in order to experience humanity as if they were observing humans from Mars or Jupiter. Voltaire is required as a Copernican to see astronomical phenomena "as if I were in the sun."[li]

It would stretch the concept of "reception history" too far if we claimed the ability to determine in the disconcerted (*befremdet*) gaze on the action of theory something like a precursor to the defamiliarized (*verfremdet*) gaze of theory itself. Its concern is much rather to find a pattern made out in the Thales anecdote, a pattern which cannot be shaken off in the history of theory. Even when using the concept indulgently, reception means something else, and it goes wrong when we leave the guiding thread of names, words, and images.

Among the authors of the early Christian period, only Eusebius has transmitted a complete extent version of the Thales anecdote, as Plato gave it in *Theaetetus*, and he also repeated the genuine interpretation of the philosopher's foreignness in the world.[4] Scholars always strain to demonstrate their high degree of literacy, in efforts to avoid the crime of neglecting or distorting extant textual material; this was also the case for the Apologist who is to preserve the good Alexandrian scholarship of the learned fourth century.[lii]

---

3   Augustine of Hippo, *De moribus ecclesiae catholicae et de moribus Manichaeorum*, I. 38, in Thomas, *The "Summa Theologica" of St. Thomas Aquinas*, 287. This passage is cited in Thomas Aquinas, *Summa theologica* II 2 q. 167 a.1.
4   Eusebius, *Praeparatio Evangelica* XII 29, 4–5 (ed. Mras, 120).

A century earlier, at the beginning of the Latin Apologetics, a completely different approach was taken by the jurist and master of a mighty rhetoric, Tertullian. To him the Greek philosophers as a whole appear as patriarchs of the heretics.[5] The protophilosopher Thales' fall into the well is at once established as the example that goes to the root of the offense. Tertullian disdains the path of Apology supported by literature; he feels himself enough of a master to speak his own language. Under no circumstance would he like to present the evidence for the truth of Christianity from heathen sources. It would have matched his style entirely to ridicule the philosophical worldview from the standpoint of the Thracian maid. She anticipates what comes to replace Greek authority for Tertullian: the "simple soul," his *"anima idiotica,"* which he had introduced to the Apologetic rhetoric with his *Testimonium animae*. But he did not perceive the opportunity to let it speak from out of the Thracian maid.

Maybe it lay in the fact that Tertullian—against his juridical colleague and rival in the literary "praxis" for the new cause, Minucius Felix—sought to build up a contrasting image to Greek philosophy and, with that, to show greater toughness. Minucius Felix had written with well-meaning ambiguity about Thales of Miletus that Thales should be called the first because "he first of all disputed about heavenly things."[6] What results from that ambiguity is a conflation of water, as the first philosophical protomatter, with the waters found in the biblical Creation account, over which God's spirit hovered; that could mean nothing other than that He created everything from water. Thus, the protophilosopher already agrees completely with the Christian teaching. And not by accident, for if he connected water and spirit, then that would be too profound and too noble for a human to have been able to invent; it is just a "delivery from God" (*a deo traditum*). This exculpation of Thales first acquires its meaning in that the heathen counter-figure Caecilius in the dialogue is, not accidentally, an academic Skeptic and would like to give probability the advantage over truth in every matter; precisely from this philosophical position, he accuses the Christians of wanting to explore the heavenly spaces and the worldly secrets. In addition, he makes recourse to the Thracian maid's formula, "it is sufficient to look before your feet,"[liii] in order to cross over to the formula, by which Socrates answered questions "about celestial matters" (*de caelestibus*)—as

---

5   Tertullian, *De anima*, c. 3. See also: Blumenberg, *Die Legitimität der Neuzeit*, 282ff.
6   Minucius Felix, *Octavius* 19, 4, in Roberts and Donaldson, *Ante-Nicene Fathers*, IV 183. "That same Thales of Miletus said that water was the beginning of things, but that God was that mind which from water formed all things. Ah! a higher and nobler account of water and of spirit than to have ever been discovered by man. It was delivered to him by God. You see that the opinion of this original philosopher absolutely agrees with ours."

Minucius Felix was already so close to Socrates in content: "What is above us is nothing to us" (*Quod supra nos, nihil ad nos*).[7] The advice, which the academic Skeptic gives the Christian, to leave the heavenly objects behind, must be understood just as metaphorically as Octavius' praise of Thales of Miletus for being the first to have concerned himself with heavenly things; to leave those things alone and instead to hold fast to the things in front of his own feet means, according to the Skeptical premise, not to look for truths in things, but to be satisfied with probabilities. It is precisely that premise, however, that the Apologist does not want to let the philosopher get away with because, as an Apologist, Minucius Felix believes that he can offer truths—whose realization was predicted to occur in the end.

It is easy to see how the lines of argumentation in the dialogue *Octavius* cross each other in the use of the expression for "the heavenly" (*caelestia*). Exactly this soft indeterminacy of the object, to which the first philosopher had already turned, Tertullian does not admit. For him, one of the roots of polytheism lies in the deification of the stars. Not the stars themselves, but their maker and mover is the divine; one must consequently investigate the invisible in order to know what the visible is.[8] As evidence that the familiarity with heaven won by Thales was worthless, Tertullian ignores its legendary accomplishment, to predict the arrival of a solar eclipse, and holds up such a darkening of the sun as a divine sign to warn the Roman proconsulate of the African province against persecuting Christians. The special threat of divine rage for the provincial authorities, which had newly set out on the harassment of Christians, mingled with the threat lurking generally around the world of its demise. It was a concern among Christians to announce the indications of God's rage, but also to restrict themselves in their prayer to a provisionally only local influence. Only by that means could enough time be won to construe the prefigurations of world-destroying divine rage in *everything* accurately and punctually.

"You have the astrologers" (*Habetis astrologos*), cries Tertullian with great fanfare to proconsul Scapula. Can his astrologers tell him what the darkening of the sun means on the Day of Judgment in Utica? Unlikely. Tertullian will not rely on established astronomy when he seeks confirmation of a future event that is only known from the Book

---

7   Minucius Felix, *Octavius* 12, 7–13, and 1, in Roberts and Donaldson, *Ante-Nicene Fathers*, IV 179. "Therefore, if you have any wisdom or modesty, cease from prying into the regions of the sky, and the destinies and secrets of the world: it is sufficient to look before your feet."

8   Tertullian, *Adversus nations* II 3 12–15, in ibid., III 132. "Rather it is necessary the more profoundly to investigate what one does not see, in order the better to understand the character of that which is apparent."

of Revelation. Even if today we accept the premise that a visible total eclipse of the sun in Utica on August 14, 212 must have been meant in Revelation, by no means do we then need to presume that Tertullian knew that eclipses arise due to natural laws or that he presumed such knowledge in the addressee of his writing. The addressee should rather ask his astronomers in order to have it confirmed that this occurrence in heaven was extraordinary and, on top of that, to hear the astronomers confess that it was a sign from Heaven.[9] The astronomical normalcy of solar eclipses is neither forgotten nor denied; otherwise the harsh cry to turn to the astronomers would not make sense. Instead, the God of great threats, in keeping with His mercy towards Christians, could also satisfy himself with the smaller threat of such a sign to the world, in lieu of the apocalyptic prefiguration, like the one he had made with the darkening at Jesus' death. Tertullian interprets that event in the manner of Mark's and Matthew's indeterminate account: solely as general darkness (*skotos*), not expressly as solar eclipse as in Luke's version. That could only have been misunderstood by those who did not know the prophecies about Christ; with that knowledge, they would have reported this "world-portent" (*mundi casum*) in their national archive.[10]

---

[9] Tertullian, *Ad Scapulam* III 3, in ibid., III 106. "All these things are signs of God's impending wrath, which we must needs publish and proclaim in every possible way; and in the meanwhile we must pray it may be only local. Sure are *they* to experience it one day in its universal and final form, who interpret otherwise these samples of it. That sun, too in the metropolis of Utica, with light all but extinguished, was a portent which could not have occurred from an ordinary eclipse, situated as the lord of day was in his height and house. You have the astrologers, consult them about it."—On dating the solar eclipse and the fragment "To Scapula," see J. Schmidt, "Ein Beitrag zur Chronologie der Schiften Tertullians und der Prokonsuln von Afrika," in *Rheinisches Museum für Philologie* N.F. XLVI, 1891, 77–98. Schmidt does admit the "possibility of a rhetorical exaggeration" by Tertullian. But although Tertullian successfully dates the eclipse in Utica and thus the text, Schmidt overlooks the fact that Tertullian cannot have intended to predict the ordinary "due date" of the event—if that were the case, everything would have arrived at the goal with an astrological authorization. Let us remember that the Gnostics wanted under no circumstances to consider the star of Bethlehem as an astrological constellation of cosmic inevitability, but rather as a sign of Fate interrupting the cosmic order.

[10] Tertullian, *Apologeticum* 21, 19, in ibid., III 35. "In the same hour, too, the light of day was withdrawn, when the sun at the very time was in his meridian blaze. Those who were not aware that this had been predicated about Christ no doubt thought it an eclipse. You yourselves have the account of the world-portent still in your archives."—On this passage, see: A. Demandt, "Verformungstendenzen in der Überlieferung antiker Sonnen- und Mondfinsternisse," Mainz 1970 (Akademie der Wissenschaften und der Literatur. *Abhandlungen der Geistes- und sozialwissenschaftlichen Klasse*, Jg. 1970 Nr. 7, 19). Demandt does not draw any comparison with *Ad Scapulam* passage c. 4.

Solar eclipses are evidence for Tertullian against the divinity of the stars, on the one hand; for they demonstrate that "the sun too is often put to ... trial."[liv] On the other hand, having pre-determined such darkenings shows that they are no proofs of self-willing power among the heavenly bodies; instead, they must be regarded as "appointed in the way of a law."[11] But then a God still stands over them, a God to whom they are subservient and who can use them against their own lawfulness, in order to give His signs. Thales is in the wrong here, and this time in a higher sense. Against the "normalization" of phenomena in the sky, a process which Thales introduced, Tertullian salvages a repertoire of pre-apocalyptic signs. His God has a powerful rhetoric—after his own image. Tertullian considers divine rhetoric capable of striking fear into Roman state power, so that they let the arm fall, which they lifted against the Christians.

Tertullian alone furnished the Thales anecdote with the variant where it was an Egyptian who laughed when the philosopher fell into the cistern. Rightly did Thales tumble so ignominiously into the well when he examined and traversed all of heaven with his eyes, and he was laughed at forcefully by that Egyptian, who asked Thales, do you still believe that heaven is given for your perception (*Anschauung*) when you cannot see anything distinctly on the earth? Thus Tertullian lets Thales' tumble imagistically characterize the philosophers as those who turn their obtuse curiosity to the things of nature, instead of first to its Creator and guide, and thus they grasp at emptiness.[12] Here the key word "curiositas" occurred, with which a restriction of theory's scope would be erected for the Middle Ages.

How does the Egyptian enter the picture? For a Christian author of the arriving third century—and even for a Tertullian—the change to the treasury of figures cannot be an accident: Egyptians, in the Greek tradition, are representatives of ancient wisdom. Fetching something back from them belonged to the obligatory program of any Greek philosopher's biography. From the position of the Bible, Egyptians are

---

11   Tertullian, *Ad nationes* II 5, 16; II 6, 3, in Roberts and Donaldson, *Ante-Nicene Fathers*, III 134.
12   Tertullian, *Ad nationes* II 4, 18–19, in ibid., III 133. "It therefore served Thales of Miletus quite right, when, star-gazing as he walked with all the eyes he had, he had the mortification of falling into a well, and was unmercifully twitted by an Egyptian, who said to him, 'Is it because you found nothing on earth to look at, that you think you ought to confine your gaze to the sky?' His fall, therefore, is a figurative picture of the philosophers; of those, I mean, who persist in applying their studies to a vain purpose, since they indulge a stupid curiosity on natural objects, which they ought rather (intelligently to direct) to their Creator and Governor."—On this passage, see L. Alfonsi, "Talete e l'Eglizio," in *Rivista di filologia classica*, 28, 1950, 204–22.

certainly representatives of the most despicable form of the idolatry: worshipping animal-shaped idols. The power of Moses and the forty-year desert diet had scarcely sufficed to liberate the world from the fascination with animal idols. Defending Egypt thus always belongs in the argumentation of the philosophers against Christianity. Origen, for instance, tells how his opponent Celsus accused the Christians of laughing unrightfully at the Egyptians and their animal deification, because they did not know the secret teaching associated with them; this cult was, in truth, one of the eternal ideas itself.[13]

Tertullian evidently knows nothing of that; the Egyptians surface in his work in an even more nebulous form than as representatives of animal worship. For Tertullian, they are those who committed the mistake of deifying the stars due to their capacity for self-movement, as "objects moved by themselves" (*"per se mobilia"*). Yet in his variant of the Thales anecdote, the Egyptian, as representative of ancient wisdom for the Greeks, is juxtaposed with the Greek, as typical of a novel impertinence. He does not laugh out of a lack of understanding, but out of better knowledge. The element of a trip to Egypt had been transferred to Thales as well; from thence he should have connected his geometrical and astronomical teachings. Then Tertullian could intend to pit the authority of the teacher against the immaturity of the pupil. The Greek inauguration of theory, in any case, is revealed as nothing but a badly adapted import. By thus denying Greek theory's originality, not only is an all too autonomous accomplishment of human reason shoved earlier in time, but the possibility is also kept open that it had its origin in the same divine revelation from which Moses had drawn. This reversal of the influence and priority relations between the Bible and Greek philosophy plays an important role again and again in Apologetics, and we easily see in retrospect that it ultimately had to do with measuring the scope of reason.

A Thracian woman would have been of no use for Tertullian's purpose because her laughter could not have had a definitive judgment behind it; Tertullian could not use any figure, who watched and mocked the astronomer from the lowly standpoint of realism. Much more, he needed one, who was able to devalue the beginning of philosophy, as defined by the Greeks, "from a higher standpoint."

---

13 Origen, *Contra Celsum* III 19, in ibid., IV 645. Another passage is unclear in its reference: *Contra Celsum* VIII 15: "How comes it, that while so many go about the well, no one goes down into it? Why art thou afraid when thou hast gone so far on the way? Answer: thou art mistaken, for I lack neither courage nor weapons." Celsus summoned a Gnostic source, the *Heavenly Dialogue* by the Ophites, as evidence that the Son of God is not more powerful than God himself (as the Christians had claimed). Why does Origen not go to the source?

The wise Egyptians, from whom travelling Greeks fetched advice and lessons, were, after all, priests, and that is also to be presupposed in the pealing laughter of Tertullian's Egyptian, no matter who his gods may have been and what derogatory things one could say of those gods. If the maid laughed in Plato because Thales seemed to her to have reached too high, then the Egyptian laughs in Tertullian because Thales had not reached high enough. Given its position in the world, the spirit would need to have turned upwards, not downwards into the uncertain: "It were better for one's mind to ascend above the state of the world, not to stoop down to uncertain speculations."[14]

To presume that the Egyptians partook in the divine knowledge of Moses and the patriarchs is not only to claim Truth's exclusive right to revelations; it is also a suggestion about the contents of possessions from a higher origin. Tertullian does not only want to know truths considered in the smaller sense of the state of awareness necessary for salvation, but rather those considered a help for reason's knowledge-seeking about the world. Expressed otherwise: Egyptians and Christians have something in common like a secret science. Measured by that standard, whatever is achievable in Thales' fall seems worthless. Thales' goal becomes especially laughable when we apply two Classical quotations to Epicurus: the first is the statement otherwise attributed to Socrates, that what is above us does not concern us; then, Heraclitus' proposal that the investigation of heaven has yielded nothing but that the size of sun equals the width of a foot. To that Tertullian adds laconically: at this point a lack of ambition reigned, even towards the sky.

Tertullian overlooks the Thracian maid from the Thales anecdote even where she seems to fit undeniably into his conception: as he rejects the Platonism of the soul. Against the metaphysical overextension of Nature's foreignness and the soul's particularity, Tertullian posits an idiosyncratic realism, in which he accepts their subtle materiality—a theory borrowed from the Stoics, where the soul copies the bodily form as ethereal matter; in this way, the difficulties of the dualism of mind and matter are avoided. Above all, though, this makes it imaginable that human beings inherit the damage wrought through sin—which is so indispensible for the history of salvation. In this context, the mention of Thales must be made, who represents the philosophical escalation with his gaze towards heaven, which overlooks what lies before his feet—here the nature of the soul as most personal—and thus falls into

---

14 Tertullian, *Ad nationes* II 4,13–15, in ibid., III 133. "Epicurus, however, who had said, 'What is above us is nothing to us' (*quae super nos, nihil ad nos*) wished notwithstanding to have a peep at the sky, and found the sun to be a foot in diameter. Thus far you must confess men were niggardly (*frugalitas*) in even celestial objects."

the well. The one short sentence has all the impact of which Tertullian is capable: "Such, however, is the enormous preoccupation of the philosophic mind, that it is generally unable to see straight before it. Hence (the story of) Thales falling into the well."[15]

The transformations of the position of the Thracian maid in the anecdote could derive from a harmless deformation, which we get to comprehend right where the denomination of the maid's origin has become her own name. When she is introduced in Hippolytus' *Philosophumena* as "a certain maid, by name Thratta" (*"famula Thratta nomine"*), the corresponding attribute in Plato's text has evidently been misunderstood.[16] This error could have aroused the feeling that simply imparting a name offered too little characterization; thus Hippolytus's contemporary, Tertullian, could have conceived his Egyptian solely in order to amplify the maid's significance. In Hippolytus' work, an immediate link is established between the events of the anecdote, observing heaven and falling down—and his allegation that Gnostic mythology, which he fought, sprung from philosophy and especially from the Greeks' astronomy. The Gnostic speculations are now the equivalent of the distant: they neglect the pursuit of salvation as a consequence of overreaching desires for knowledge.

Where the quotation shrinks to a mere reference (or, better said, where it is *refined* to one) the author must presuppose the reader's familiarity with what is supposed to be awakened in memory. Epochs of compendia and readers, of transmitting simplified elements of knowledge from second- and third-hand sources, promote the consciousness of assured ownership and tend to avoid sources that would unsettle that consciousness anew. Tertullian knows exactly what Platonism is and what a Platonist is, but he does not give the impression that he has ever read a text of Plato's. Asserting this does not imply a disparagement; it could be said for many greats of philosophy, even for Kant. This tendency does have consequences for texts' quality: any refined discussion of the positions represented is invalid due to ignorance of the genuine literature, because only seeming confrontations arise against the doxographical resolutions of the opponent; -isms stand against –isms, as we would say today. With regard to the reception of the Thales anecdote, a degree of familiarity

---

15 Tertullian, *De anima* VI 8, in ibid., III 186.
16 Hippolytus, *Philosophumena* I i, in ibid., V 11: "and a certain maid, by name Thratta, remarked of him derisively that, while intent on knowing things in heaven, he did not know what was at his feet."— In the fifth century, Stobaeus' *Florigium* still shows how the Greek text must have looked, back when Hippolytus misunderstood it: *"therapaina thrâtta oûsa ..."* (ed. C. Gesner, 420).

with the story does still appear in the background, a familiarity which the patristic authors evidently presume by making mere references without reviewing the event for their readers.

As a Syrian, Tatian construes the new opposition between pagans and Christians according to the old model of Greeks and barbarians in his *Speech to the Greeks*. He cultivates barbarian pride against a cultured world, which seems empty and dilapidated to him, whereas he masters their rhetorical toolkit professionally with a sophist's skill. This novelty, the "barbarian philosophy" to which he first found his way at a mature age, combined with his weariness over his own educational experience. That provides an insight for every theory about the occasions for reception: weariness with the given is a stronger motive than attraction to novelty, reaching for which takes even weaker forces of attraction in the case of weariness. For Tatian even this novelty was just an episode in the transition to a radical re-establishment of Gnostic sensibility and one with far more decisive barbarisms. Modern admirers of ancient civilization have paid back this disdainer of ancient values with harsh judgments and called him a "sad original," an "Oriental anti-intellectual," a "wild stylist."[lv]

That would not require mention here, had Tatian not taken on the role of the Thracian maid in his reference to the Thales anecdote. Within the framework of a barbarian tirade against the Greeks, spanning from their language to their poetry all the way to their philosophy, the reference to Thales' mockery by a barbarian woman fits as closely as possible. In addition, Tatian expresses laughter, apparently at those who still clung to Aristotle's doctrine that there is no predicting anything underneath the moon's sphere of movement—a doctrine which becomes even more laughable when the same people (closer to the earth than the moon and lower than its path) play at prediction in the same place where they deny its possibility. Aristotle also deceived when he claimed there is no happiness for those who were denied beauty, wealth, physical strength, and nobility. Here Tatian polemically infers that the cosmic God of philosophy, made into the mover of the heavenly spheres, could mean nothing other than the arbitrariness of humanity's natural conditions for happiness. Tatian's purpose in referring to the Thales anecdote is to notice the lack of concern for the potential happiness of all human beings by the philosopher concerned with heavenly things.

Surprisingly, he goes so far as to incorporate inquiry about God when cursing philosophers for their neglect of human affairs. Falling into the ditch is radicalized from the viewpoint of that "barbarian philosophy:" "While inquiring what God is, you are ignorant of what is in yourselves; and while staring all agape (*kechenotes*) at the sky, you stumble into pitfalls."[17] Throughout this work, reminiscences on readings from heterogeneous origins are put on the same level: "The reading of your books is like walking through a labyrinth, and their readers resembles the cask of the Danaids." With his pleasure at grotesque exaggerations, Tatian belongs to the few authors of the time for whom laughter, even if it is ferocious, at the least ought to be overheard on occasion. For other early Christians, what John Chrysostom had claimed about Jesus was considered exemplary: he never laughed. But did Thales? Was that not rather the privilege of the Thracian maid?

Without names, it cannot always be determined how definitely the anecdote stands in the background at the mention of theory's self-elevation and resulting tumble into the depths. In the case of Irenaeus of Lyons, the issue is with those truth-seekers who still believe that they have can find the truth until they tumble into the hidden ditch of ignorance; evidently, nervous feelings during the search for truth raise the probability of such accidents. Horizontal movement now suffices to enhance the risk.[18] Relations of distance and proximity repeatedly seem to demand the apostrophe to the unnamed Thracian maid and to her criticisms, and calling something near or far (*nah oder fern*) from humanity can be construed as a decision spanning the epochs. What lies before one's feet is still only the metaphor for that which is more internal and closer to the self than it is to itself: "closer than the spirit is to itself," as Bonaventura would say and thereby exceed everything familiar to the Church Fathers including Augustine a millennium later.[lvi]

Augustine had worked on redefining the close at hand. When he promotes reflection on to the concept of *memoria*, he finds that memory and forgetting are not simply antithetical, because there could not have been consciousness of having forgotten otherwise: *memoria* is consciousness of memory itself and of its opposite.

With the application of *memoria* to reason (*ratio*) and will (*voluntas*), not only did Augustine indulge his Trinitarian passion by devising an

---

17   Tatian, *Ad Graecos* II 8–9; XXVI i, in Roberts and Donaldson, *Ante-Nicene Fathers*, II 76.
18   Irenaeus of Lyons, *Adversus haereticos* V 20, 2, in ibid., I 548. "Now, such are all the heretics ... as blind men are led by the blind, they shall fall deservedly into the ditch of ignorance lying in their path, ever seeking and never finding out the truth (*iuste cadent in sublatentem ignorantiae foveam, semper quaerentes, et nunquam verum invenientes*)." The search cannot yet enjoy the advantage of the finding attained only much later. The movement is still the self-sufficient value that yields the "side-benefit" of everything else attained "on the way" along the endless path to the ultimate—which simply does not yet matter or which still promises nothing.

anthropological Ternar,[lvii] but he also thematized a structure that undergirds the intentionality of reason and will; that would not be forgotten about him even by his detractors in the dark Middle Ages. And as he described it: "Certainly, O Lord, I am working hard on it, and my work is being done on myself; I have become unto myself a soil of difficulty, and of too much sweat."[19] Already fully present in that statement is the connection, uncommon in antiquity, between theory and work, reflection and effort, whose rhetoric Husserl would finalize;[lviii] but also present is the play on the biblical sweat of the brow, with which the earth should be worked. Here sweat becomes a metaphor for the close at hand and cries out for the confrontation from the Thales anecdote.

There is no longer any need to speak of a fall, because the self-explorer and self-knower gazes upwards from the depth reached from the standpoint of *memoria*. He already acts within the closest at hand possible and has moved beyond probing heaven's spaces, measuring the distance between the stars, and inquiring about the equilibrium of the earth. He is completely by himself because he stands in the immediacy of self-exposure before his Creator. He does not need to be reminded that he must remember himself and that everything else is at a distance from him: "It is not so astonishing if whatever I am not is far distant from me, but what is nearer to me than myself?"[20] Although closest to himself, if the power of memory traverses beyond this nearness, it cannot be comprehended: "yet I cannot speak of myself without" memory.[lix] Those who desire knowledge, on the other end, are already firmly lodged in the catalogue of vices under the heading of "curiositas."[lx] They can and must fall because they relocated themselves to be under the stars and consider themselves enlightened by the stars; thus they only ever arrive back on earth—which has turned into a metaphor for self-knowledge—at the moment of their fatal fall.

If Augustine is supposed to have killed off ancient philosophy by reformulating the command to know oneself in his own rhetoric, then he may have inaugurated—or at least greatly contributed to—ancient philosophy's notorious uniqueness: even when overcome and ostracized, it never fails to be rediscovered and never lacks a rousing effect. Ultimately, Scholasticism is nothing but a resumption of the interplay

---

19 Augustine, *Confessiones* X 16, 25, in Augustine, *Fathers of the Church, Volume 21*, 284.
20 *Confessiones* X 16, in Augustine, *Fathers of the Church, Volume 21*, 284, V 3,5: "They consider themselves to be exalted as the stars and heavenly bodies. Behold, they are cast down to the earth." Ibid., 105. A propos: *Sermo* 241,3: "Falling just as low as they had been carried aloft in their investigations, they were sunk in the depths, for the greater the height from which an object falls, the more deeply it is submerged." Augustine, *Sermons on the Liturgical Seasons*, 258.

between Christianity, now firmly established, and the antiquity that had been "overcome" a millennium earlier. The enthusiasm with which it was rediscovered and newly recognized derives largely from the intellectual situation of the previous century, of the Dark Age (*saeculum obscurum*). That enthusiasm explains the Scholastic love of overstatement, which increases under the name of "dialectic" and produces the figures of wandering "sophists" and "peripatetics."

With the revival of philosophy in the eleventh century, the conflict reemerges about theoretical behavior's place in the world; with it, the figure of the heaven observer returns. Reactionary theology sees a danger in him, which represents the threat of the dialectician. Moreover, a topic comes to the foreground, whose threat shall surface first in its entirety centuries later: that of divine omnipotence with its destructive potential against rationality—not so much *of* theology as *in* theology. Tertullian had already enlisted this procedure against Scapula, when he marshaled the metaphor of the lawfulness of world events against the divinity of the stars. The heaven watcher has become the representative of the conflict between theology and dialectic, to the extent that the latter insisted on the universality of reason's laws and did not want to treat omnipotence as an exception. The astronomer was the prototype because his theory could never abide by conceding the durability and order of its phenomena to the prerogative of a higher power: it refused to incorporate signs and miracles, acts of omnipotence, into its calculations. Constitutively, astronomy formed itself in an essential connection with a metaphysics, which, even if not derived from admiration of the world's order, still could not surrender that admiration to unfamiliar advice without self-loss. The observer of heaven is not imbued with the thought of divinity's limitless possibilities and cannot be. In this respect, he remains an anthropocentrist.

In light of this conflict, it will no longer appear accidental when the heaven observer's plummet down a well occurs in a tract "On divine omnipotence" from the eleventh century by Peter Damian.[lxi] As in the Aesopian fable, the philosopher remains anonymous; in a new turn, the maid receives a name, Iambe, which puts her in a surprising relationship with the origin of iambic meter and thus of poetry. Iambe had a supporting role in the myth of the earth goddess Demeter, whose daughter by Zeus, Persephone, the underworld god, Hades, had abducted in secret contract with her father and had made into the queen of his shadow kingdom. The inconsolable Demeter tirelessly seeks her missing daughter when she comes upon early humans in the forest, who live by hunting and to whose hospitality it belongs that this very Iambe seeks to cheer Demeter up with funny and taunting verses, whose "iambic" meter is devised on this occasion. At the very least, iambic meter proves its value at this point, since, according to

Pausanias' report, Demeter thanks these primordial humans with the gift of grain, through which they turn from hunters into sedentary farmers. In a variant version, Iambe belongs to the founding myth of the mysteries of Eleusis, in whose royal court Demeter takes respite; there the serving girl Iambe's poetry makes her smile and even brings her to laughter. The founding myth refers to the cultic function of poetry to assuage the raging divinity, even through whimsy like Iambe had mastered. The barbarian maid's mockery at the Milesian cistern is moved over into art when the one who remained nameless for so long—with the exception of Hippolytus' false attribution—is called by the name of Iambe and thus poetically combines mockery and consolation.

The way in which the astronomer figures into this tract about omnipotence results from a special quality, which involves the relationship of omnipotence to time. The astronomer works over time and especially with the future; for him, the past is the absolute limit of omnipotence, which cannot make undone what is once done. Questioning any capacity of the Omnipotent Being is an irritation for theology indeed as soon as it is spoken; moreover, time belongs to created nature and its order cannot be an impediment to the divine will. The astronomer of the fable is the metaphor for the objection that philosophy takes with the unlimitedness of omnipotence over time. For the theologian, the philosopher is more unknowing than ever when he understands that which he admires and studies as a law and not as reason's obedience.

Damian forces dialectic, as a mere way with words (*ars verborum*), into an irreconcilable opposition with divine power (*virtus divina*) as the true reality. Even the principle of contradiction, for him, belongs in the realm of matters that only emerge through the means of language and remain confined to the lawfulness of language, because such matters rely on the temporal condition of simultaneity, inexorable within language. The concept of time renders the link to human arrogance—which is represented by the philosopher who conducts astronomy and falls into the slimy well (*in limosum repente lapsus est puteum*)—beyond the ancient grotesquery of foreignness to the world, which took on traits of prostration by someone possessed by a spirit. The figure of the maid is raised to unique dignity, since she does not just mock and laugh, but rather poetically articulates (*poetata est*) the misfortune of her master and the lesson to learn from it. If the female inventor of poetic meter is thus ranked against the inventor of philosophy, we might attribute this to an unknown tradition, but we must, above all, understand that he no longer judges the woman as a fool across from the philosopher, but rather in the image of the "*idiota.*"[lxii] Her new traits give urgency and credibility to her warning that sacrilegious efforts to access the secrets of heaven through investigation violate the measure

(*Maß*) of the human power to comprehend: "My master did not know what was under his feet and fell into some foul mud, as he was trying to investigate the secrets of the heavens."[21] The author of that tract against dialectic in support of omnipotence employed the Thales anecdote in another context. In a missive to Archbishop Andreas, Cardinal Peter Damian complains about the coarse and libelous use of his own statements from the pulpit. Here, he claims, one must proceed by vulgar means (*rustice*). In order to dramatize the situation, he gives an adorned version of the philosopher's tumble: as some philosopher carefully observed the paths of the planets and the course of the stars at night, he fell by accident into a ditch, which, as Damian says, yawned enormously deep and stank of disgusting muck. Now this philosopher had a house maid named Iambe, who frankly and skillfully (*libere ac prudenter*) assaulted her master in iambic verse (which would later be named after her), and she said the following about him, which deserves applause (*plausibiliter*): "'My master,' she said, 'did not know the filth lying under his feet, as he tried to learn about the stars.'"[22] This application, which draws on the scene drastically intensified by the contrast between filth and stars, is alien and uniquely ambiguous; with the transition to the statement that such a thing could happen "even in our times," it looks as if the maid's lack of understanding has come up against the philosopher's high aspirations, although she had just been praised. What the correspondent seizes on, in a crude turn, is the theology of the unknowing, of those *rustici* who have hardly learned anything else but how to till the land, to watch over pigs and over grazing animals' fold yards. They do not hesitate to dispute about the Holy Scripture on streets and intersections in front of wenches and fellow plebeians. As degrading as it is to say it, they would spend the whole night between wenches' thighs and not be ashamed during the day to deal with the conversations of angels and to decide in this way about the proclamations of holy teachers. In exhibiting such beautiful neighbor love towards the abusers of pearls from his sermons, the Cardinal lost sight of the anecdote's structure. He still owes his addressee an account of how he wishes to have the collapse of the philosopher be understood as comparable with the self-overestimation of those who believe that

---

21 Pietro Damiani, *De divina omnipotentia*, c. 12 (Migne, patrologia latina CXLV 615): "They pay attention to things beyond the extent of their capacities, and they are bursting with arrogance to discover what is above them" (my translation).

22 Pietro Damiani, *Epistola* V 1 (Migne, Partologia latina CXLIV 336 sq.): "Dominus, inquit, meus ignorabat stercora, quae sub euis pedibus errant, et nosse tentabat sidera."

they are allowed to rise to angels' conversations after their lowly days' and nights' work. The reader shall not at all be able to avoid equating the writer's pilfered rhetorical gems with the preciousness of illicitly overheard heavenly conversations. This language of the letter is one of a harsh theology, as has repeatedly been spoken in the Christian tradition, where the distance between the world and God shall appear so hopeless that it can neither be traversed by falling nor by elevating oneself.

In both uses of the anecdote, its disfigurement is recognizable. For the indeterminate secrets of heaven, to which the movement of the stars only stands in the foreground, the earthly is not confronted as the reality close at hand and belonging to life-skills, but rather the lowly muck, into which he falls, who does not declare himself satisfied with the offer in the Revelation. The well comes to resemble the pit of sin, and not without reason (*Grund*), since the sky explorer's theory has been written up in the catalogue of vices as curiosity. Then, in light of the repellant circumstances of the sinner's fall, the figure of the maid appears particularly excessive with her lyric. Lacking a precise function in the anecdote, she gains that of poetic invention in order to keep her role at all. It becomes clear how heterogeneous this is when one considers that crediting a poetic meter with her name does not make her into the saintly figure who could then present the true contrast to the philosopher who fell in the filth.

Six Astrological Predominance

The most important change that medieval reception tends to make to the Thales anecdote is the introduction of an astrology reference. This reference is not a matter of the label for the stargazer's profession; despite the differentiation declared by Peter of Spain, the Middle Ages apply the terms "astrology" and "astronomy" synonymously in most cases. Practicing the latter art became the precondition for the former ability. Formerly the astronomer was the figure for depraved curiosity, for whom objects at a spatial distance distorted his relationship to those in earthly proximity, but that figure became the astrologer in the specific sense: someone who penetrates the future's distance, reserved for divine wisdom and foresight, and therefore appears baffled in his contact with realities in temporal proximity to his present time. Temporal futurity substitutes for spatial distance as the negatively marked direction, a change which appears on first glance to signify intensified derision towards that figure within the Christian system; however, a further analysis of the epoch's characteristics reveals that not to be the case. Tolerance towards astrology expressed an ineradicable need, whose gratification was determined by nature's libidinous underground. There was greater tolerance towards astrology than towards the purely theoretical urge, which had come to be seen as arrogance and as alienation from the elementary concerns of human beings (*Daseinsbesorgnisse*). Sometimes, when the Thales anecdote does turn against astrology, the transition from astronomy's spatial reference to astrology's temporal one only emerges in the "moral" of the story, appended in the style of fables.

One example is the version from Venice of 1520 printed in Gaspar Schober's fable collection: the nameless astronomer is found in the well by a likewise nameless pedestrian, who hears his cries for help, and the Aesopian allegation is imparted: "He said, 'Hey! You endeavor to perceive what is in the sky, and you cannot discern what is on Earth, not even near your feet.'"[1] After this ancient moral comes the new lesson to draw from

---

1   *Aespoi Phrygis Fabulae* CCVIII e Graeco in Latinum conversae, Venetiis 1520.

the fable: that most people claim to know the future right when they do not know what is happening in the present: "The fable contains a hint for the many who claim to know the future while ignorant of the present."

Plato's version of the Thales anecdote gained influence later than the Aesopian fable and also later than the version by Diogenes Laertius, whose work was already extant in Latin translation in the twelfth century and determined ancient philosophy's image along with Augustine and Cicero. Already before the middle of the fourteenth century, Walter Burley, the "clear and transparent teacher" (*doctor planus et perspicuus*), transmitted a version of the anecdote in his history of the philosophers' lives and lifestyles first published in 1472 in Cologne and then in many editions afterwards; that version tells the tragedy of the philosopher who was blinded after being led out of his house by an old lady.² The old lady advised him to let his misfortune convey the insight that the theoretical urge reaches its limits in time rather than space—rather through age and the loss of sight than through its objects' mere unattainability. As an opponent to the nominalists, the old lady warns philosophers, more to convince than to deride; this may have worked as an admonition that such a desire to know was incompatible with the finitude of life. For in the future's lap there still lies an idea of method, which will make theory's program invulnerable against the disappearance of the individuals who conduct it.

Walter Burley's *On the Lives and Deaths of the Philosophers* also found its way into German.[lxiii] We must recall how starkly such a depiction of the philosophers contrasted with the characteristic impersonality, even facelessness, of Scholastic theory production, in order for us to imagine both the interest in the wealth of anecdotes and its influence on the concept of philosophy in the following centuries. In Hans Lobenzweig's version from the mid-fifteenth century, the Thales anecdote reads unusually: "One time, [Thales] left his house at night and wanted to watch the stars, when he fell into a wolf pit (*wolfsgruebenn*). There he screamed and cried. There came an old woman and said: 'Dear Thales,

---

Fab. XIII: De Astrologo et viatore. "The observer is knowledgeable about the stars and heavenly bodies, and he spends his days and the beginning of his nights investigating them diligently ..." (my translation).

2   Walter Burleigh, *De vita et moribus philosophorum*, ed. H. Knust, Tübingen, 1886, 6. "And it is said of him that at night he would be escorted out of the house by an elderly woman (*vetula*) in order to watch the stars. He fell into a ditch (*foveam*), and as he was moaning, the elderly woman said: 'O Thales, you certainly cannot see what is before your feet. How can you identify (*agnoscere*) what is in the sky?'"—German versions from the late Middle Ages: R. Wedler, Walter Burleys 'Liber de vita et moribus philosophorum poetarumque veterum' in zwei deutschen Bearbeitungen des Spätmittelalters. Heidelberg, 1969 (Phil. Diss.) (my translation).

you want to see what is in the sky. Why did the firmament not also show you the wolf pit before your feet?'" The transition to the following statement from the threefold thanks by Thales is charmingly procured with the expression: "Thales thanked his fortune," which we can relate to the previous scene and to the following sentiment. The three privileges worthy of gratitude are: having become a human and not an animal, a boy and not a wench: "thirdly, that he was born a Greek and not a German." Moreover, the untranslated *"barbarus"* from the original is left to the side; Lobenzweig "Germanized" it. His rendition of the oil-press story also deserves attention: "Thales was very poor when, out of his great love of wisdom, he did not want to have the prosperity that he considered inferior to the good. Thus he was heckled from all sides. And the people said that his art was useless." That is his paraphrase of the opening situation. Thales contemplated "how he would bring his hecklers to shame forever." The stars do not promise him just a fat oil harvest for the next year, but something beyond that, which would not be inserted into the story anywhere else: "and afterwards for a long time, no more oil shall come." For the first time, the philosopher's triumph through public demonstration comes from a long-term speculation: with such trickery, he put a lot of pennies together, showed the money to the hecklers, and said: "Wisdom is useful. A wise man becomes rich when he wants to, but wisdom is nobler than property. Therefore I have selected learning and wisdom."

Chaucer enlisted the anonymous fable in *Canterbury Tales* for an attack on astrology. The knight's narrative, with its anachronistic mixture of ancient and courtly elements, makes a burlesque contrast with the story that it follows about the drunken miller who follows the pilgrim group. The story is about an Oxford carpenter and his very young wife, who have rented a room in their house out to a student—with the inevitable consequences. The poor student, called the "fine Nicolas" (*heende Nicolas*), does not just distinguish himself through his weakness for secret love affairs, but also through passion for astrology. With the laboratory of almagest, astrolabe, and mechanical calculator, which he maintains in his attic room, he promises himself and others answers to every possible question. The amorous and the astrological element get artfully interwoven in accordance with the motto of the prologue: "A husband should not be inquisitive about God's secrets or his wife's. So long as he finds God's plenty there, he should not ask questions about the rest."[lxiv] The motif of *curiositas* presents eroticism and astrology parallel with one another, making the astrologer the doppelgänger of the erotic hero. For the student, the halo of his clairvoyance helps him huckster the prognosis of a second Deluge to the carpenter. The skillful performance of an astrologer, who stands transfixed as he watches the apocalyptic signs from heaven, awakens fears in the simple mind of the carpenter, fears which he articulates through the story of the ancient astronomer and his tumble:

> I always thought this would happen! Men should not pry into God's secrets; yea, ever blessed is the ignorant man who knows only his creed! It happened like this to another cleric who practiced astrology. He walked in the fields in order to determine future events by gazing at the stars, and he fell into a fertilizer pit; he didn't see that.[3]

The carpenter is another *idiota*. He is in the right when he predicts the outcome of Nicolas' astrological trick. Despite his gullibility towards what is preached to him, he is a representative, like Plato's maid, of a realism free from illusory perspectives. For reality is what can be ignored, on the one hand, but what then returns as inescapable all the more painfully. The condition for our ability to observe heaven is the earth under our feet.

The image of the star observer who falls in the well might have appeared too harmless, too private, too idyllic to illustrate the arrogance of the astrologer who wants to see the future. This is understood when Icarus' crash from his flight near the sun procures the appropriate image in André Alciato's emblems: "Icarus falls down into the sea by raising himself too high. Whoever wants to master Heaven is too full of presumption. According to this fable, the astrologers should beware, lest their overweening investigations take them where God brings rogues."[4] Only the unhappy father Daedalus sees what happens;

---

3 Chaucer, *Canterbury Tales*, 71. In the original:
   I thought ay wel how that it schulde be!
   Men schulde not know of Goddes pryvety.
   Ye, blessed be alwey a lewed man,
   That nat but oonly his bileeve can!
   So ferde another clerk with astronomye;
   He walked in the feeldes for to prye
   Up-on the sterres, what ther schulde bifalle,
   Til he was in a marle pit i-falle;
   He saugh nat that. Chaucer, *The Canterbury Tales of Geoffrey Chaucer*, 138.
4 *Les Emblemes de Maistre Andre Alciat*. Paris 1542. 116 sq.: LIII.
   Icarus cheut dedans la mer
   Par trop grande exaltation:
   Cil qui ueult le ceil entamer,
   Est trop plain de presumption:
   Doncques sur ceste fiction,
   Doibuent garder les astrologues,
   Que leur haulte discußion,
   Les mette ou dieu reduit tous rogues.

no unaffected or mocking spectator would be commensurate to the demonic yearning and the deathly image. This is a matter of cursedness (*Unheil*), not misfortune (*Unglück*). Alciato seeks the same effect when he alters Aesop's fable of the bird catcher and the viper; that fable also mentions the astrologer who overlooks present danger on earth as he scrutinizes heavenly objects and studies their significance for the future.

The transmission of the story about the heaven watcher's plummet noticeably separates into two types: one type stigmatizes metaphysical overreaching, and another deals with the realist–moralist contrast. The sin of desiring knowledge ends in a different dimension than the offense against the rules of everyday temperance. The return of the anonymous passerby from the Aesopian tradition or of the maid from the Platonic one is primarily an indicator that the theologically reprehensible has been traced back to the realistically and morally inadvisable. This is the case when Guicciardini begins the story with the moral: researchers who study the future almost never comprehend anything about the present.[5] He is not so much defaming something reprehensible as offering a maxim for prudent deliberation in the face of our restricted access to the world, where we must decide for this or that option, since we cannot have both as one person. Moreover, well-intended lectures about human nature tend to be accorded increasing validity in this period, and universal validity can only be had at the expense of content, which "morality" (*abfabulatio*) levels into mere platitude: "This can be applied to those who gloat of their absurd deeds without being able to do the things people do normally."[6] Thales' name even appears in collections that expressly claim the title *Aesop's Fables*.[7]

---

5 Francesco Guicciardini, *Detti et fatti piacevoli et gravi di diversi principi, filosofi, et cortigiani*. Venedig, 1566, 27: "Those who profess to know the future are almost always ignorant of the present. An astrologer (*astrologo*) fell into a pit (*fossa*), while contemplating and eyeing the sky. When his wife (*la moglie*) saw him, she said, 'this all went very well since you wanted to see and to know what is in Heaven, and you did not see and do not know how to walk on your feet'" (my translation).

6 I. N. Neveletus, *Mythologia Aesopica*. Frankfurt, 1610, 226, is a dual language text that does not mention Thales' name: "An astrologer (*astrologus*) was of the habit of leaving in the evening to observe the stars. At some point when he had gone to the suburb and had all of his spirit intent (*intentus*) on the sky, he fell down unwittingly into a well (*puteum*). Some passerby (*praeteriens aliquis*) heard the sound of his voice sighing earnestly and screaming. And he confirmed his understanding of what had happened, 'You were undertaking to see inside the sky; you just did not see what was on the earth.' The 'moral' (*adfabulatio*) is very non-specific: 'For those who stand out by gloating at their absurd deeds, and who cannot do what people do normally (*obuia*)'" (my translation).

7 C. Barth, *Fabularum Aesopiarum* libri V. Frankfurt,1623, 49: XIII. Thales. "As he

Astrological Predominance   51

It is obvious how the story about the astronomer's plummet coincides with skepticism: risky, fruitless overreaching for truth is illustrated and shown to carry disastrous consequences. The Middle Ages, although in possession of at least one translation of Sextus Empiricus, took little interest in doubt; when truths were literally "summarized" (*summieren*) like an inventory of possessions, it is not obvious to ask the question of whether truth itself is attainable or compatible with human nature, whether we might not live more calmly with less certainty. Furthermore, no one will be able to say that the turn away from the Middle Ages bore predominantly skeptical traits: indeed, Descartes is no thorough skeptic because he already knows what certainty he stands to gain when he takes on the horrors of the most pervasive doubt. Only his provisional morality—although it maintains the promise of future definiteness—participates in that type of skeptical satisfaction with what is reliably present as probable, normal, and reputable.[lxv]

The moralistic movement is saturated in skepticism from its beginning; it no longer observes the human as a utterly well-conceived, privileged creature. Reason becomes restraint. Remnant medieval forms of doubt about science of the Scholastic type are Nicolas of Cusa's revival of the *Idiota* and the justifications of magic as a form of resignation towards theory. Magic is the subversive exploitation of the human's privileged position in the universe, of his participation in the elements and stars, of his attribute as microcosm in the macrocosm.

Magic attempts to undermine nature's regularities, and how closely that relates to skeptical resignation can be detected in Agrippa of Nettesheim's satire "On the uncertainty and vanity of the sciences" from 1527. Criticism of scholarship almost always was and remains a domain of scholarship. An argument is raised, which contains the hidden motivation of the idea of method—which becomes the core of the modern problematic a century later—in that it rigorously dispenses

---

camped outside with the stars above, he drives after their starry paths. Thales fell down backwards in an open pond (*lacu patente*), and there almost came to ruin. 'How clumsy!' [someone] said, 'you take pains to see the heavens, and cannot see the earth.'" The moral uses the formula: "Celestial thinking often drives us away from understanding ourselves" (my translation; see original below).

In asta dum superna totus excubat
Viasque siderum exigit.
Lacu patente ponè decidit, Thales,
Ibique penè perditus,
Inepte dixit, et polos dein studes
Videre, non potens humum.
Superna saepè cogitatio catos
Scientiâ exigit sui.

with the medieval expectation of achieving the attainable whole of knowledge: the disproportion between knowledge's demand for time and life's propriety over time.[8]

But astronomy and astrology, theory and occult wisdom, part ways precisely over this dilemma. Although astrology depends on the reliability of astronomy, time never grows short for the astrologer; he is the master of time. Agrippa understands astrology as interpreting the sky's effects and thereby smashing apart confusions in astronomy about cycles and epicycles, which are consequences of theory's inability to catch up with its object in time. He has been acquainted with astrological practices since childhood, but has known for as long that "the whole art had no other foundation than the mere figments and trifles of imagination: and it very much repents me of the time which I have wasted, and I wish I could absolutely forget and abolish the memory thereof in my mind."[9] The only difference between astrologers and poets is supposedly that they do not share an opinion about the morning and evening star; the poets would insist on letting both morning and evening star rise on one and the same day. For that, they too met with trouble, according to Agrippa, since unlike the astrologers, who could get rich with their art, poets suffered hunger and anxiety from theirs.

What is expressed here—almost simultaneously with the first draft of Copernicus' system modification, with the same pathos, and with nearly the same formulations—is reproach towards others' confusion about heaven, which they evoke through constructions that are unnatural and unworthy of the divine Creator's objects, through "the Fiddle-faddles and Trifles of Mathematicians, taking their beginnings from corrupt Philosophy and the fables of the Poets."[lxvi] That is how astrology builds a false connection between heaven and earth. It presents itself in the form of the ancient theorist from the anecdote, which is taken up with double attribution to the masters of the Ionian School: "These Astronomers a Serving-maid of Anaximenes very reasonably tax'd with a sharp reply. The Maid was wont to walk with her Master, who one day going out a little later than ordinary to look upon the Sky, while he was gazing among the Stars ne're minding the scituation of the place, fell into a Ditch. Then quoth the Maid, I wonder Sir how you can pretend to foreknow things in Heaven, that cannot

---

8   Agrippa of Nettesheim, *The Vanity of Arts and Sciences*, 6. "The knowledge of all Sciences is so difficult, if I may not say impossible, that the age of Man will not suffice to learn the perfection of one Art as it ought to be."
9   Agrippa, *Declamatio*, XXX *De astronomia* in Ibid., 87 (German translation by F. Mauthner, Munich, 1913, 116–23; Mauthner uses an old translation: Cologne, 1713).

tell those things that are just before your Nose?"[lxvii] The transference of the story onto Anaximenes is otherwise unknown; its genuine attribution to Thales by Plato follows immediately: "Thales Milesius was reprehended with a like witty saying by his Maid-servant Thressa."[lxviii] Cicero supposedly makes almost the same point; and Agrippa knows about it from life experience: "I myself learnt this art from my parents."

This variant of the tradition is dear to us because it borders so closely on Copernicus. Not only the date, but the subject matter, since what Agrippa disregards and scorns is not so much the astrologers' excessive zeal to see the future as their "careless curiosity"—their initiated action, "as if they had just recently fallen down from the sky and had been there for a long time"—that is to say, he sees their art's constitutive befuddlement as concomitant with astronomy's monstrous degeneration and sees astrology as the demise of astronomy. It is evident that he still would not give astrology a chance, if that were not the case; but the stronger argument against it is that no good wisdom for human needs can be built on top of a bad theory.

Authors who take up the encyclopedic task show the least consideration as they transmit the story's content. A nice example occurs in Sebastian Franck's *Chronicles* from 1536. Here the anecdote is equipped with every transmitted fact available about Thales as one of the seven Greek wise men; presented on the same level with the preciously Christianized statement, "the world was haunted and full of devils" (*geseilet und voll teüfel*).[10] The anecdote is then delivered in accordance with Diogenes Laertius' version, but it pulls an inconsistent element out of Plato's version: that the old woman makes her statement while "laughing," which makes little sense in the tragic revision of the scene. It speaks against esteeming encyclopedic and chronologistic works any more highly in reception histories that they almost completely give up on determining the context of the very element that reception history seeks to observe. In the case of Franck's *Chronicles*, as a result of the slackened context, there is hardly any further insight to win. Such widespread and widely utilized "handbooks" must still be considered reception events, for their part, albeit ones with uncontrolled material.

---

10 Sebastian Franck, *Chronica Zeitbuch und Geschichtlibell*, 1536 (Ndr. Darmstadt, 1969), 28 (my translation).

Seven   Applause and Reproach from the Moralists[lxix]

Montaigne created a distinctive variant of the Thales anecdote, which broke from the atomistic transmission of fables and emblems, so that he could fit it consistently within the genre of his *Essais*. Plato's maid has now crossed over from berating Thales verbally after the fact to helping instigate the philosopher's plummet. Plato's skeptical successor shows himself agreeing with her duplicity:

> I have always felt grateful to that girl from Miletus who, seeing the local philosopher Thales with his eyes staring upwards, constantly occupied in contemplating the vault of heaven, made him trip over, to warn him that it was time enough to occupy his thoughts with things above the clouds when he had accounted for everything lying before his feet. It was certainly good advice she gave him, to study himself rather than the sky ...[1]

Here it looks as if Montaigne too wants to set up the alternative between studying nature and knowing oneself; for him, however, the futility of astronomical exertions are only the paradigm for skeptical resignation towards every kind of truth. Our human peculiarity includes understanding that what we hold in our hands lies beyond our grasp and above the clouds, just like our knowledge of the stars.[2] Astronomy is

---

1   Montaigne, *The Essays of Michel de Montaigne*, 604 (*Essais* II 12, ed. Didot, 274 AB): "Ie scay bon gré à la garse milesienne qui voyant le philosophe Thales s'amuser continuellement à la contemplation de la voulte celeste, et tenir tousiours les yeulx eslevez contremont, lui meit en son passage quelque chose à le faire bruncher, pour l'advertir qu'il seroit temps d'amuser son pensement aux choses qui estoient dans les nues, quand il auroit prouveu à celles qui estoient à ses pieds: elle lui conseilloit certes bien de regarder plutost à soy qu'au ciel ..."
2   Ibid. "But in fact the human condition is such that, where our understanding is concerned, the things we hold in our hands are as far above the clouds as the heavenly bodies are!"

Applause and Reproach from the Moralists 55

no longer the epitome of an overshooting curiosity, which one only needed to relinquish in order to gain the ability to turn one's attention to a realm that promised more than hypotheses and assumptions: the nearby. That message of the Thales anecdote is misleading. The maid's attendant has good intentions, and the maid does not even laugh any more. Yet her realism is not that of the moralist who sees—prefigured in the form of the astronomer—that even self-knowledge is hopelessness. The study of the sky is not the exception to the situation of human knowledge, there is no near-transcendence of the far off; it is normal with the human situation regarding an unknown nature. Even he remains unknown to himself, however much literarily authenticated self-knowledge the moralist might acquire.

It is immediately informative for understanding this standpoint of Montaigne's that he can hold astronomy and medicine—as disciplines of the farthest (*Fernstliegenden*) and of the nearest (*Nächstliegenden*)—to the same criterion. For both, the object of their toil is unattainable, whether outward or inward. It offers no advantage to reason to be the object oneself which is also supposed to be given over to reason.

The philosopher should only stumble, not fall; and certainly not into a well, for that has completely disappeared from the story. In lieu of *Schadenfreude*, the somewhat obtuse—perhaps owing to a loss for words—reproach emerges: to try it first with easier matters. We notice clearly that Montaigne undertakes these changes so that he can still agree with the maid. Among the changes belongs the most important virtue of the moralist: timeliness of intervention.

Here medicine enters the picture and removes all possibility of misunderstanding what Montaigne could have meant by taking sides with the maid's procedure. The danger of both disciplines lies in doing what would characterize any thinking as philosophy, taken in its broadest sense: supplying fictions for irresolvable problems. Philosophy supposedly offers us nothing that is, not even what it believes to be, but rather whatever it contrives for the sake of appearance and pleasure: "Certainly, philosophy is poetry adulterated by Sophists."[lxx] The philosopher would be greatly deceived if he thought philosophy had mastered even one single object properly and in correspondence with its essence; and when he departs the earth, he will leave behind ignorance even greater than his own was. This conclusion he reaches about philosophy also goes for our knowledge of humanity's closest concerns (*was… am nächsten liegt*), our own selves and our bodies:

> Philosophy does not only impose her ropes, wheels and contrivances on to the high heavens. Just think for a while what she says about the way we humans are constructed. For our tiny bodies she has forged as many retrogradations, trepidations,

conjunctions, recessions and revolutions as she has for the stars and the planets.³

Montaigne both mourns and mocks the helpless state of medical knowledge of the human body. The limits of medicine also present him with the surest indication that knowledge of the world—of the whole and of the part that humans represent—is a hopeless undertaking, so that the starry sky's inaccessibility only repeats itself in our close range knowledge. Rejecting cosmology for its complications is therefore not identical with realism that focuses on the earth. Despite expressly evoking Socrates, no reference is implied to the Socratic turn towards questions about human nature:

> As Socrates says in Plato, you can make against anyone concerned with Philosophy exactly the same reproach as that woman made against Thales: he fails to see what lies before his feet. No philosopher understands his neighbor's actions nor even his own; he does not even know what either of them is in himself, beast or Man.[lxxi]

Here Montaigne is not referring to the figure of Socrates who asks different questions than Anaxagoras had asked, but rather to the Socrates who claimed to know that he knew nothing. Knowing nothing became all the more difficult once the world around us started believing it knew so much when in fact it had just begun to make gains in knowledge that could be hoped to endure; such gains could still only be measured against the first glimpses of an unknown land.

At another point Montaigne quotes from Diogenes Laertius that Thales responded to the question, "What is hard?" with the answer, "To know oneself."⁴ This assertion, supposed to be historically plausible for the founder of natural philosophy, could only have meant that he devoted himself to observing the sky because another knowledge, that of himself, was too hard for him. That sounds exactly like someone revising history in one's own image by insisting on positing self-knowledge as *the* topic for philosophy precisely in opposition to branching out to natural philosophy—and by insisting that *he* could achieve self-knowledge. Montaigne recommends drawing the opposite consequence from Thales' statement: that he wanted to call knowledge of human nature hard, while claiming that the knowledge

---

3   Montaigne, *The Essays of Michel de Montaigne*, 603.
4   Ibid., 628. "When Thales reckons that a knowledge (*cognoissance*) of Man is very hard to acquire, he is telling him that knowledge of anything else is impossible."

of everything else is simply impossible. Then, the task ahead of him consisted in the program of combining skepticism and moralism: we do not need to know anything, but we do have to know a little about human nature lest we come to ruin.

Montaigne is not a dogmatic skeptic.[lxxii] Not once does he come near the thought that everything might be purposefully designed to rebuff humanity's knowledge-hungry nature by exiling humans in the realm of their illusions about the world. Likelier to him (*liegt ihm ... nahe*) is the thought of a merciful sheltering from the abysses of natural secrets: if we knew what we longed to know, it would hardly sit well with us. Nature favors humanity by denying its most insistent wish. It would be a cheap modernization of Montaigne to have him predict or even imagine what consequences and implications knowledge about the natural world would have in store within a few centuries. His foundational thought is rather that of economizing the short and precious lifespan: not using it on second-rate goals and pursuits.

Because he is no dogmatic skeptic, he does not let the stargazer plummet into the abyss. Because all knowledge appears only arbitrary and incidental due to his skepticism, which removes him from every linear procedure, his sympathy goes out to the maid's intercession, as she just lets the philosopher stumble with a little trick and interrupts his concentration on his work to remind him of something else. Carefully conducted mischief, not a prank that evokes metaphysics and conflicts over gods. For: "human understanding in its strivings to plumb the depths of everything and to give an account of it, destroys itself, just as we ourselves, tired and exhausted by life's long race, fall back into childishness."[5]

Even before theory could programmatically settle on a method, Montaigne would have advised humanity against endowing theory with independence by crafting a method that would apply to all of the lives under its purview. In place of the theoretical seeker, he places a "new character" (*nouvelle figure*): that of a demurring, patiently attentive sage, "a chance philosopher, and not a premeditated one!" (*philosophe imprémédité et fortuite*).[6] Truth, if there should be any, can only come from life already lived, not from life turned into an instrument for truth—as the *Essais* themselves show. Philosophy does not preempt life, does not form it with norms, but descends from it like a fruit. That beginning of all things theoretical was therefore justly disrupted, if not even prevented.

The realist regarding the finitude of individual life has the Milesian maid see as well what he himself finds awry (*unheimlich*) in the

---

5   Ibid., 626.
6   Ibid., 614.

rigorous discipline of the sky watcher: the beginning of a history where theorists are forced away from the object of their theory into a wide-cast toil overextended to span all lifetimes; whoever completes the portion of work they can do for this project must forego its benefits. This insight was still foreign indeed to the ancient sky watcher. It first emerges from the vantage point of an astronomy that already has access to recorded data by which it can measure its hypotheses. Astronomers thus benefit from the pioneers of a future knowledge and reject them. That is not yet the form of skeptical abstention that Montaigne recommends for elevating the value of individual life in its incomparability, which he brings to the formula: it is all about exposing humanity to itself, that is, exposing our reason to our reason.[7]

A century after Montaigne, La Fontaine took up the Aesopian fable in the first part of his collection. It stands out for being strikingly out of place among the other fables. As an explanation for its erratic placement, one scholar has suggested that the great comet of the winter 1664–5 was the contemporary occasion for an attack on astrology, since it roused the interest in star interpretation among a broad public and the susceptibility to charlatanry.[8] Despite the winter chill, the streets and plazas of Paris at night were packed with people who wanted to see the spectacle of the heavenly body. An almost automatic connection was made to political events of the day, especially the trial against Foucquet and its possible outcome.[lxxiii] It was an instruction on how to see (*Anschauungsunterricht*) what the new science could procure for reason's benefit: once again the sky could manifest itself unimpeded as the canvas for the great sign.

Theorists at that point had not yet suspected this comet of drawing a consistent path around the sun and thus of lacking any role in the course of history. As soon as 1682, Halley would summon evidence that this year's comet was identical with the one from 1607, 1531, and 1456 and returned along its path. In Halley's *Cometographia* of 1705, the appearance of the same comet in 1758 was predicted and its meaning as a sign was destroyed along with its every relevance to human fear. It was reason repeating its achievement of predicting a solar eclipse, an achievement initially connected to the name of Thales. Shortly after reason's optimism had taken its hardest blow from nature with the earthquake in Lisbon of 1755, the announced arrival of the comet in

---

7   Ibid., 628. "This suffices to demonstrate that Man has no more knowledge of his own body than of his soul. We have shown Man to himself—and his reason to his reason, to see what it has to tell us. I have succeeded in showing, I think, how far reason is from understanding even itself."

8   Jasinski, *La Fontaine et Le Premier Recueil Des "Fables,"* 359–65.

the sky emerged as the triumph of that same reason and took on the name "Halley's."

La Fontaine—known as the tree that fables grow on—could not yet know in 1668, when he published the first issue of his collection, that these discoveries would neutralize the sensitivity to signs from heaven. The "moral" of his astrologer fable was ahead of its time in striving to demystify the putative signs from Heaven. The success of this effort must not have met his expectations. At the arrival of the next comet, whose adherence to scientific law Halley demonstrated in 1682, it was evidently necessary to make a royal edict denying right of residency in France to all persons who engaged in astrology and clairvoyant predictions. This was not just a matter of craft fairs or swap meets, as shown by the fact that even the statutes of the Academy of Sciences had to explicitly forbid their members from including astrology among their objects of inquiry.

La Fontaine's quatrain, which presents the fable laconically, reads like the explanation of an emblem only showing the result of an accident that occurred "one day:" an astrologer at the bottom of a well. It is a faceless and genderless "moral" that speaks to him like a banner hanging over the scene: "Poor dog, you cannot even see what's in front of your feet and you think of reading what is over your head?"[9] This plain story is not applied to the astrologer in the well and his trade; the contemporary charlatan, who had edged his way into the courts and academies, did not lend himself to comparison with a figure lacking realism. The target is the majority of people, those who think they can master their fate and yet still tumble down the well shaft of chance or of their foreordination.

Providence did not inscribe the future on heaven's outer surface. That would have offered no use to humanity since inevitable evil was still inevitable and knowing about it in advance would also have to ruin the anticipation of future pleasures. To comprehend heaven's disinterest in human life, one does not have to be a Copernican or even to speak like one:

> The firmament goes silent, the stars make their paths,
> The sun lights all of our days.

---

9   La Fontaine, *Fables II* 13, Pléiade edition, 62: "An astrologer took a fall to the bottom of a well. Someone told him: 'poor beast, while you can barely see to your feet you think you can read what is over your head?'" (my translation; see original below).
   Un astrologue un jour se laissa choir
   Au fond d'un puits. On lui dit: "Pauvre bête,
   Tandis qu'à peine à tes pieds tu peux voir,
   Penses-tu lire au-dessus de ta tête?"

Because the heavenly movements are homogenous, they are too monotonous and dull to be able to foretellingly depict earthly life in its color and complexity:

> Why respond in ever varied ways to the process
> so steady by which the universe moves?

As a reader of La Fontaine's fables in verse, Voltaire expressed dissatisfaction with the astrologer bit. He takes umbrage at the curses addressed to the tumbler. Voltaire evidently no longer takes the attack on astrology seriously. Past the fallen astrologer of the previous, still unenlightened century, he sees the astronomer of ancient tradition reappear. As evidence that astronomers can "read" what is over their heads very well, he names Copernicus, Galileo, Cassini, and Halley; the last of whom just because Voltaire saw in Halley the occasion that had depotentiated the relevance of La Fontaine's fable. The best astronomer, according to Voltaire, could tumble once and still not be a poor dog. Astrology was a most ridiculous quackery indeed, but not because it had made heaven its object, but because it believes or wants to spread the belief that one can read in the sky what is not written there.[10]

Did Voltaire remember, when he wrote this addendum to his dictionary article on the fable, that he himself had been in the situation of the fallen star observer in the years of his friendship with Émilie du Châtelet? Indeed, he discovered in her an observer whose enlightenedness was more refined than the ancient astronomer's. Their witness recorded the night scene in his own memoirs. Voltaire's coach broke apart underway to Cirey, Émilie's estate, in 1747, and the travelers were flung outside. While Voltaire's secretary, Sébastien Longchamp, was going to the next town for help, he saw a constellation whose ridiculous lack of realism was matched by its exquisite disregard for earthly realities: Voltaire and his friend were sitting side by side on the coach cushions that they had taken out and laid in the snow and observed the beauties of the starry sky. He knows, writes the memoirist, that astronomy was always one of the preferred interests of both philosophers; but even now they are enraptured by the greatness of the spectacle over their heads and around them, shivering with

---

10 Article "Fables" in Voltaire, *A Philosophical Dictionary*, 317, 1771 addendum: "[La Fontaine's] astrologer, again, who falling into a ditch while gazing at the stars, was asked: 'Poor wretch, do you expect to be able to read things so much above you!' Yet Copernicus, Galileo, Cassini, and Halley, have read the heavens very well: and the best astronomer that ever existed might fall into a ditch without being a poor wretch. Judicial astrology is indeed a very ridiculous charlatanism, but the ridiculousness does not consist in regarding the heavens: it consists in believing, or in making believe, that you read what is not there."

cold in spite of their furs and still conversing about nature and the stars' courses, about the orderliness of the countless globes in space's expanse. Compassionately, the secretary adds that they were only missing their instrumental fortifications for their full happiness: "They were only missing telescopes to be completely happy. With their spirit lost in the depth of the skies, they did not even notice their sad position on earth, or rather on the snow and surrounded by ice."[11] Only their much needed rescue interrupts the cosmic contemplation and conversation over worlds. The connection between theory and happiness (*theoria* and *eudaimonia*) has become anachronistic and no longer has its ancient self-evidence; this lost connection is recognizable in the strangeness of its conditions here: a mishap must precede happiness in order to induce it.

Voltaire must have thought of the scene of our anecdote a quarter-century later when, taking offense at La Fontaine's fable, he reclaimed the fallen astrologer as a legitimate sky watcher and sheltered him from his onlooker's barbaric cursing. He had experienced first-hand what an enlightened century he lived in when not even a servant had found cause for laughter in people's enthusiasm for the starry sky. Theoretical reason was established, and so much so that its self-styling as humanity's rightful interface with the world was effective even in the most eccentric (*ausgefallensten*) situation in the world.

If we endorse the strong probability that humanistic Copernicus knew the fable of his astronomical colleague's tumble down the well, then we would hardly leave that probability's horizon if we accepted that he conceived the foundational thought of his system reform as dependent on its "moral." As I have tried to show already, he could have formulated it thus: the obscure (*Fernstliegende*) can only be recognized in the obvious (*Nächstliegende*); the truth about the sky can only be attained through a true theory of the earth and its movements.

Everybody knows nowadays that this was not modern theory's last word about the universe. Next, Galileo's telescope opens up an epoch of reflexive optics that see in the heavenly bodies what must also be valid for the earthly body. Modern theory will only exceed these triumphs through spectral analysis when it stumbles upon the discovery of nuclear fusion while explaining the sun's energy production.

This surprising turn away from the principle grasped by Copernicus is not its dismissal: the sky becomes the mere detour for understanding what is no longer or not yet occurring on earth. To read something like an *epimythium* into Copernicus' theoretical fable in this way, or to append one, is obviously just a metaphorical construction meant

---

11 Longchamp et al., *Mémoires sur Voltaire, et sur ses ouvrages*, 166–9. See also Strauss, *Voltaire*, 78.

to illustrate how the tendency of the upcoming epoch is latent in the simplest remark made during the theoretical action of one of its protagonists.

This excursus on Copernicus' underlying principle does not amount to a history of influence (*Wirkungsgeschichte*) as normally conceived; this is clear when we observe how a decisive opponent to Copernicus such as Francis Bacon could not resist applying the principle whose consequences he rejected in order to become a kind of latent Copernican in spite of himself. The way that Bacon expresses his irritation at the configuration forged in the Thales anecdote reveals more about him than does any doxographical evidence from the vague collection of his supposedly empirical science.

In the autumn of 1624, while Bacon was recuperating from a serious illness, he dictated a set of apothegms from memory; among them, a variant on the Thales anecdote. It emphasizes the polysemy of Thales' doxographically eminent relation to water: he did not need to fall into the water to observe the stars; looking at the water and seeing their reflection would have sufficed. Doing what he did, however, he would not have been able to learn anything about water since he only looked upward at the stars.[12] The impression is barely avoidable that Bacon alters and extends the anecdote through associations that evoke the protophilosopher's double character: both as the star gazer who dismisses the mediated optics of reflection and as the inventor of the first cosmogony from one unifying principle, that of water, the confirmation of which he experiences in a crude way, by falling into it.

As a jurist Bacon was acquainted with the practice of citing case history (*Spruchpraxis*). The purpose of his own collection of sayings (*Spruchsammlung*) was not to produce rhetorical ornaments but rather "precedent cases" for an everyday citizen's practice (*ad res gerendas etiam et usus civiles*).[lxxiv] He saw before him a canon of human situations conditioned by the return of standard cases (*occasiones autem redeunt in orbem*). A selection of preserved solutions can orient us to whatever returns, and the power of human nature reveals a resemblance between whatever returns and what Bacon called nature's "common course" (*cursus communis*); in keeping with his empirical theory of nature as a whole, Bacon treated nature as if it observed customary legal procedure. The astronomer's plummet into the water illustrates both the punishment for metaphysical speculation and a practical rule for life: better to prefer the indirect path when the direct one comes along with risks. Since it comes down to this harsh bit of wisdom, the figurative situation is neglected; wisdom is not expressed within the

---

12 *A Collection of Apophthegms, New and Old* §57, in Bacon, *The Works of Francis Bacon, Lord Chancellor of England*, Vol. I, 111.

scene itself through the eye-witness or the laughing maid, but rather by clever people who ponder the event in retrospect with an interest in its general applicability.

Unfamiliarity with the anecdote is not the issue here; Bacon had known it well for a long time. Already twenty years before his collection of sayings, he used it in the piece *Of the Proficience and Advancement of Learning* to call for the study of mechanical arts (*artes mechanicae*). As applied knowledge of nature, the mechanical arts represent the realism of the claim that knowledge is power (*nosse = posse*) against a theory of objects, which left no possibility of mastering them and which could not contribute to humanity's hope of reacquiring Paradise as an earthly one. It seems to Bacon that it would injure the pride of learned people if they were expected to take on the investigation of mechanical phenomena, unless the investigation were also simultaneously about secret arts or irrelevant, hairsplitting objects which could win their investigator scholarly honor. The best and surest instruction cannot be found among the great paragons (*grandia exempla*). Precisely that fact is given expression in the widely known fable—and not unemphatically (*non insulse*). Bacon does not name the philosopher who falls in the water. But in place of it, he claims to impart his own opinion of what he later lets someone else say to the sufferer: the sky watcher would have been able to observe the stars in the water reflection if he had directed his gaze downward, whereas he could not see the water while directly viewing the stars in the sky.[13] This is supposed to mean: cosmogony from water could not be corroborated in the place where the philosopher had gazed so self-forgottenly.

What unites the generation that founded modernity, that of Galileo, Bacon, and Descartes, more than any dogmatic characteristic, is their reevaluation of liberal and mechanical arts. They did not reevaluate in the same direction by any means: Galileo and Descartes discover a thesaurus for still unacknowledged pure theory in known and established technical powers, particularly the defensive use of ballistics and arsenals; Bacon pushes in the other direction, for the deconstruction of theoretical "purity" in favor of the norm of its applicability, of equating the most useful (*utilissimum*) with the most true (*verissimum*).

---

13 *Of the Proficience and Advancement of Learning, Divine and Human II*, in Bacon, *The Works of Francis Bacon, Lord Chancellor of England*, Vol. I, 188. "But the truth is, they [ancient sages] be no the highest instances that give the securest information; as may be well expressed in the tale so common of the philosopher, that while he gazed upwards to the stars fell into the water; for if he had looked down he might have seen the stars in the water, but looking aloft he could not see the water in the stars."

Unmistakably, this is a form of anthropocentrism once again: if paradise consists in laying truths bare for humanity, then whatever is supposed to help humankind return there must have the highest truth status. The Thales anecdote need not be taken as a figure for pure theory; it does, however, illustrate the contempt for instruments devised through mechanical engineering in favor of an unarmed theoretical orientation that brings the image of the fallen Greek up to date. Astronomy stands for *artes liberales* and their distance from their objects.

Let us not forget that the programmatic thinker out to recuperate paradise has in mind that paradise was a garden and not a world—even if he did not yet know that there was no starry sky over this garden, because the light of the newly constructed fixed stars did not have enough time to reach the earth. Astronomy transcends the provenance of magic—to which Bacon still largely belongs—even of magic transformed into the scientific. The stars are the negative of the unity of science and power that hovers before Bacon: "for man cannot act upon, change, or transform the heavenly bodies."[14] Reflection has a magical trait in this context: *making* the far off (*Fernliegende*) into the near at hand (*Naheliegende*) instead of playing the one against the other as in the traditional anecdote. Bacon's own reading of the Thales scene is that small, close things assist more in recognizing large, distant ones than the other way around. He believed that he could appeal to Aristotle, who recommended leaving one's family in order to recognize the essence of the state; he could just as well have thought of Plato's *Republic*, which recommends fathoming the concept of justice by observing it magnified in the polis.

When Bacon extols the compass as one of the great inventions—the one that had allowed him to evoke the image of transcending the *Plus Ultra*, of sailing beyond the Pillars of Hercules, for the new science—the magnetic instrument also comes to illustrate indirect methods of conducting theory.[lxxv] Had someone spoken before the invention of the compass about a device with which we can precisely determine the poles of heaven, without looking up at it itself, then people would have thought of wacky astronomical instruments and speculated long about how such a thing could be invented since they would consider it impossible for its movement to coincide with the heavenly movements although it does not come from heaven, but is just an earthly substance of stone and metal.[15] On the one hand, only mechanics can set theory

---

14 *New Organon II* in ibid., Vol. III, 373: "neque enim ceditur homini operari in caelestia, au tea immutare aut transformare."
15 Bacon, *The Works of Francis Bacon, Lord Chancellor of England*, Vol. III, 358. *New Organon I* §85.

in motion: as the example illustrates, unfree skill (*unfreie Fertigkeit*) brings liberal arts (*freie Kunst*) to life; on the other hand, the paths opened up by technical trickery only lead to more and more technical tricks. Domination over nature comes from an obedience that no longer entails bowing to the higher power.[lxxvi]

Bacon's paradox could read: the sky observer fell in the fable because he failed to realize that he was already fallen. Bacon is pervaded with the loss of paradise and only therefore interested in human possibilities: paradise could become ours again because it was already ours once. In the interim between exile from paradise and its recuperation pure theory has no place; theory is tied to the demand for happiness, whose conditions are unsatisfied—if they are satisfiable at all. In Bacon's language, the philosopher lost in the image of the sky would typify whoever does not want to admit that paradise is lost; he makes it his task to recuperate the leisure of theory, a lost but nevertheless recoverable human condition. Bacon describes our lost paradise as a region where man still worked, but where the work had not been conducted out of necessity: "man was placed in the garden to work therein."[lxxvii] The world as garden is a site of culture, not of wild growth. Not even in paradise is nature completely willing to comply on its own; after our exile more so than before it, nature offers itself for the taking since it is now in the clutches of our necessary way of proceeding with it: "the passages and variations of nature cannot appear so fully in the liberty of nature, as in the trials and vexations of art."[16] Between science and its objects there exists a tense situation, in which glances towards the sky always bear the risk made known by the Milesian astronomer.

The ancient concept of theory stands within a horizon of optical metaphorics, approximately in the range spanning between the uninvolved spectator and the self-forgotten observer. Bacon favors an acoustic orientation for his concept of knowledge, across the variety of tolerances between impartial listening and stressful, forced interrogation. Science comes to resemble the archiving of whatever nature—willingly or unwillingly—gave as protocol.[17] Even when Bacon seeks to win *The Wisdom of the Ancients* for his side in 1609 through the method of mythological allegoresis, that wisdom is hidden fortuitously in names and stories that have something to do with nature's speaking up. As if by accident, a relationship to that strange element in the transmission of the Thales anecdote emerges: the moment when Peter Damian named the Thracian maid "Iambe."[lxxviii] There she was brought

---

16 *Of the Proficience and Advancement of Learning II*, in Bacon, *The Works of Francis Bacon, Lord Chancellor of England*, Vol. I, 189. On this passage, see: Wolff, *Francis Bacon und seine Quellen*, 52:I 26; I 204f.
17 Blumenberg, *Die Lesbarkeit der Welt*, 86–91.

into connection with the origin of iambic meter. Iambe, according to Bacon, is a daughter of Pan, whom the only mortal god conceived with his spouse Echo. She is supposed to have pleased visitors with her laughter-inducing banter.[18]

The hinge that would link the daughter of Pan and Echo to the Thracian woman in the Platonic anecdote: the incidence of laughter. A notable reference to the mythic background of the astronomer's plummet can be construed: if the laughing maid is supposed to be the daughter of the god Pan in an otherwise lost transmission, the conflict would be between the sky observer's world and her world of pre-Olympian deities, of the Earth, of caves, of the Arcadian landscape and of the heaviness still surreptitiously present in a heaven forsaken by Earth. This link invites association between Plato's mention of the Thracian woman and the fable by a Phrygian or Thracian Aesop. In Bacon's allegoresis, he identifies Pan's daughter with philosophy, whose chattiness produces endless, fruitless theories about the essence of things.[19]

Daughter Iambe only signifies what she does for Bacon in contrast to mother Echo; in Echo's name he construes the idea of an empirical philosophy that makes itself the echo of nature. Pan already stands for the universe according to his name, which leaves nothing further beyond itself that could be linked with him. Only the echo provoked by the whole turns into its equal: Echo still lasts solely to be conjugally united with the world, in which she represents philosophy. Her truth is the most faithful copy of the voices of the universe itself: "for that alone is true philosophy which doth faithfully render the very words (*ipsius voces*) of the world." Had Thales the sky observer lost his right to theorize because he walked around as if in an unlost paradise, then there would be nothing to laugh at in the Thracian woman's chatter about him—not if she had been called Iambe. True philosophy, the wisdom of the ancients (*sapientia veterum*), was already lost by the time Thales turned away from the world too full of gods, instead of depleting and then renewing the wisdom hidden in mythical names and events. The original suspicion of all Romantics—the end of truth entered with the beginning of history—runs throughout modernity since modernity claims to know how to go about beginning anew.

---

18 *The Wisdom of the Ancients VI*, in Bacon, *The Works of Francis Bacon, Lord Chancellor of England*, Vol. I, 290: "... a little girl called Iambe, that with many pretty tales was wont to make strangers merry."
19 Ibid., Vol. I, 292. "... for by her are represented those vain and idle paradoxes concerning the nature of things which have been frequent in all ages, and have filled the world with novelties; fruitless, if you respect the master; changelings, if you respect the kind; sometimes creating pleasure, sometimes tediousness, with their overmuch prattling."

Eight In the Grip of Historical Criticism

At this point, whoever still considers the wisdom of the ancients attainable, even recoverable, must be sure that he is working with well-transmitted sources. This condition, under the name of "criticism," will definitively separate the early Enlightenment—even before the end of the century that Bacon introduced—from the Renaissance's assurance about historical materials. Criticism will relinquish the possibility of wisdoms hidden within historical transmission by developing suspicion about "history's lies." History becomes whatever makes it through criticism.

Astonishingly, the Thales anecdote passes this test. In the article "Thales" from Pierre Bayle's *Dictionnaire historique et critique* of 1697, it claims the rank of approved historical fact. Even the typesetting of this most consequential dictionary of historical criticism showed how little remained left over when the full ledger of methods had been applied: below the thin, often only two-line entries of ascertained facts hung the forceful, much-admired critical apparatus. The version that Diogenes Laertius had given of the anecdote of the fallen astronomer stood clearly in the best stead according to Bayle's penetrating gaze: "an old woman bantered him (*se moqua*) very merrily, for having gone abroad with her (*étant de son logis*) to look at the stars, and falling into a ditch."[lxxix]

In the early stage of historical criticism represented here, it is characteristic that the optically observable event, the raw fact of the philosopher's accident, gains entry into the catalogue of the reliable, but not the maid's comment. The unity of the anecdote is torn apart. The accompanying adage, which does not seem to be an "event" in the physical-phenomenal sense, is suspected of contamination because its wording is not transmitted consistently, and the disparities between the versions are not sufficiently explained by the diversity of positions held by observers and reporters.

Historical transmission and fictitious amplification interpenetrate by a mechanism recognizable when we see imaginative elements enter precisely where a hole had remained in the authentic material, and the result meets the later critic's criteria for fabrication. The Milesian incident requires a witness to mark the disparity between theory and the lifeworld because no criticism would believe that Thales himself spread the story of his misfortune. But the witness does not need to give meaningful statements about himself or herself. Bayle's finding thus includes leaving it open as to whether the philosopher's chaperon actually said what she was thinking at all: "People have twisted that woman's thought in many ways."[lxxx]

Bayle refers next to Alciato's *Emblemata* (Augsburg, 1531) where he finds an epigram by Thomas More against a "horned" astrologer (*contre un Astrologue cocu*). This epigram takes up Chaucer's tradition again insofar as it thrusts the anecdote into the association between astrology and eroticism totally foreign to antiquity. This version could be called the oriental one since already in 1258 the *Gulistan* of Sa'di had introduced the astrologer, who finds his wife with a stranger when he returns from a trip; the surprise has professional ramifications for the astrologer because the future is not supposed to have kept anything unknown from him.[lxxxi] Bayle is discernibly glad to mock the humanist Alciato, who is entirely unsuspicious to criticism and who depicts astrologers seeing entire erotic constellations play out in front of them among their mythical star-images in the sky without ever knowing how to interpret and apply the signs in the sky to their own marital situation. The effect of historical criticism and its peeling away towards the hard kernel of facts is to free up the soft surroundings of history's variability for aesthetic demands.

The erotic moment is not just a poetic touch. It represents the "realism" of what gets in the way (*im Wege Liegenden*) on Earth, and it completes the "reoccupation" of the position occupied by various antitheses to obscurity (*Fernliegenden*) within the whole tradition of the anecdote. The sky is not just distant and unattainable to the grip of human hands, it also stands there indifferently and in contemptuous unmovedness over the fates of human beings, what matters for humanity most of all (*am nächsten gehen*). Thomas More's epigram, which Bayle quotes with the gratification of someone who had to fight against the fear of comets, portrays the sky as keeping silent about the problems so obvious to the astrologer, for whom it is otherwise so informative: "Hence when the wife receives her lover,/ the stars, so taken up, can ne'er discover."[lxxxii] Precisely because Bayle was passionately committed to the historical destruction of this side of the tradition—whose subtraction required him to excavate the rest of the history in order to write it off as unacceptable—he could have

In the Grip of Historical Criticism   69

produced a kind of reception history of every mocking statement that had ever been put in the maid's mouth with regard to the philosopher's tumble. But his concern is neither with establishing a context nor with the epochal significance of such products of free variation, but it is rather with their fungibility as an indicator for their tradition's lacking reliability. Reading this as material for a reception history—which manifests the potential of an inaccessible moment of inaugural invention and updates that invention for ever new applications—requires a precondition of appropriate distance from the historical "criticism" of the early Enlightenment.

Once we perceive the anecdote's deformities in light of the materials Bayle cites, the counter-position to astronomy and astrology stands out as crude. Bayle recognizably favors one formula for the maid's statement, and it is useful for him to look back over the available body of texts in order to give a profile of this preference. Plato's version had the maid charge the philosopher with desiring knowledge of the things in the sky while what lay at his feet remained concealed to him. No association gets made between the success of astronomical efforts and any struggle for the earthly; there does not seem to be any skepticism about the *possibility* of higher knowledge. Problematic is that version's demand for exclusiveness. For Diogenes Laertius, the sequence of both perspectives is reversed. In the context of a skeptical turn, one perspective's failure becomes an argument for the other's illusory supposition: "O Thales, when you cannot discern what is at your feet, do you think to make discoveries in the Heavens?"[1] An *argumentum a fortiori*: earthly clumsiness is the indicator of celestial hopelessness. The only one who formulated or reported the anecdote neutrally in this regard is Stobaeus in his *Florilegium*; he only has the Thracian maid say that the tumble served the man right who watched the sky while he overlooked what lay at his feet.

Here it is characteristic that Bayle selects Laertius' statement by the "woman of ripe age" (what he calls a *"bonne femme"*) out of possible versions on offer. It suits his purpose to befriend, even to intensify, the explicitly skeptical formulation, so that the ability to recognize stellar objects appears completely discredited by the accusation of inability to perceive what is close at hand (*Nächstliegende*): "How can you know what passes in the heavens, said that good old woman to him, since you do not see what is just at your feet?"

A connection between theory's archetype and theoretical curiosity's guiding concept first gets established in one of the early encyclopedias

---

1   Bayle, *An Historical and Critical Dictionary*, Vol. IV, 2864. "Comment pourriez-vous connoître ce qui se fait dans le ciel, lui dit cette femme, puis que vous ne voiez pas ce qui est proche de vos pieds?"

by Johann Heinrich Alsted in 1620, in that it marks the Thales anecdote with the keyword *curiositas*. From a purely formal point of view, the encyclopedist's attention turns to making a comparison between problems of theory's origins in distant times (*Zeitenferne*) and the problems of justifying the rise of scientific curiosity in recent times (*Zeitennähe*). The bounty of aphorisms presents the reader with the medieval repertoire as well as the ancient texts that were familiar again since the Renaissance. The finding—unexpected for the encyclopedia's contemporary (*zeitgenößischen*) user—is that divine will can account for an object's natural inaccessibility in the world, and this finding demands that one quit submitting it to inquiry; the manifest clarity of circumstances warns against ignoring them in our haste. The world is no longer just the order of its members' ranks and values, but also the guide to accessibilities and clarities for theoretical observation: "God wanted some things to be hidden; however, He made other things manifest, and those are not to be neglected."[2]

This maxim, delivered at the beginning of the seventeenth century, makes the Thales anecdote sound thoroughly medieval. The text is repeated in Bruson's *Facitiae et exempla* and resembles Stobaeus' terseness. Only one hint of deformation is recognizable. The maid also indicts the sky observer here and says that it serves him right, but not for making the wrong choice of object in the face of other possibilities to consider, but for not noticing the state of things in front of his feet *before* he starting observing the sky. In this *non prius* lies the charge that he made a mistake that would best be called methodological; for a philosopher, a considerable shortcoming, but no longer a metaphysical offense.[lxxxiii] What the maid utters is burgeoning moralism: good advice rather than reproachful *Schadenfreude* across the abyss of misunderstanding. There is no trace left of the hiatus between divine provenances (*Götterwelten*); the one God stands for them all since He made His Creation to express what He allows and what He forbids.

Philosophy's early historiography loves anecdotes. One reason why is that it counts all reports that withstand historical criticism as equally valid: statements and stories, biographical and doxographical accounts alike. Inevitably, the Thales anecdote appears within the work of the first and most influential historian of philosophy of the whole eighteenth century, whom even the philosophy-disparaging Goethe claims to have read diligently and on whom all knowledge of the history

---

2   Alsted, *Cursus philosophici encyclopaediae*, 2005. "Thales, while looking upwards, fell into a chasm (*barathrum*). A maidservant who saw it happen, said that he deserved to have fallen, because, while he observed the sky, the things in front of his feet had not been looked at first (*non essent prius perspecta*)" (my translation).

of philosophy depends into the following century—mostly without acknowledging him: the great "second hand," Jakob Brucker.

The way Brucker sees Thales the protophilosopher fits the context of his more general question of how the Greeks came to acquire the beginning of philosophy. As befits the type of his work, which seeks to give short and formulaic answers, he dubs the quality of that philosophical beginning "pretty slight, and moreover very dark."[3] This lowly qualification is the price for the fact that the otherwise so gladly perceived Greek dependence on the Orient, especially on Egypt, is devalued in favor of the stand-alone Hellenistic achievement. For Brucker, derivations cannot be said to reveal much because he sees a totally foreign principle of thought at work in the philosophy of the barbarians: that of received philosophy (*philosophia traditiva*). This consists of a trusted and erudite relaying of fixed answers to constant questions. By scrutinizing this dogmatic type of thought, the Greeks were able to set up their new beginning. Philosophy's Oriental inheritance need not be denied, but its effect has a different specificity than putting Greek philosophy's origin in the context of a tradition: the Oriental tradition became a spur to original thought, something to object to, rather than something to adhere to.

Brucker diverges from one of the Greeks' most persisting self-interpretations regarding the beginning of philosophy, that it originated in the astonishment at the cosmos and from the discovery of hidden allegorical meanings in myth. Instead, Brucker evokes "the curiosity of the Greek nation" and highlights the way that political circumstances supported this trait. In a "form of government in which everyone may think, say, and teach what he wanted," genuine curiosity's impulse towards science flourishes.[4] In the "Addenda and Improvements" that accompany the second volume of *Short Questions from Philosophical History*, the theoretical-political complex is clarified: with the beginning of original thought and of theory formation that consisted not only of claims, but of justified connections between sentences, the investigation of truth among the Greeks came "down from the priests and eventually landed among politicos."[5]

Brucker does not discernably fall in line with the traditional report that Thales secured freedom for the city of Miletus by offering political advice, and that, when this freedom fell to the Persians, philosophy too was over. Philosophers saw the theoretical orientation as contingent on leisure; they needed no other public conditions than the negative one of freedom from the compulsion of needs. They did not grasp the need for

---

3 Brucker, *Kurze Fragen aus der Philosophischen Historie*, Vol. I, 350, 354.
4 Ibid., Vol. I, 221f.
5 Ibid., Vol. II, 880–3.

a further condition, that of satisfying their desire to know in the context of political matters which would provide everyone the protection they needed to question everything. No one had thought of a way to guarantee science its freedom. The figure of Thales revealed the energy of the authentic beginning rather than the success of his astronomical and mathematical inventions; these were "pretty poor and meager by the standards of our time." Brucker's repeated emphasis on philosophy's minimal initial value goes together with his decoupling its origin from all predecessors and influences; wherever something is supposed to have emerged by itself, it can only come to light in the smallest early successes. Only when an inheritance is being claimed does the wealth arise in the beginning.

The maid's lack of understanding refers to the originary difficulty of something strange coming to light, according to Brucker. She is the public for the as yet unforeseen about Thales: "he lusted so much for study that he not only gave the management of his property to his sister-son, but also dug in so deep that he fell into a ditch once while ardently watching the sky, and got laughed at for it by his maid." In a comment, completely in Bayle's style, the exaggeration gets turned back into tragedy so that the first adventure of newly founded theory turns deadly. That Thales "tumbled down from a height and broke his neck is openly a fable." This disqualification follows from the source's inferiority relative to all others—though no version allows the philosopher to speak a word after he tumbles. But how do such "fables" come about on the other side of fable? We learn through Brucker's judgment that Anaximenes' letter to Pythagoras, retained by Diogenes Laertius, transmits just such an embellishment of the anecdote's ending. What goes too far and ends up contradicting an otherwise consistent transmission "is only drafted *exercitii gratia* by Sophists." The sophists, who fabricated documents with beautiful twists on the facts for the sake of practice, play a large role in purifying the tradition through "historical criticism." They create leeway around the core material of the historical and make the latter provable through the recklessness of their inventions.

Brucker makes no use of the possibility of finding confirmation, in the apocryphal correspondence presented by Diogenes, for his thesis that philosophy requires the precondition of freedom. Negligence towards the standards of criticism could no longer be afforded; that is so even if Brucker means to demonstrate how the life and death of philosophy's founder seemed to his pupil Anaximenes to have occurred in a circumstance of politically secured leisure because he could only regard the past from the altered situation that emerged when the threat of the Persian king hovered over Miletus. That stands in contrast with the situation at theory's starting point with Thales.

Faced with the choice between death and servitude, no one could dream of a life devoted to researching the sky. And yet it was through applied astronomy that Thales managed to foresee the right path among the political options.

To show an example of how formulae that Brucker forged get brought into circulation by "multipliers," I exhibit Johann Heinrich Zedler's *Universal Lexicon of All Sciences and Arts*, which presented itself as "complete" and appeared in a total of 68 volumes with 67,000 pages between 1732 and 1754 which adopted Brucker's passage—about Thales' dogged study and the accident that accompanied it—almost verbatim in the article "Thales" from volume 43 in 1745. Recognizably, the anecdote is there to cleanse the autoptic sky observer of the suspicion that he primarily took his knowledge from Egypt: "And he may have build his erudition upon such first foundations, even though the destitute quality of Egyptian knowledge may leads one to believe that he had his own thought and diligence to thank most."[6] That is also why he takes the account seriously that was transmitted by Plutarch, Pliny, and Diogenes Laertius. In that account Thales showed the Egyptians how to measure the height of a pyramid and wins their great admiration. That can only be taken relative to the low estimation of Egyptian measuring abilities; Thales' own inventions in this field are seen as "poor and meager," in Brucker's words, due to their primordiality. But just making that argument required the self-oblivious objection that brings into view the event in the anecdote. To sharpen the case, Brucker is almost quoted verbatim; the only thing left out is the sophists' forgeries. Instead, Zedler speaks up about the anecdote of Thales the astrologer's fortune with oil tree speculation: that the philosopher "made an uncommonly large capital gain is a fiction that is told one way by some and other ways by others."

For this critique, Zedler's *Universal Lexicon* refers to another standard work, Thomas Stanley's *History of Philosophy*, which had first appeared in 1655 in London and then in 1701 in the third edition. The protophilosopher's financial success roused the acumen of the first English historian of philosophy to a Puritanical defense, although he too considered it to be invented for the sake of vindicating philosophy against the accusation that it lacked realism. The astrologer's nocturnal

---

6 Ibid., Vol. 43, 372–82. "He was so set on his studies that he not only left the management of his property to his sister's son, but also plunged himself in so deeply that he once fell into a ditch during the assiduous observation of the sky, and was laughed at by his maid, who put the accusation to him that he wanted to know what was in the sky and yet could not see what lay before his feet. That he tumbled down from a height and broke his neck ... is obviously a fable."

tumble had not awakened him to reflect on the contradictory transmissions; he privileges Diogenes Laertius' version, but adds without qualification that the old woman was a Thracian—although her inventor, Plato, had imagined her as still young. After reconstructing the maid's age and origin, Stanley gives the event a turn towards cruelty of his own invention. The old lady conducted the philosopher where he would have to fall in the ditch: "wherein she purposely led him."[7] There we see the thought introduced by Montaigne—that the maid actively participated in the philosopher's stumbling—transposed into a crudified form: at play was cruel duplicity and not just rousing him to pay attention. Wherefore does the old lady do it? Stanley gives us a clue: Thales had drawn the disdain of some people by practicing astrology ("became obnoxious to the Censure of some Persons"). We can see her resemblance to the woman in Montaigne's version: the dissembling woman had a mission to carry out, either to wreak revenge or to issue a harsh warning.

For modern historical criticism, the anecdote seemed generally less malleable than the doctrinaire element whose changes they attributed to readers' misunderstanding and to distorting or harmonizing disciplinary practices rather than to the narratable occurrence, the life event. But then besides Stanley, Bayle, and Brucker, there emerged a specialist in the critical treatment of the philosopher anecdote. Christoph August Heumann demonstrated his mastery in this area with the treatise *On Diogenes the Cynic's Keg*, in which he made the—admittedly still long disputed—case in 1716 that whichever texts accuse the protocynic "with the greatest seriousness" of this more comfortable form of living are "ridiculous and untrue."[8] One is eager to see how the Thales anecdote will fare at such a tribunal.

Heumann comes to Thales' plummet in an eminent place: in the introduction to his *Historica Philosophica* of 1715. In short, the history of philosophy instructs about the method of philosophy. Above all, its history encapsulates the guidelines for avoiding mistakes: "Wherever we find that philosophers before us crashed, we see where and how we have to pay attention."[9] And there he draws an analogy with the turn Socrates executed against the Ionian philosophers' wrongheaded disregard for morality: that the Cartesians went on the same wrong path of the Ionian confinement to nature "and thus simply stand in

---

7   Stanley, *The History of Philosophy*, Part I, chap. VIII, Sect. 5. "Thales, said she, do you think, when you cannot see these things that are at your feet, that you can understand the Heavens?"
8   On Heumann's tract about Diogenes' keg, see Niehues-Pröbsting, "Der Kynismus des Diogenes und der Begriff des Zynismus," 218f., note 12.
9   Heumann, *Acta philosophorum*, Vol. I, 29f. Einleitung I, 14.

need of a Socratic correction." It is just this correction that is already seen, without any critical reflection, preformed in the Thracian maid's behavior towards the first philosopher: "for even Thales' maid can teach us that the following applies to those who let the field of philosophical practice lie untilled: they are senseless with reason: they act comprehending, while they comprehend nothing."

The anecdote is taken for so familiar that no introduction to its scene is deemed necessary. Nevertheless, Heumann has Thales' predicament in mind, when he transitions immediately to discussing contemporary philosophy's lack of a method "for drawing the truth from out of Democritus' well." The association connects the two accounts where something fell in a well philosophically: for Thales, the philosopher himself; for Democritus, "just" the truth.[lxxxiv] The Thracian maid became symbolic for a constantly returning problem of philosophy: not dissipating into theory self-forgottenly, not using reason to produce nonsense. The maid is now a philosophical figure herself, meant as a complaint against forgotten wisdom (*Weltweisheit*) and morality. A century after Descartes, the Thracian maid is against his consequences, against the all-pervasive new interest in nature—she has even become Socratic.

We can already see from here that Heumann has decided on the historical reliability of the anecdote about the philosopher's tumble and would not contradict Bayle on this. That becomes even clearer when we consider the two Thales anecdotes, that of the well-tumble and that of the speculation-win, in a reversed relationship. At the site of its original source in Aristotle, Thales' prescience about the olive trees' fertility is the exact antithesis to the well-tumble: the evidence of concrete service to life in whatever had been accomplished by founding philosophy and could go on being accomplished. The errant nocturnal wanderer's misfortune comes across as the painful fee for proving himself a realist to the citizens of the polis by day. Moreover, it was pretty insignificant which theoretical instrument Thales had used, and it was pretty obvious that everyone would assume the prediction was a piece of astrology. In the meantime, however, Thales' prediction came under the most scandalous suspicion, as Heumann quotes from Carl Owen's *Theater of Deceptions* from 1715, namely, the suspicion that Thales had received his foreknowledge from "the Devil's revelation." Therefore, the lucky anecdote can only be historically false—that is imperative—in favor of unlucky history. Only if Thales had not been able to draw any daytime utility from his nocturnal affair, would it be unobjectionable as the beginning of philosophy, would his act be astronomy in its later implemented distinction from astrology.

The question now emerges in the midst of the rivalry between the two anecdotes for the prize of critical approval: "Because our Thales is a diligent astronomer and also attests to his tireless *stellatim* with the present account (*Historie*), since his maid mocked him, when he accidentally fell into a ditch while watching the stars, and she took it for foolish to see more above than nearby oneself; therefore, it is not an irrelevant question whether he was an astronomer or an astrologer."[10] There he is to contradict his predecessor Stanley most decisively: nothing proves Thales' astrological errancy (*Abwegigkeit*) besides the story of the oil-press success, and this is the kind of story "that one recognizes at first sight not to be true, but rather a fable invented by astrologers to honor their art." Due to the poverty of sources for this anecdote, no work can be done with the discrepancies between transmissions, and it is indicative about a form of thought that is gradually developing under the name of "criticism" that Heumann had already crafted his case in the theoretical introduction to his *History of Philosophy* with the argument that "this fiction grew in the brain of astrologers and calendar-makers, who have sought to make a reputation for their vain art through Thales' authority."[11] Here is someone showing an "interest" in Thales' success; he specifies this success as astrological and discredits it in the same instant as unhistorical.

Emerging unscathed from criticism, the anecdote does not win its rhetorical shimmer from the plummeting philosopher, who now falls as a pure astronomer; it wins it rather from the maid's resolve. Emphasizing her resolve permits even the offense with which the sophists are charged elsewhere, that of embellishment. In the chapter of *Acts of the Philosophers* entitled "Characteristics of False Philosophy," Heumann recommends Agrippa of Nettesheim's book on the *Vanity of the Sciences and Arts* so that the reader may get a picture of the possibility of strictly theoretical errors in arithmetic, algebra, alchemy, and astronomy, as well as in physics; along with these, another figure of theoretical "narcissism" comes into the picture: "And if it is still true that Archimedes concerned himself with nothing but his Circle drawing during the siege of Syracuse, then I can praise him as little as that maid did her master when he fell into a hole while observing the stars, and almost broke his neck."[12] Even the neck that is only

---

10 Heumann, *Acta philosophorum*, Vol. III, 173f.
11 Ibid., Vol. I, 16f. Einleitung I, 8.
12 Ibid., Vol. III, 173. The famous Jakob Gronovius committed the "clever error" of taking the maid's origin designation in Attic dialect, "Thratta," for her personal name (as Hippolytus already had in his *Philosophumena*)—but "even greater is the sophist's error, who takes up the epistle found in Laertius ... and reports of it that Thales had such a bad fall at that time that he broke his neck and had to give up his spirit" (my translation). On Gronovius' slip of the pen (*Fehlleistung*), see Heumann, *Parerga Critica*, 111f.

almost broken should be disqualified if we consider the anecdote an exact account, as Heumann does; but here his concern is—now that he has already disclosed the anecdote of the astrologer's deal with the Devil—to strengthen the maid's position rhetorically in opposition to *pure* theory as well.

Nine From Cursing Sinners to Reproaching Creation

The Baroque pulpit orator Abraham a Sancta Clara wields rhetoric of a totally different caliber through the Thales anecdote in his plain language encyclopedia of social classes and trades, *Something for Everyone*. Under the rubric of "the Scale and Sign Master," he enhances the short, ancient vignette into a circuitous philippic against astrology's "meddlesomeness" (*Fürwitz*):

> Thales of Miletus, an impeccable philosopher, once went walking on a cool evening, and while he trod, he scrutinized the sky with his yawning mouth; thus he spoke to himself: look, there's the mid-heaven circle, where the sun goes by with fiery steeds. There is the sign of Libra; whoever is born under it is fated to be a lawyer, as he should be a lover of justice. See, over there is the star called Venus; whoever has this sign in his birth is suited to chastity like a sickle in a knife rack.[1] [lxxxv]

The folk preacher savors one more tidbit of this sort so that he can paint the plummet as deserved and drastic when he gets to it:

> While he continued on with eyes raised to the sky in observation, he tripped a bit and fell in a deep manure lagoon, so that the brew climbed over him; that was an odd rabbit in the pot. After he lifted his head up from the desolate sow bath, he heard an old woman mocking him. Her nose had a wild crystal on it, like the icicles on straw roofs in the winter, and she shamed him with her unarmed mouth, so much so that, since she didn't have a very upright back before, she laughed herself a hunchback.

---

1 Abraham a Sancta Clara, *Etwas für Alle*. Würzburg: Dritter Theil, 1733, 819–21.

The subsequent defamation speech transfers directly from the ancient heckler's mouth to that of the Baroque preacher, who addresses his "smart-alecky brother Curiosity" and "overconfident sister Impudence," in order to excuse them for their rudeness in brooding over God's immeasurable work. Here for once theory's special vice takes on general human traits. His vitriolic rant almost makes a little meddling (*Vorwitz*) once more seem harmless even if it does not comply with the reliable indeed but untransparent higher plan for humanity and the world:[lxxxvi] "O, since your understanding is so empty and poor that it cannot fathom natural matters, why then do you want to anatomize natural and Divine Judgment?"

If the Thracian maid's opposition to the Milesian astronomer may still have been suitable to renew its entreaty at a time when still growing knowledge about nature delayed the announcement of a "definitive morality,"[lxxxvii] the figure of the ancient sky observer must have appeared too harmless to continue giving figural expression to the new science's access to its objects. Above all, this figure did not hold up in the situation that followed Leibniz's failure to unite theory and theodicy, a situation which generally made science into the organ of dissatisfaction with the factually given world. It would have been more obvious (*eher nahegelegen*) from the Thracian maid's standpoint than from that of the Milesian astronomer not to see the world as that which ought to be and as how it ought to be—to unleash reproach on the cosmos would have been that much more difficult because there was no authority to whom Thales could have been directed. Authorities make complaining easier.

It was compatible with theory's failure to redress such complaints, which culminated under the name "theodicy," that the world appeared to be the product of divine incompetence (or, as Voltaire put it, degraded omnipotence). Using inventiveness to bring the world to the standard of convenience was no longer merely a matter of hope for the human equipped with theory; rather, he was already on the way to proving that it would succeed. The later invented anecdote, where Thales is so arrogant to the Egyptian priests that he tries to show that they mismeasured the pyramids—which could only have been built by measurement—betrays the necessity of a more aggressive style of theory. This style demands to know, and even begins to explain, how the world must have been made.

The figure that stands for applying the principle that all knowledge implies its feasibility is Alfonso the Wise of Castile (deceased in 1284); he competes with the Thales anecdote in the modern imagination's world of figures. He takes over its function as a theoretical self-assessment bordering on self-consciousness. He would have been able to advise God on how to set up the universe better, went the blasphemous statement of the king's supposedly, had he been around for the Creation. He is not yet the Demiurge himself, who needs to be able to have made what he wants to have known;[lxxxviii] but he is also no longer the ancient theorist type, for whom the farthest objects (*die entferntesten Gegenstände*) are the most suitable because they exclude the thought of ever laying a hand on them. That would have unintentionally turned the free citizen's "art" into a matter of the unfree. The Thracian woman would have had nothing to laugh at. But reproaching the world lay outside of the scope of ancient relations with the cosmos. In any case, what happened between gods and humans in his antitheodicy could call the critique of philosophers back to life.

The theorist, not the moralist, destroys theodicy at its core; he rivals Creation by using its own principle. Humanity takes matters into its own hands, not in order to relieve God, but in order to replace Him. Alfonso of Castile had only wanted to advise an unreal God (*nur im Irrealis*). Leibniz was of the view that Alfonso spoke in the absence of better theory. Leibniz's syncretic mind (*irenischer Geist*) found the excuse for blasphemously reproaching Creation: the Castilian king just did not know about Copernicus yet.[2, lxxxix]

It became more important than the historical excuse for the royal haughtiness that the king was seen as exemplifying the conflict between theory and realism. Again, it was Bayle's preliminary work on the sources for this prefiguration that predetermined the modern viewpoints: on the one hand, the generous, royal sponsor of astronomy who ordered the restoration of Ptolemy's astronomic tables and esteemed that work; on the other hand, the reproacher of Creation who had to pay the political price of decline and failure for his turn to the starry sky and now incurs the afterworld's reproach through the pen of the most influential historical critic. Even for the honor of the sciences, he would have had to rule his people with more fortune and wisdom: "It were to be wish'd, for the Honor of Learning, that a prince who was so adorn'd with it had governed his people more fortunately and more wisely."[3]

---

2   Leibniz, "Sur ce qui passe les sens et la mateire (c. 1702)," in Leibniz, *Die Werke von Leibniz gemäss seinem hanschriftlichen Nachlasse in der Königlichen Bibliothek zu Hannover*, 153: "… all of our complaints come from our lack of knowledge, somewhat as King Alfonso, to whom we owe the astronomical tables, thought to recast the system of the world since he did not know Copernicus' system, the only one capable of allowing sane judgment on the greatness and beauty of God's work." For more on this passage, see Blumenberg, *The Genesis of the Copernican World*, 259–63.

3   Bayle, *An Historical and Critical Dictionary*, Vol. II, 902. From the article "Castile, Alsonso X King of)." For the current state of research on the astronomer Alfonso the Wise, see Cesare Segre in *Grundriß der romanischen Literaturen des Mittelalters* VI/I, Heidelberg, 1968, 124f.

Bayle musters all of his perspicuity to relieve Alfonso of the accusation that he wasted resources on his astronomical passion. He proves that the sum spent to develop the astronomical tables is based on a printing error if it totals forty thousand ducats and not four thousand, a quantity hardly worth mentioning. The king lost a portion of his wealth evidently, not due to his astronomical dilettantism alone, but due to his disinterest in the duties of his station altogether. To show this, Bayle quotes the rant by a contemporary that most precisely befits a follower of the Thracian maid: "he was skilled in letters and managed civic affairs, but when he sat and watched the stars in the sky, he parted from the earth."[xc] The disjunction, *heaven or earth*, stands only as an example, or even as a symbol, for the plain state of affairs that the king found *everything else* more interesting than his office and duty.

What Bayle does not utter with the same clarity is the state of affairs, easily perceptible when conducting historical criticism, that the king's political collapse—like Thales' plummet from the Thracian maid's perspective—was also seen as a punishment for a misstep that could only be an insult to divine majesty from a king's status, as if from throne to throne. There is no source for the king's notorious statement, ascertains Bayle; "For the whole Proof of this Fact, [Mariana] alleges but a vulgar Tradition that has been preserv'd from hand to hand."[xci] By considering the state of the sources, it was easy to salvage a little piece of historical reality by taking the statement as merely modifying the earnest conclusion that has since become permissible to draw: if God had made the world the way Ptolemy's system had presumed, then He could indeed have been given better advice. Although Bayle articulates this harmless variant, which Leibniz evidently had under his eyes, Bayle gives own accusation against the king its sharpness with the rebuke that the king would have needed to manage his affairs better if he wanted the sciences he sponsored to deliver evidence for their compatibility with the highest office.

Bayle knows very well, of course, that a medieval ruler neither conducted astronomy nor let it be conducted for its own sake, but sought advice and help by applying it to the future. It belongs to the image of the haughty king that his collusion with this dubious art earned him odium for distrusting Providence and let his political misfortune come as punishment for that. That is how the case of Alfonso of Castile shows the most beautiful similarity with that of Thales of Miletus.

The historian cannot permit conflating breach of faith with world history in this way; he makes it into a psychological showpiece to reveal the link between character and action. The story goes that, after the prediction that he would lose his throne, the king became so distrustful and monstrous that he made an innumerable host of enemies. That was precisely what led to his downfall; and that sort of thing was well possible if a divination, nothing but raving in and of itself, turns into a real misfortune through the behavior it causes. From that follows a very general law of historical criticism: "The Examples that are alleg'd of Predictions that have been accomplish'd are almost all built on that Foundation."

Nearly all of the concerns raised by the Castilian king's point of view, which historical criticism rationalizes, amount to concerns in the modern period that theory is getting away with something. The effort now dissipates that once sought to dispose of the medieval astronomer's blasphemy or to excuse it, and the effort expands that divorces his political failure from his reputation in the history of astronomy. Fontenellle commemorates the king in "The First Evening" of his *Conversations on the Plurality of Worlds* as a great mathematician, but clearly one lacking humility, and considers his thought of Creation's ability to improve too free-thinking since the contemporary reader also has to admit that the disorder of the world system of his time presented an opportunity for the sinner.[4] [xcii] Fontenelle's fundamental thought on the matter would still persuade the Göttingen mathematician Abraham Gotthelf Kästner, who dealt with the Castilian king more fundamentally than anyone.

In keeping with the now further advanced Enlightenment, Kästner did not feel satisfied to let mitigating circumstances explain the king's dissatisfaction with the world; instead, he tracks down the source behind the folk transmission that Bayle used for the king's judgment: Alfonso had retracted the Archbishop of Compostela's ecclesiastical assets. There is the solution for Kästner:

> When I read this, I thought I knew what Alfonso's insult to God consisted of. Indeed, with this engagement with ecclesiastical assets, Alfonso did so well that people could only say that against him; or rather, it is convincing evidence of Alfonso's impunity that nothing nastier can be told about a king, who had done business with popes and archbishops, than a funny notion, which a strict moralist rightfully derides, but his deed that only insulted clergy is made into an assault on God.[5]

---

4 Fontenelle, *Conversations on the Plurality of Worlds*, 14. "The thought is too libertine, but it's amusing to think that the system itself provoked his sin because it was too complicated (*trop confus*)." Bayle already quotes Fontenelle's *Conversations* in his 1695 Castile article and corrects his mistake that Alfonso was the King of Aragon, as Fontenelle emends.

5 Kästner, "Worin mag König Alfons des Weisen Gotteslästerung bestanden haben?" in Kaestner, *Gesammelte poetische und prosaische schönwissenschaftliche Werke*, II, 131. Even in his 1751 essay contest entry for the Berlin Academy of

What Kästner found is a piece of history as deception by priests; it was not the political mistake of a king, who apparently still made some others.

In addition, Kästner poses the simple question as to whether the accusation was correct that passion for astronomy transferred over into politics as Alfonso of Castile's fate. The standing accusation runs that this king "to the extent that he watched the sky, lost sight of the earth (the German Kaiser's honor)."[xciii] But this, Kästner maintains, "is the joke of a historian who is glad to mock a science that he does not understand." Indeed, the Göttingen colleague of Lichtenberg also only knows the single, and for him persuasive, piece of evidence that such could not have been the case: Julius Caesar, between battles, took up the study of stars, according to the witness of Lucan the poet—and with astrology won a greater kingdom than that which the Christian king Alfonso later lost: "There are indeed examples of kings hunting their lands to death, wrecking, and bedeviling (*verjagt, verprasst, verh-t*) them, but not easily of a king ruining his land by observation (*verobserviret*)."[6]

Here an antagonism takes shape, which the following century will first be able to name when the great unifying titles "natural science" (*Naturwissenschaft*) and "human science" (*Geisteswissenschaft*) become available. Kästner's lament targets historians' careless misunderstanding about what natural science can or cannot do when they assign astronomy the blame for the king's unwelcome political end. Yet again the cruelty of invention is afoot; it attributes to theory the failure of a practice that cannot at all be traced back to it. This invention portrays the former as a mere distraction from the latter and makes the royal astronomer's reproach of Creation into an expression of his lack of political realism.

Sciences, entitled "Treatise on the duties, which unite us in the knowledge that no blind chance occurs in the world; rather, everything is ruled by divine foresight," Kästner treats the Alfonsian verdict on the Creation. Ibid., III, 63.

6   Kästner, "Worin mag König Alfons des Weisen Gotteslästerung bestanden haben?" in ibid., II, 132f. "Julius Caesar, whom Lucan has say:—'I was always free, in the midst of battles, in the regions of the stars and sky above,' whose calendar lasts much longer than the Alfonsian tables, won an even greater empire through his revelries than the one Alfonso lost."—It is illustrative of the emphasis put on the royal astronomy's political background that the French *Encyclopedia* includes an article on Alfonso without mentioning the anecdote until its supplemental part (Vol. I, 1776, 321), while maintaining the airiness of his imperial aspirations outside of any association with his theoretical passion: "It started with murmurs in Castile, then conspiracy ... He returned to his estate, won over the malcontents with gifts and promises; but he left a germ (*levain*) of rebellion in their spirits." The point worth noting is that the article (about all Spanish Alphonsos) comes from Diderot.

It is historiography that does not abide when its figures, consigned to acting, participate in anything more deeply than making their history. If they clash with this postulate, they are punished with invented history: "A great lord's love of astronomy alienated the unastronomical historiographers; therefore they write this love off as bound up with the way that war and the rulers' deaths relate to comets. And the whole story of Alfonso's reproach of Creation is a totally unfounded saga." If we could still see the Milesian primal scene (*Urszene*) shining through here, then the historical orientation's complete disdain for the triumph of the natural sciences would have manifested on the side of the Thracian maid.

Kästner does not wonder what there is that remains unwarped by his discipline and what must be punished such that history keeps the tool of inexhaustible invention readily available. His interpretation of the anecdote about Alfonso is displaced into the position of the theoretical alternative between giving nature or history primacy as an object (*den Primat der Gegenständlichkeit*).

Through this transcendent dimension, the process is inhibited whereby a configuration arises from the king's apothegm like the configuration that belongs to the anecdote. No one ever discovered to whom Alfonso of Castile and Leon said what he is supposed to have said. He is no Job, who holds his complaints and accusations to God, as to a perceptible partner. The anecdote about reproaching Creation remains incomplete because the situation in which Alfonso would have or could have had an addressee is impossible; the Creation took place without him, and a future one is not in sight.

If the analogies with the Thales anecdote are nevertheless accessible in the reception of this anecdote, that is the case because the fragmentary residue of the Alfonso anecdote reflects the modifying of ancient preconditions. The maid can scold the observer of the cosmos because he is not fair towards the reality that matters to her; but the observer of the cosmos would have had no one to scold if his research had given him the chance. Thales saw the world filled with gods and saw himself urged to a timely philosophical epiphany by them—but these gods only filled the world in, they did not answer for it. Alfonso of Castile is observer of the sky and reproacher of heaven in one (*Betrachter und Tadler des Himmels ineins*). He goes as far as imagining the situation in which he would have made the world differently or prompted it to be different than it had become. By having his political demise cited in connection with his reproach of Creation, Alfonso becomes the very thing that history attacks from the position of realism: having failed the world's demands while he thought that he could live in a world other than the real one.

Just this conjoining of two originally unrelated elements, the statement and the plummet, creates the full congruence with the Thales anecdote because now the same principle of realism takes the stand for the reproachers' side. Kästner chose an unsurpassable way to make that point: disputing the existence of the king's reproach of Creation on the basis of one of his political mistakes and presenting evidence for a planned historical lie about him. What matters is that, in the original configuration of the Thales anecdote, a framework is pre-given, whose positions are reoccupiable (*umbesetzbar*). The anecdote thus takes on the function of standing for something that neither the anecdote itself nor its reception can use up.

Ten   Tycho Brahe's Coachman and the Earthquake in Lisbon

We have shown that an imaginative potential was available in the Thales anecdote that permits us to expect not only distortions of its pool of figures, but also reoccupations. Kant thus narrates approximately the same story, this time about Tycho Brahe from whose *Vita* an association with Thales is induced insofar as Brahe only made his turn to astronomy, away from his vocation to become a jurist, because someone's prediction of a solar eclipse had affected him.[xciv] Kant then tells about Tycho that he once felt himself capable of finding the shortest way for his coach to travel by the stars; at that point his coachman set him right: "Good sir, you may well understand the heavens, but here on earth you are a fool."[1] No reproach, but reconciliation through a division of competences.

In making this variant on the Thracian maid's speech, Kant refers to the alleged talent in metaphysics that claims the power to go beyond experience by perceiving spirits as symbolic manifestations of the invisible. The symbolic nature of ghosts would not be worth mentioning and relating to metaphysics, were there not "certain philosophers," who called on comparable abilities for themselves when they "assiduous and engrossed, train their metaphysical telescopes on distant regions and tell of miraculous things there." Although to be imagined as better equipped than the ancient astronomer through the metaphorics of the telescope, they have still remained the addressees of a realist scorn that is rerouted towards them from the mouth of Tycho Brahe's coachman. Metaphysics of such a sort can only be conducted at the price of losing reference to the world. For Kant, "intuitive knowledge (*anschauende Kenntis*) of the *other* world can be attained here only by one losing some of the understanding one needs for the *present* (*die gegenwärtige*)." This formulation has been available since 1766.

---

1   Kant, *Dreams of a Spirit-Seer*, 27.

Fifteen years later, Kant found an extension of this main idea in an unforgettable footnote to *The Critique of Pure Reason* to the effect that the ignorant can have no concept of their ignorance. The consciousness of their shortcoming must thus be delivered to them from outside, in that they bump against a reality which it could not have occurred to them to consider. Now the roles are indeed reversed; not the earthly reality giving the unexpected shove towards realism, as with Thales' well plummet, but the theory of heaven, now taken for science, takes the person towards believing in the paltriness precisely of the reality of the closest at hand (*des Nächstliegenden*):

> The observations and calculations of astronomers have taught us much that is worthy of admiration, but most important, probably, is that they have exposed for us the abyss of our ignorance, which without this information human reason could never have imagined to be so great; reflection on this ignorance has to produce a great alteration in the determination of the final aims of the use of our reason.[2]

"Abyss of ignorance" (*Abgrund der Unwissenheit*)—almost a Pascal formula. How does this enter Kant's language if not as pure rhetoric of admitting suspicions tending towards faithlessness? Is it a caption for an experience? We must go back to the thirty-year-old Kant, who is executing that stroke of genius, known as *General Natural History and Theory of The Sky*, and there we find an experience that exemplifies the tension in the antagonism between heaven and earth, as it had been illustrated in the Thales anecdote and returns in the warning of the coachman to Tycho Brahe. It was the most sensitive year for reason, which had just started considering itself capable of anything when the earthquake in Lisbon sufficed to send it plummeting into the most extreme doubt about the quality of the world[xcv] and about itself at the same time. In a certain sense, Kant's *Theory of the Sky* had been a document of reason's one-time self-assurance that it could encompass objects and problems spatially and temporally distant from itself with *one* broad grasp and to explain it in *one* natural history of the world.

This was the vulnerable intellectual moment when nature itself could take on the role of the Thracian maid and remind the theorist what was under his feet and belonged among the overlooked self-evidences (*Selbstverständlichkeiten*) of the lifeworld, as long as it remained at rest. In three treatises on earthquakes Kant sought to salvage what could be salvaged. In attempt to console the widely upset European temperament, he forced unrest into the habitus of reason, showed it

---

2   Kant, *Critique of Pure Reason*, 555f.

as an expression of theoretical curiosity: "Great events that affect the fate of all mankind rightly arouse that commendable curiosity, which is stimulated by all that is extraordinary and typically looks into the causes of such events."[3] Theory remains in the right, even if mankind's is affected at the core with regard to its assurance about the world and seems to demand everything else but the explanation for the far-reaching causes of its unhappiness.

Kant not only explains what emerges from the fact that "the ground under us is hollow;" he immediately draws consequences for the application of reason against blind submission to the hardness of fate. Lisbon would then have to be rebuilt where it was, but this time with attention to the earthquake's recognizable direction of attack. But then he does not even spurn the consolation that he can grant his Prussian countrymen from the insight—which certainly cannot be brought into harmony with the intention to improve morals through fear—that the surface of their flat country did not show any indication that it intended to treat its residents to such strikes.

That such a treatise would also have to contain a chapter called "On the uses of Earthquakes" is nearly self-evident (*versteht sich fast von selber*).[4] Kant sees their utility in the renewal of the soil materials, which in turn enable plant growth and mineral development. But above all he sees humanity exposed to a lesson that it undergoes with difficulty: not being the purpose of all things and thus not being able to make a valid claim to possessing the Castilian king's insight as to how it would have been able to be made better. In Kant's formulation "we imagine that we would better regulate everything to our advantage, if fate had asked for our vote on this matter."

When the aftershocks of the tragedy in Lisbon refused to relent, Kant reached for his feather once again in April of 1756 and began: "The fire of the subterranean vaults has not yet subsided."[5] Above all, though, the minds and spirits of humanity have only just begun to process the events that gripped all of Europe; speculative minds wanted to make the sun, comets, and planets into causes of the tellurian unrest. Kant's third earthquake-writing thus also serves to put a damper on theory's cosmic folly. That is now the point at which he stands up against reason's lust for explanations that connect the nearest at hand to the

---

3   Kant, "On the Causes of Earthquakes on the Occasion of the Calamity That Befell the Western Countries of Europe towards the End of Last Year (1756)," 330.
4   Kant, "History and Natural Description of the Most Noteworthy Occurrences of the Earthquake That Struck a Large Part of the Earth at the End of the Year 1755 (1756)," 359.
5   Kant, "Continued Observations on the Earthquakes That Have Been Experienced for Some Time (1756)," 368.

farthest off (*das Nächste mit dem Fernsten zu verbinden*). He can take on the role of the Thracian maid and vary her classical formula for reproaching theory: "It is a common extravagance to import the source of an evil from several thousand miles away when it can be found in the neighborhood (*in der Nähe*) ... People are reluctant to perceive something that is merely close at hand. To detect causes at an infinite distance is the only proper proof of a[n] astute understanding." The topos of the Thales anecdote—that it does not matter what can be seen in the sky, but what lies at our feet—thus found the pressing occasion to be staged anew in the very event that should have killed off the link between theory and theodicy. And not by accident is it Kant, in the year of his youthful cosmogonic feat, who "applies" (*anwendet*) the formula to the earthquake as the most threatening way to announce the priority of human and earthly reality.[xcvi]

He also applies the formula to himself. Now the composer of "Universal natural history and theory of the heavens" has need of relief and begs his readers' pardon "for having led them so far around the firmament to enable them to judge correctly the events that have taken place here on our Earth."[6] Viewing comets and planets only distracts from the one elementary fact that can be validated against all of the lifeworld's consistency: "the fragility of the ground we stand on (*unseres Fußbodens*)."[7] In light of the turn from speculation to realism, from the universe to the earth—almost the Socratic turn again—the experience of the year 1755 sets the standard for Kant's own further work, for which the earthquake could have become the foundational experience (*Urerlebnis*). He cried out soberingly into the speculative discussion about the earthquake: "Let us therefore look for the cause in our place of habitation itself, for we have the cause beneath our feet."[xcvii]

Could this possibly have been the imaginative background by whose orientation the path could ultimately have led to the *Critique of Pure Reason*? Indeed, that must remain an unprovable conjecture. Such conjecture might lie precisely on the margin of what could be allowed through "a certain good taste" in philosophy, as Kant had accepted and validated that taste for natural science precisely in order not to expose himself to the "humbling reminder, which is where [man] ought properly to start, that he is never anything more than a human being."[xcviii]

In the meantime, after a whole century of historical criticism introduced by Bayle, criticism received a second thrust: criticism towards the critics. Almost simultaneous with Kant's *Critique of Pure Reason*,

---

6   Kant, "Continued Observations on the Earthquakes That Have Been Experienced for Some Time (1756)," 371.
7   Ibid., 372.

Dietrich Tiedemann's *First Philosophers of Greece* appears. He also uses Thales to show how to proceed with an autodidact's understanding in the absence of the great apparatus of educated role models. The oil-press story cannot be reliable, which follows neatly from the fact that "even today, after so many thousands of years of new experiences and so many failed calendar prophecies, we still cannot predict the fruitfulness of particular years at all, not to mention knowing about particular crops in advance; how much less must they have known back then?"[8]

The main anecdote too undergoes appraisal through considerations that are not derived by confronting sources: "Plato's reputation proves the antiquity of this tale, but not its truth." The anecdote seems concocted more for the sake of the humorous idea than the other way around, with the idea having emerged from the event. Tiedemann's explanation looks at the realistic circumstances at the scene, in order to show what would have to be expected for such a thing to be possible: "For Thales could very well have known the wells at his birthplace, and the wells were also not so completely lacking in fencing."[xcix] That Thales lost his life in his tumble is also the rhetorical escalation of a sophist, who had found it meaningful "even to let him die watching the stars." More reliable, according to Tiedemann, is that he died of old age from heat and thirst as a spectator at the Olympic Games, as Diogenes reports. It is improbable for someone to die abnormally; that even goes for people that are significant enough to be treated in books.

One last observation on the eighteenth century reveals that the Aesopian fable of the fallen stargazer made an entry into pedagogy, specifically by way of Samuel Richardson's widespread collection *Young Man's Pocket Companion*, introduced to German by Lessing. Considering the influence of this author and publisher on Rousseau and on *Werther*, that is, on youthful emotionalism with its background in the Puritan family novel, the piece "The Astrologer Admonished" must be accorded secondary influence, which the publishers of widely known works exert with whatever they produce on the side.[9] [c]

The hero of the story is no longer "a certain star-gazer," the one who stumbled into a fairly deep ditch during his business and who tries to help himself out again. A "sober fellow" (*nicht unvernünftiger Mann*) passes him by and chides him by combining nearly all of the usual variants in the tradition: "make a right use of your present misfortunes; and, for the future, pray let the stars go on quietly in their courses, and do you a little better to the ditches; for is it not strange, that you should tell other people their fortune, and know nothing of your own?"

---

8 Tiedemann, *Griechenlands erste Philosophen*, 120.
9 Aesop and Richardson, *Aesop's Fables*, 61.

This surprising conclusion especially recalls the cuckolded stargazer, who is met with mockery for not having recognized his own marital misfortune in the stars.[ci] Richardson is concerned with the story's lesson, and so it comes immediately after the fable's self-reference: just punishment comes to those "who neglect their own concerns to pry into those of other people." Besides the lesson, there is yet another "Reflection," which deals with prophecy of various types; it is "one of the most pernicious snares in human life." This goes particularly for gullible women and children, among whom the imagination is so strong, since imagination is like soft wax that takes on every impression. The "Reflection" is overtly intended for educators working with the fable pedagogically. The utmost caution is laid on their hearts: to protect the spirits entrusted to them against "the impudent pretentions of fortune-tellers." The verbose quality of this warning is far removed from the allure of the twist that Richardson gave to the fable itself. Looking backwards from this highpoint in the epoch of pedagogism, we see Montaigne as the first to have found an educational principle in the fable's moral: "There is great folly in teaching our children ... about the heavenly bodies and the motions of the Eighth Sphere before they know about their own properties."[10]

---

10 Montaigne, *The Essays of Michel de Montaigne*, 179.

Eleven Absentmindednesses

The expression "absentmindedness" (*Geistesabwesenheit*) has an unprecedented meaning in Ludwig Feuerbach's language. He designates Idealism's exoticism as a way of life: between the *risk* that Idealism distorts reality and the *humor* of its involuntary distance from life. The writer is the professional incarnation of this way of life, which Feuerbach describes as "humorous-philosophical."[cii]

From a perspective situated in the year 1834, that very absentmindedness lands him near the configuration that has shown up in the ridiculed misstep of equating existence and mind since Thales and the Thracian maid. By no coincidence, Feuerbach chooses, instead of someone tumbling into a well, someone drifting out onto high sea with risky prospects as a metaphor for what has also been called losing-the-ground-under-one's-feet (*Den-Boden-unter-den-Füßen-verlieren*). Where the loss of reality and of realism is supposed to be lamentable, the ground under one's feet is the most common metaphor; if this is meant to describe leaving the lifeworld, it turns into the metaphor for the inconspicuous assurances which comprise the syndrome of lifeworldliness—the thematizing of which will be one of philosophy's latest insights. Feuerbach thus prefers to describe his authors' "absentmindedness" with the unfathomability (*Unergründlichkeit*) of the sea rather than that of the well: "On the high sea of mental productivity, where the idea of infinity is present to the human ... he loses sight of those landmasses on which the human otherwise sets a firm foot and builds his petty Philistine world."[1]

For those absent *through* their mind or *with* it, real life, familiar life is nothing but a burdensome and shameless beggar; that beggar rips them out of their imaginings and meditations with his impertinent demands at the most inconvenient time. A great portion of these

---

1 Feuerbach, "Der Schriftsteller und der Mensch," in ibid., I 341. On the metaphor of the "high sea," see Blumenberg, *Shipwreck with Spectator*, 7–10.

people's actions turns into a kind of disengagement in attempts to get such pestering off their throat.

Here is the passage where the association with Thales and the maid is formed. The protophilosopher's "absentmindedness" is the early parable for the relationship to reality of the theorist's latest professionalization in the form of the writer:

> Thales, with whom the light of science rose over Greece, once did not notice a ditch in front of his feet, since he was just observing the stars, and fell in. An old woman, who was his maid or possibly just happened to be there completely by chance (which I no longer know, though it is completely insignificant), mocked him for it, and did well to do so, for it was an old woman, and common folk still mock him today for it, and she has the indisputable right to do so as common folk.

The right to laugh goes to the maid; yet this no longer instantaneously means that the philosopher rightly plummeted into the ditch and got mocked. The situation has become perspectivistic, can no longer be measured by one standard. That is the perspective of the nineteenth century; in its pure form it is dismissively called historicism.

Common folk, who laugh and take it as their right, are called into the archaic scene for their realism; but the absentminded one has his own right that no longer needs to be confirmed by fulfilled solar eclipse prognostications or oil mill successes. It is grounded in his willingness to abstain from success and applause of all kinds of realism and to withdraw himself from the pestering of common life. The theorist is a humorous sort, but laughing at him cannot do him justice—that is the laughter of another kind of absentminded people. Thus the prototypical scene, still in Bayle's wake, gets treated like a piece of history (*Historie*); but now only in order to dispense historical amnesties to all parties involved.

To ask for the moral of the story now means: the moral for whom and when? The case in the absentminded one's defense now lies in the temporal sequence of his absences and presences—he is not permitted to be observed synchronously in relation to the reality of those who mock him, but diachronically in relation to the reality that will always only become shared in the future and will eventually become everyone's common reality. An object of experience cannot be everything at every time—a triviality that will be time-intensive and painful to discover. What makes the star observer as ridiculous as the philosopher is his view towards "realities" beyond the reality *of today*. To put it otherwise: what had passed for transcendent until then proves for him to belong in the horizon of future experience.

That has to do with the unique time relation between seeing and thinking. The protophilosopher is the following state of affairs, manifest in anecdotal form: one can think without seeing, but cannot see without thinking—this most consequential original fact (*Urfaktum*) of philosophy. The first philosopher is not defined by his still being far (*Noch-Entferntsein*) from becoming all head, but by his getting away (*Sich-entfernen*) from being all eye. Something happened there, which Feuerbach first described towards the end of his life as the ultimate intensification of "absentmindedness" through an example from his own experience: "When I once suddenly noticed a majestic meteor while observing the starry sky, I wanted to call the people in the nearby room over to share the pleasure, but I could not call out; I was speechless."[2] There is the ridiculously absentminded person whom no one laughs at; not just by chance, for his bodily absence protects him from the odium of speechlessness, to which he is condemned by a perception that demands his attention without his premeditation. The objectively trivial experience of the meteor can become what the solar eclipse could no longer be since Thales.

Feuerbach too sought to relate his philosophical achievement to astronomy's exemplary historical track. Almost inevitably, this blooms into a clarification of his outlook on the Thales anecdote once again:

> I made an object of empirical science out of what was considered until now to lie beyond knowledge, even by the better ones only as a matter of uncertainty, of faith. To make what did not pass for an object—first of *real*, then even just of *possible* knowledge—into an object of knowledge, as in the case of astronomy, is the course of science itself. First comes physics, then pneumatics. First the sky (*Himmel*) of the eye, then the heaven (*Himmel*) of the spirit, of desire.[3]

The relationships of far and near (*Ferne und Nähe*) that play against each other in the Thales anecdote are still the conceptual aids by which Feuerbach's realism determines the beginning of philosophy and its distance from this beginning. No longer is what lies in front of the feet and gets overlooked there the epitome of the real, but something more brutish, what is "incorporated" (*einverleibt*): breathing and eating. The nearest comes so close that it can only be the farthest in time: the last approach by human wisdom to humanity itself, that "you are what you eat."[ciii] The Thracian maid would never once have thought of that: "The

---

2 "Spiritualismus und Materialismus," 1863–6, in Feuerbach, *Sämmtliche Werke*, X, 211.
3 "Nachgelassene Aphorismen," in ibid., X, 343.

near is precisely the furthest from humanity, because for us it does not qualify as a secret, and just for that reason it is a secret to us, because it is always, and thus never an object."⁴ Near and far are not ultimately disjunctives: the starry sky's unreality, which the Thracian maid's laughter reflects, is the future reality, still meaningless at its beginning, but assured as future reality by the turn to theory.

Feuerbach could not once divine theory's "nearness," entirely still awaiting construction by theory. What matters to him is that, before the stars become scientific objects, they had been "beings (*Wesen*) that reveal themselves as untouchable, unfeelable, only optical, only for the eye as light, purely mental, superhuman, divine beings, i.e. beings of the imagination."⁵ This imagination is akin to an intellectual instinct; it is no longer the organ for mounting the rudiments of past perceptions into new collages; rather, it is the organ for preconceiving the expansion upon sensation (*Sinnlichkeit*), the organ for anticipating reality.⁶

If humanity is "the living superlative of sensualism," a concept of perception would not befit humanity if it explained perception as a system of adaptation to an environment comprised of preservation signals; rather, perception should make "the world, the infinite" into the referential whole of the senses "and purely for its own sake, i.e. for the sake of aesthetic enjoyment."⁷ The difference between the gaze raised to the stars and attention turned to the earth in the interest of self-preservation—the dualism of theory's Milesian primal scene (*Urszene*)—is negated (*aufgehoben*). Sensation's end in itself and its self-enjoyment are manufactured only more purely "through the purposeless gaze at the stars" and thus anticipate the wide-ranging purposiveness of the drive for knowledge as it extends across history. What divides the protophilosopher and the Thracian maid is a hiatus, which time would close with sensibility's reach outward, a reach which over time becomes an end in itself.

If a person is ridiculed at the beginning of a particular history, and that person represents the impetus for that history, then the ridicule comes across differently in that we must ascribe to the ridiculed person that he pursued his goals according to the traits of the human species[clv] and is thus determined by the species' prescience about its own future.

---

4 "Einige Bemerkungen über den 'Anfang der Philosophie' von Dr. F. J. Reiff," 1841, in Feuerbach, *Gesammelte Werke*, II, 144.
5 "Die Unsterblichkeitsfrage vom Standpunkt der Anthropologie," 1846, in Feuerbach, *Sämmtliche Werke*, I, 125.
6 On Feuerbach's concept of the "drive for knowledge" (*Wissenstriebes*) as precondition for a new notion of "beginning" in philosophy, see Blumenberg, *The Legitimacy of the Modern Age*, 440–7.
7 "Wider den Dualismus von Leib und Seele," in Feuerbach, *Sämmtliche Werke*, II, 349.

Realism, like that of the maid, is then only a matter of dull simultaneity. The true realist is the one who is already caught up in time, stands in the unrecognized service of history. Thales' ridiculousness in the maid's eyes is based on the fact that he does not live in simultaneity with her concept of reality. Humanity, by nature of its species, does not want to know "what it cannot know," as we could hear and construe in the maid's laughter.[8] Humanity only wants to know what is "now not yet" factually known and can be. The drive for knowledge does not want to intrude ahead into the inaccessible, which is meaningless to the human; the human wants insight into the perspective on what is possible in time: "Humanity has nothing less than a supranatural drive for knowledge, as Christianity or Platonism muses; it has no drive that steps beyond human nature's measure, which is indeed not finite, not measurable with the circle of a philosophical system; his drive for knowledge extends just to the knowable for the human, that is, to human objects, to objects that achieve their effect in the course of history."

The model articulated here only repeats what Feuerbach had discovered about the relationship between theology and philosophy: just as theology is the historical form of an anthropology still to come, which for now is only metaphorical, so Classical astronomy is the projection of an ideal of comprehending the reality of the unattainable and thus of "pure" admiration. The view (*Anblick*) of the stars is the prospect (*Ausblick*) of retrieving the metaphor that has become enacted in that viewing. The Thracian maid laughs because she cannot perceive that it is her concern that Thales almost breaks his neck for.

The danger entailed by a history of covert projections—occurring behind humanity's back, through the genre of deceptively wrought metaphors—is that the projections might achieve independence: the absolutism of metaphors, as Platonic forms or as divine attributes, their retrievability ultimately remaining forgotten.[cv] The Thracian maid's role remains occupiable (*besetzbar*) again and again, in order to make new distances of ridiculousness palpable. In his enthusiasm for astronomy, Feuerbach almost feels caught in the old thought that astronomy has to do with a higher reality, with a more pure reality, with the part of nature closer to thought itself (*gedankennäher*).

It is fitting to remember the lower gods wherever the tendency arises to take Idealism at its word. The present has its analogy with Copernicus' cosmic call to order, to seek the conditions of the furthest removed phenomena in the unremarkable things nearest at hand: nutritional science as quasi-ontology that equates being and eating. It

---

8   "Der rationalistische und ungläubige Unsterblichkeitsglaube," in Feuerbach, *Sämmtliche Werke*, I, 172–4.

enables contemporary philosophy to come forward in *one* person on both positions: the position of presumption and of the call to order:

> But why do I presume to go to the far sky of astronomy, in order to denounce the natural sciences for their revolutionary tendencies in our governments? We have a much more relevant, urgent, timely case for natural science's universal, revolutionary meaning in a newly published piece: *Theory of Nutrition: For the People* by Jacob Moleschott.[9]

And the philosopher—plummeting into the depth of reality because he is called back as species-being (*Gattungswesen*) from his somnambulism—can still exclaim between astonishment and outrage: "Thus it is a matter of eating and drinking when we question the ideality or reality of the world? ... what commonness!"

From the other wing of Hegelianism, Eduard Gans, having just been promoted to juridical professor in Berlin against Savigny's protest, built the Thales anecdote into his lecture on natural rights in the winter semester of 1828–9. The nocturnal loneliness of the protophilosopher under the stars and the barbarian laughter at his plummet down the well now stand for the traits of the Greek world—and of history and theory themselves along with it—as it emerged from the Oriental world. "Before Greece there is no philosophy."[10] That is not its misfortune, but the precondition of the rupture that is inevitable if more is to become than the immediacy of the human being's meaning in the world (*der Sinn des menschlichen Daseins in der Welt*).

The Thracian maid is not some Oriental woman, but she does come from Europe's crossroads with the Orient and can imagine the anecdotally fixed moment when the worlds separate. "The Orientals are in themselves still all in being. But no thought about their being has come to them yet. They are not yet divided within themselves (*zerrissen*), they are pure children." The first philosophy is natural philosophy; humanity has not yet arrived at the idea "of observing itself as nature."

This state of affairs is legible in Thales, and Socrates himself ironically strengthens the case against this connection of philosophy with nature, since he first invented metaphor of the fallen and ridiculed Thales. It is not self-evident to Eduard Gans that the citizen of Miletus and the political advisor for his polis overlooks his state in order to see the stars, because he is a philosopher. For in the meantime that

---

9 "Die Naturwissenschaft und die Revolution," 1850, in Feuerbach, *Sämmtliche Werke*, X, 11.

10 Gans, *Philosophische Schriften*, 47 (from an anonymous postscript to the lecture on natural right).

state has become the epitome of what the maid claimed for the most obvious concern (*das Nächstliegende*), as little thought as she may have given to state affairs. Thales "is not troubled by the state, but by water, the ground of all things ... Yes, how little he thought about the state is witnessed by the anecdote where he, looking at the stars, fell into a wellspring." If we do not expect playful language from Eduard Gans even a little, then we would have to regard falling (*Verfallen*) into the water—without falling (*Nichtverfallen*) for the state—as a fall into the ground of all things. The ongoing play of the image lets the philosopher fall on the water that is here *called* "wellspring" (*Quelle*) and is supposed to *be* the "ground" (*Grund*).[cvi] The spring instead of the cistern—that cannot come from pure linguistic chance in a moment at the lectern.

The laughing maid is of no interest to Eduard Gans. And yet she is thoroughly present. The quality of her non-understanding as a historical role is insinuated such that the figure is not even necessary. She supposedly does not understand individuality confronted with nature and laughs rightfully, although this right must remain hidden to her—as Feuerbach's Thales had his right hidden from him at the beginning of history, because beginnings with consciousness of what they begin and set in motion would be false beginnings. Eduard Gans is already dead when Feuerbach writes the following, and it does not refer to Thales, but to Luther: "Whosoever already sets his goal preemptively from the beginning as that which can only result from a purposeless, non-arbitrary development process misses his goal."[11]

Eduard Gans gives the maid's laughter its late articulation; as an observer more than a little familiar with the historical attitude, he deemed the following formula appropriate to describe the founder of natural philosophy and his turn to the starry sky: "the first philosopher was outside of all reality."[12] He went his own way outside of the neighborhood of the polis without Gans having to make any use of the other, seemingly trivial trait from the tradition: Thales "left the city" at night to conduct his theory. That the maid was also outside of the city, in order to be able to become a witness to the scene, is excused from the opposite direction. She had not yet acquired the free realm of the state and of the conditions of thought created in it alone: "without free individuality, there are no thoughts. A slave is not capable of free thoughts."

Behind the historically given hiatus at the origin of natural philosophy, another one already stands, which robs laughter of its

---

11   "Fragmente zur Characteristik meines philosophischen Curriculum Vitae," 1846, in Feuerbach, *Sämmtliche Werke*, II, 385.
12   Gans, *Philosophische Schriften*, 48.

juvenile harmlessness, if one may say so. In the eyes of the Berlin legal philosopher, it only follows logically that the maid's gracefulness gets lost in the course of the anecdote's tradition. Grown old, she is now just the blinded philosopher's angel of death.

With a late demand, if not the latest, for a totality in the image of nature (*Naturanschauung*), Alexander von Humboldt practiced unprotected, risk-prone observation of the sky on his great travels, where he was exposed to irate glances from the unenlightened outside of the observatories that had already become bulwarks of theory. He only became a legendary figure as a sky observer in the end: through a political satire that had appeared for the first time in 1874 in the Polish newspaper *Gazeta Narodowa* in the form of a report, that was probably fraudulent, though it did not neglect a core reality. Then it was taken up in the same year in the *Glasgow Weekly Herald* and from this source wandered right off to the German magazine *Aus allen Weltteilen*, only to turn back to Russia finally in 1889, whence it must have emerged.[13] It deals with an episode that is supposed to have occurred in a small city of the Tobolsk government during Humboldt's trip in 1829 to the Ural and Altai Mountains and to the Caspian Sea. In the satirical text, the episode turns into the content of a report by the local police officer to the general governor.

If we view the episode as a variant on the configuration of the Milesian philosopher with the Thracian maid, then the insinuation changes. The establishment of science in the modern world has proven decisive: the laughter that unfailingly erupts is that of the imagined observer of the nightly scene, the reader of the fictional piece. For a civilization familiar with the ritual activities of the theorist, the work-related annoyance of a state officer towards the sky observer has no chance of being taken seriously. The satire—or the satirical exploitation of a real event—targets a public whom one can no longer expect *not* to place themselves on the side of theoretical action. Especially as this action has decisively removed itself from the suspicion of ruling class leisure, has long been recognized as solid "work." What plays out is the switching of sides through realism's concession to theory on the one hand and its doubt over what constitutes healthy understanding on the other.

Due to this "reoccupation" of the archaic schema, it is worth inspecting the police report in its full scope:

---

13 Humboldt, *Gespräche*, 103. On the historical truth content, see: Beck, *Alexander von Humboldt*, 122. "It could be precisely that the place names, which are evidently incorrect were purposefully forged in order to conceal the story's originator" (translation varies from cited edition; citation not found).

A few days ago, a German by the name of Humboldt came here, frail, of short stature, insignificant by all appearances, but important ... Although I showed him deference as duty requires, I must still note that this person seemed suspicious and very dangerous to me. From the very beginning I did not like him ... The whole time he granted the higher personages of the city no regard and occupied himself with the Poles and with other political criminals whom I keep under surveillance. I dare report that the sort of conversation he had with the political criminals did not escape my attention, especially since after his long conversations he went to the peak of a hill that dominates the city. They dragged a box up there and drew an instrument from it that had the look of a long tube that seemed to me and to the whole society to be a cannon. After he had steadied the tube on three feet, he directed it right at the city and everyone went over to him to see if he had aimed it properly. Since I see a great danger to the city in all of this (for it is completely made of wood), I promptly ordered the garrison, which consists of a deputy and six common men, to head for the same spot with loaded weapons, not to let the German out of sight, and to observe his shenanigans. If the fraudulent deceptions of this person justify my suspicion, then we will give up our life for the Czar and Holy Russia.[14]

Although the exaggeration of the police action and the pathos in the language of the report are presumably satirical, the core of the distrust towards the expedition and its activities is reflected in a journal entry from May 1851, where Karl August Varnhagen von Ense notes about the Czar's visit to Berlin: "The Czar did not speak a word with Humboldt while in his presence, which the latter took badly, but which [would have been] a delight for a courtier ..."[15]

For Humboldt, the experience of 1829 could not have been surprising if he had considered past experience and the absolutist zeal for the state on top of it. The theorist's position as eccentric in a cultural sphere held back from scientific progress at the turn of the nineteenth century was in fact already familiar to him from his first great trip from 1799 to 1804 through the viceroyalty of pre-revolutionary South America. There as

---

14 The fact that it was not unobjectionable everywhere in the world to engage in the astronomical theorist's stance and to use the appropriate instruments comes up in the travelogue of G. Rose regarding his contact with a Chinese border-guard in Bachty on the Irtysh River in the same year of 1829, where Humboldt takes special precautionary measures in order to arouse no suspicion among the Chinese with his procedures for determining the height of the sun. Humboldt, *Gespräche*, 108.
15 Varnhagen von Ense, *Tagebücher*, IX, 232–3.

here, the equipped sky watcher was a suspect figure. For determining his geographical position, Humboldt preferred the mirror-sextant in whose artificial horizon the sun was reflected more clearly as a star and which enabled easier reading during the day. Nevertheless, according to Humboldt's own report, there was an incentive to switch to performing position determination at night when a certain population had a distrustful orientation towards operations performed during the day.[16]

When Humboldt embarked on his South American expedition in 1799, he must have waited until nightfall the first time he made observations, due to the population's distrust:

> I have observed the sun and the stars of the first magnitude as often as circumstances have allowed. In the Kingdom of Valencia, I have had to suffer a lot of nasty hisses from the rabble ... I have often had the pain of seeing the sun go down without being allowed to unpack my instruments. I was required to wait for the quiet of night in order to satisfy myself with a star of the second magnitude, which showed up sadly on an artificial horizon ... In Martorell, I made observations in the middle of the road surrounded by 30 onlookers, who cried that I was praying to the moon.[17]

The Thracian maid had already perhaps mistook the theory of the stars for their cult—and may have supposed her gods to be the stronger ones on this basis.

After the strange rituals of theory were long integrated into the lifeworlds of Europe's cities, as misunderstood as these rituals may have remained or still would for a while, the theorist's outlandishness was renewed again as soon as he left the fixed positions of his mustered instruments and the daily discipline of their use and set off on an expedition. Here he did not just find the unfamiliar, but became it as well. Humboldt's passport to visit the Spanish colonies contained the precautionary note that he was allowed to use his instruments "with full freedom" and could "conduct astronomical observations in all Spanish territories."[18] The alienated response to the alienating behavior (*Das Befremden über das Befremdliche*) takes on alternating forms and degrees. It is comparatively harmless among the young ladies of Quito, who do not see the gallant cosmopolitan dally longer than is

---

16 Beck, *Alexander von Humboldt.*, I 88.
17 Ibid., I 120–1. Humboldt reports this in his observation journal to the Gotha astronomer Franz von Zach, who had introduced the mirror sextant in Germany and had instructed Humboldt in its use.
18 Ibid., I, 128.

necessary to pay them compliments and to satisfy his appetite, only in order to return immediately to looking at the rocks outside again and to collecting plants: "At night, when we had long gone to bed, he was staring at the stars. We women could understand that all much less than the Marquis, my father," one of those beauties, Rosa Montúfar, tells the geographer Moritz Wagner more than a half century later.[19]

Humboldt came closest to the Milesian philosopher's situation in 1801 in Bogotá when all sorts of gossip and rumors about himself were shared with him just outside of a reception held for him by the local nobles. In a sketch of his lost journals, he notes the discrepancy between the beautiful speeches about the scientist's self-sacrifice for the interest of humanity and the disappointment that he did not meet the expectations directed toward him of a stiff and awkward scholar about whom the rumor had circulated all around that he observed the stars from the depth of a well.[20]

The century of the Enlightenment had fundamentally ended. Not only had it never penetrated these parts of the world, it had not even penetrated the traveling scholar's motivations, who perceived no opportunity to enlighten the surroundings, particularly not the ladies' world, as he attended to his procedures; so little did the thrill of teaching seem to surge in him. It would only take a quarter century for Humboldt's lectures in Berlin—the precursor to *Cosmos*—to become the talk of dinner tables and salons. But that was Berlin, where people felt the need to enlighten the world so little that they thought they could give themselves over to the pleasure of the whole. Humboldt's success becomes one of the last highpoints for expectations satisfied by the theorist, his plummet becomes impossible, the laughter decisively falls silent.

---

19 Ibid., I, 196.
20 Quote from Schumacher, *Südamerikanische Studien*, 102–4. "Now people from all corners were making beautiful speeches about the interest of humanity and the sacrifice for science; compliments flowed in the names of the viceroy and the archbishop. Everything sounded so endlessly grand, only they found the man himself very small and very young. They have imagined instead of a thirty-year-old, a fifty-year-old, someone stiff and awkward. Besides, the most contradictory reports had been spread from Cartagena: I could not speak Spanish well, I always observed the stars from inside a deep well, I had a chaplain and a mistress as part of my entourage ..."

Twelve Where Thales had Failed, According to Nietzsche

"How was it even possible for Thales to renounce myth? Thales as statesman! Something must have occurred at this point."[1] [cvii] Nietzsche expresses astonishment rather than explicating a question when he drafts his notes on the problematic of the protophilosopher in 1875. By looking back on the first member of his guild, he already sees the last of them: the last philosopher, whom he had already envisioned in 1872 as the one who would relinquish philosophy for a new myth of art.[cviii]

Combining the first and the last in this way only made sense if there was something like a teleology for the story between beginning and end, which would have to be recognizable at the beginning, at least as an insinuation. The same Thales of Miletus, whose break from myth had been the entire purpose of his more rebellious than insightful water-cosmogony, held himself to a criterion for a realism whose concept of reality made it incomprehensible to the maid. She cannot perceive "profundity" in Thales' forceful turn from the cosmos and his plummet into the sole primal element. Modernizing that feature of this construction does not require Nietzsche to mention the anecdote of the well plummet, whose Platonic version he had traced back, during his philological days, to a collection of Thales' sayings (*apomnemoneumata*). The anecdote must have been "very old" and was treated "as plausible" by Aristotle.[2] For Nietzsche, then, the Platonic version

---

1 Nietzsche, "Vorarbeiten zu einer Schrift über den Philosophen," in *Gesammelte Werke*, VI, 118.
2 Nietzsche, *The Pre-Platonic Philosophers*, 29, in *Gesammelte Werke*, IV, 268–75. A lecture series beginning in 1872. "Finally that there was a set list of attributions to Thales is proved by Plato" in section 174 A of *Theaetetus*. *The Pre-Platonic Philosophers*, 29. It is clear: what Aristotle possessed must have been available to Plato as well, and "Aristotle is the only reliable source of Thales' fundamental principle." *The Pre-Platonic Philosophers*, 27. A reminiscence on the anecdote could be contained in the poem "Declaration of Love" printed in the appendix

was more faithful to its source than what is found in Diogenes Laertius, whom he simply took for a dubious hack. He forges no connection, however, between the anecdote and the aspect of the figure of Thales most important to him, an aspect contained in one sentence of that early treatise: "[Thales] must have been an extremely influential man politically," for he putatively advised the Ionians to unite as a confederation in order to repel the Persian threat.[cix] The connection with the turn away from myth is then only established in the text through juxtaposition; the impulse is still expressly connected with the fundamentally mathematical orientation: "It was a great mathematician who gave rise to philosophy in Greece. Thence comes his feel for the abstract, the unmythical, the unallegorical."[cx] Nietzsche found it peculiar that he remained in Delphi "despite his antimythological sentiments."

Nietzsche brings two testimonies into conjunction with Thales' great "departure:" the assumption of his Phoenician ancestry among the Alexandrian scholars, an assumption that achieved foundational significance, and the legend of his time spent in Egypt. The decisive trend against claiming the autochthony of theory and philosophy is marked impressively by two short sentences: "Now, for the first time, Greek philosophy is said to have not originated in Greece. The Phoenician still had to seek education among the Egyptians."[cxi] It is almost tempting to read another line into this: and to be laughed at by a Thracian woman.

It thus remains undecided whether Thales found myth repugnant primarily as a mathematician or as a politician, who wanted to extinguish the particularizing effect of the local myths with the goal of achieving higher unities. Nevertheless, the only reliably transmitted sentence from Thales, that the origin of everything is water, can also be read as a unifying ersatz myth for the Ionian coastal cities. It should not only have presented them with their common origin, but also with the condition of their common survival. Nietzsche places weight on the rationality of this one sentence as "a hypothesis of the natural sciences of great worth."[cxii] Thence he also finds worth in the lasting, established relationship between that sentence and the

---

of *The Gay Science* and whose subtitle reads "(whereby however the poet fell into a ditch)." Nietzsche, *The Gay Science*, 253. The poem appeared in 1882 and on the whole portrays the contraposition to the subtitle's stance, for instance, in the second strophe: "Star and eternity, / he lives now in the heights that living shuns, / forgives all jealousy—: / Who see him fly, they too are soaring ones." Ibid., 254. The Thales configuration is even more clearly marked if one adds the strophe that Nietzsche crossed out in the manuscript before the one quoted above: "He flew to the highest—now the sky / lifts him in glorious flight: / Now he rests motionless and hovers by, / forgetting glory and who is glorified."

image of Thales the astronomer: the facts would have proven him right insofar as the present day celestial bodies must have derived from less stable aggregate states, back to the gaseous primeval form of the world, familiar from the hypothesis of Kant and Laplace. The natural philosophy founded by Thales was then "certainly on the right path."[cxiii] Something had been done there, which would neither require a complete correction nor be possible to repeat or supersede at a later time: "To conceive the entirety of such a multifarious universe as the merely formal differentiation of *one* fundamental material belongs to an inconceivable freedom and boldness! This is a service of such a magnitude that no one may aspire to it a second time."

For Nietzsche, Thales was a realist, but not as the man behind the oil-press speculation, which Nietzsche does not mention once in his early treatise; nor is Thales a realist in foretelling the solar eclipse, which Nietzsche deems the only stable point for dating Thales' lifetime, but which he sees as unrelated to theory's important anti-terrifying role. That Thales was successful with his prediction, but failed in his vision to confederate the Greek cities on the coast of Asia Minor, did not hinder Nietzsche from accentuating Thales' character as a statesman. His statement of burnout, that everything is full of gods—whose universally quantifying form competed with the new founding sentence about the ubiquity of water—showed up as an indicator of a stronger fact: the first philosopher failed right away with the first political concept that emerged from philosophy's first step.

Nietzsche says Thales failed due to the endurance of what he believed he had left behind him: "he failed due to the old mythical concept of the polis." [3, cxiv] The only way in which theorists stay successful in the long run is in their perspective towards cosmogonies, according to Kant; the statesman had underestimated what he had gotten into and overestimated what he was able to offer with his ersatz myth. The precondition for his vision was simultaneously the impediment to its realization: "If the polis were the cutting edge of Hellenic will, and had it relied on myth, that would mean giving up myth along with giving up the old concept of the polis." That was what philosophy was not able to accomplish. The universalizing power will either come from a place where myth is genuinely weak, namely from Rome, or it will arise from the great religions' dogmas, which entitle them to their recklessness in demanding unity.

We do not know to which segment of Thales' biography the anecdote of the well plummet refers. Only late is the elderly and

---

3   *Wissenschaft und Weisheit im Kampfe* in Nietzsche, *Philosophy and Truth*, 145 (translation modified) (*Gesammelte Werke*, VI, 118). The last drafts date from 1875.

blind theorist brought into view, whose demise Nietzsche translates according to Anaximenes' alleged letter: "he fell from a cliff at night."[cxv] His fascination with the composite of philosopher and statesman—no less with the reason why this composite failed—is relevant. Thales, who watched heaven and was mocked by the maid, could be a figure for resignation; he who fled into the nights of star observation also fled into philosophy as the long-term instrument for grappling with myth, which remained un-overcome at that point. When Plato showed Thales his highest reverence, in that he blended him with his image of Socrates, the Persian Wars had already taken place, Athens had already exhausted the success of its hegemony, and philosophy had failed in the political once again in the person of Plato himself.

Nietzsche called the Greeks "the counterpiece to all realists." They supposedly only believed in the reality of humans and gods, whereas they observed "all of nature equally only as a disguise, masquerade, and metamorphosis of these god-people."[4] With the sentence, *everything is full of gods*, Thales must have meant that for nature—or for something like a nature—there was no more room; to accomplish this, he reduced the cosmogonic instrumentarium to a single element. What Nietzsche attributes to the Greeks and where he lets Thales go against the grain is nothing other than the anthropomorphism of his own assessment of the world: the disappearance of nature, or of what nature would have been, among the projections that humanity cast over her and in which humanity recognizes nothing other than itself in nature. Nietzsche has once again followed the overwhelming Docetism, which resides in Greek myth *and* lives on in Greek philosophy—even in that of a Parmenides, who had only agreed to the unity of the one existent reality, who returned everything to what it was in the form of "belief" (*doxa*), and who ostensibly treated it all with disproportionately more thoroughness than he had treated that which had been said about that one being.

The failure of the contradictory approach towards myth taken by Thales of Miletus is only superficially his individual catastrophe; the miscarriage of Thales's demythologization only exhibited more drastic consequences than elsewhere, because the Ionian cities were subordinated immediately following their philosophical hardness of hearing and their stubborn refusal to see themselves as exceptions in history. The beginning of philosophy already decided what would not be possible for it—even with more nuanced distinctions between appearance and reality.

Nietzsche's earliest surviving encounter with the Thales anecdote occurs in a text which does not belong in the repertoire of classical

---

4   Nietzsche, *Philosophy in the Tragic Age of the Greeks*, 41, 1873 (*Gesammelte Werke*, IV, 165–7).

philology and not even in that of the Diogenes scholar. Nietzsche counts as one of those not so rare intellects who appear to exist only in order to write about themselves.[cxvi] Already as a thirteen-year-old, he wrote "From my life," and we also have the fortune of another early self-thematization in the "Retrospective on my two years in Leipzig." The latter describes his second winter there, from 1866 to 1867, when he entered a writing contest with an essay on Diogenes Laertius' sources.[cxvii] In the retrospective, he reports about a discovery in the Leipziger Rathsbibliothek, whose mention already sheds light on his later interest in the anecdotal within philosophy: "From the rich mass of older prints, a Walter Burley stood out to me, which the bibliographic handbooks do not know: Walter Burley, *De Vita Philosophorum*."[5] At an early age, Nietzsche ran into evidence of the late medieval interest in ancient philosophers' famous situations and sayings, an interest which had died out by his own century despite the revived historiography of philosophy—or precisely because of its preoccupation with concepts (*Begriffsfreudigkeit*).

Of Pierre Bayle it could be said that his excisions from the inventory of extant literature formed part of the precondition for overrating its historical accuracy, a misjudgment cultivated through the Renaissance. And thus freedom from contradiction sufficed for transmitted anecdotal material to achieve historical credence, according to Bayle; for Nietzsche, the guiding premise of historical study works exactly the other way around. For every datum and fact, the burden of evidence already lay completely within the historian's safeguarding work. It is was thus obligatory that Nietzsche accredit the Thales anecdote in its Platonic version to the source of the protophilosopher's sayings from which Aristotle had produced the most reliable of Thales' dogmatic propositions. Moreover, the anecdote's narrative quality can hardly be characteristic of such sketches: even during the Milesian well plummet, the philosopher is not allowed a single word.

With this construction, Nietzsche had authenticated the historical accuracy (*Historizität*) of an event that could have amounted to the Greeks' first tragedy, their real tragedy, the only tragedy of their philosophy. In Nietzsche's view, the figure of Thales alone could decide about a successful way to introduce the new form of thought: whether the unity of reason could ever prevail over the pluralism of myths. That would take more than the weak motivation of thought alone. Never could a situation more opportunely render political survival such a powerful motivation for philosophical thought about the origin and unity of reason than when the Greeks came under threat of enslavement by Asia.

---

5   Nietzsche, "Rückblick auf meine zwei Leipziger Jahre," in *Gesammelte Werke*, XXI, 59.

The foreignness of theory in the lifeworld did not only mean its foreignness in front of foreigners from Thrace. Even the Greeks had not comprehended what was ascribed to them there, nor what had been offered them. Plato's correctness in seeing Socrates prefigured in the protophilosopher's plummet has become part of the history of the philosophical genre from Nietzsche's perspective. The tragedy of philosophy results from the fact that the situation of its beginning is simply unrepeatable. If the decisive aspect of this story could not be completed in a situation or in a process, but rather had only been acute in *one* moment of *one* single person, then no genetic derivation helps in comprehending the leap, the hiatus, the assumption; instead, it is an image, a scene, an anecdote.

In the initial lecture of his Basel professorship in May 1869, Nietzsche defended classical philology with the paradigm of the Homeric question against the accusation of having set out in "a destructive, iconoclastic direction."[6] It is recognizable that he not only wants to win back this figure against the Romantic misunderstanding of folk poetry (and other folk accomplishments). Without naming any other names, the text reads thus: for Thales, who clashed with myth and failed due to its power, the image of the well plummet and of its misunderstanding witness may not go lost for the sake of something like "historical criticism."

Nietzsche views Thales of Miletus as an erratic occurrence among the Greeks. He is the realist, not the Thracian maid. In that claim, Nietzsche performs the reception-technique of switching sides within anecdote. Thales is the realist, because he "began to look into the depths of nature without fantastic fables about it," in that he recognized a requirement for the survival of his polis. Again, a form of "unconscious" beginning: someone founds philosophy and science although he only wants to find the organ against the loss of freedom. The sentence, "everything is full of gods," will be read differently depending on whether we see the ultimate goal of *logos* as demolishing *mythos* or as only serving to replace myth's distaste for unity. It should have been the closing sentence of myth and the link to its replacement, but instead it became the beginning of an endless chain of new claims, which distanced themselves again from radical restriction and all of which operated with the expression "everything."

As Nietzsche saw it, this "everything" only works in the sense that Thales intended if a "nothing" remains included as part of it. The philologist's attitude makes it understandable that Nietzsche did not bother with a different and very late, thus poorly verified Thales anecdote, which first added a sharp antithesis to the statement of

---

6 Nietzsche, *Homer und classische Philologie*, 1869, in *Gesammelte Werke*, II, 7.

god-filledness: when King Croesus asked Thales what he thought of the gods, Thales repeatedly requested time to think, and finally answered laconically, "nothing."[7]

Against our preferences, perhaps, we may only relate both statements to one another fittingly if we think back to the Thales of the oil-press speculation and the earthly condition for his competence: only because there were differences in the scarcity and abundance of harvests in the world over the years, could he observe and exploit intermittency—the business cycle—in a way that was useful and led to income. The mythic world was not a world where changes occurred regularly; as one filled with gods, it was one where occupations (*Besetzungen*) lasted, occupations which, however clement and influenceable they may have been, did not offer assistance for predicting solar eclipses or oil harvests. Achieving that did not depend on saying what everything was already full of, but rather saying whence it all came forth and how everything obtained the guarantee of its lasting concern for human affairs (*Daseinsstoff*). It was therefore "efficient" in the highest degree to assign nothing to the gods, in order to adorn the question of "whence" with one answer: "from the water."

Whoever considered—as the descendants of Thales did in the Ionian natural philosophy—that this answer depended on the content and one needed to test more closely whether water deserved this rank, had already distorted what had or should have been won in that statement. The Athenians may at least have grasped this fact when they sought a beginning for their philosophical tradition that was simultaneous to that of the Ionians and let their protophilosopher, Musaeus, say: "all things proceed from unity and are resolved again into unity."[8][cxviii] This sentence—still exemplary today as a theory of the universe—makes clear it what Nietzsche was devising here. In turning to Thales the statesman and his relationship to myth by way of the transmitted sentence in its singularity, Nietzsche found a satisfying demonstration for the fact that no further sentences were necessary to understand the restrictive function of philosophy for the return of myth. The factual failure of philosophy, as again on much later occasions, appears unable to overpower the impressive force of its self-presentation as lacking any historical confusion about its beginning.

Indeed, in order not to obfuscate the origin's manifestation, Nietzsche makes no use of Herodotus' nuanced defense of Thales' ambitions as a statesman. The historian tells how the Ionians gathered in the

---

7   Tertullian, *Ad nationes*, II, 2,11, in Roberts and Donaldson, *Ante-Nicene Fathers*, III, 130. "When Croesus inquired of Thales what he thought of the gods, the latter having taken some time to consider, answered by the word, 'Nothing.'"
8   Diogenes Laertius, *Lives of Eminent Philosophers*, Vol. 1 I, 3, 5.

Panionium after their defeat and the loss of their freedom in order to hear the speech of Bias of Priene, who gave them the advice to sail together to Sardinia and found a single all-Ionian city there. In so doing, they would escape servitude, come to wellbeing, and additionally win rule over others from the position of the largest of all the islands. Had they followed this advice, Herodotus adds, they could have become the happiest and richest people in all Greece. But they only needed this advice in the first place because they did not listen to Thales of Miletus before their oppression: for he had advised them to found a single political midpoint (*bouleuterion*) and to make all cities dependent on it.[9]

Herodotus simply does not say why the Ionians followed neither that advice before their misfortune nor his other advice after it. Nietzsche explains it with his insight into Thales' way of thinking and its relationship to Ionia's political reality. This gives the first philosophical treatment of myth its situation-specific edge: in order to establish the *one* center of political power, Thales sought to eliminate the local stubbornness about gods by means of *one* theory of the world from and on water.

Nietzsche did not find anything comparable in the other report we possess through Herodotus about Thales, although the first of all historians gives free rein here as well to the finesse of his affinity for depicting human relationships.[10] Only indirectly does he show what meaning it must have had that a citizen of Miletus had been able to predict a solar eclipse. It is explained through the case of the barbarians: with the same darkening of the sun, the Medes and Lydians, who had been waging war with one another for years, were seized with such a panic that they immediately made peace. Granted, the side-effect of conquering fear had been a good one this time, yet an accidental one resulting from lacking insight. Thales had effected the lasting transformation of the human conception of the world by liberating his fellow citizens from this very fear.

When Nietzsche's *Birth of Tragedy* appeared at the beginning of 1872, and in the same year the young Ulrich von Wilamowitz-Moellendorff spoke out against Erwin Rhode's exuberant advertisement of the work under the disdainful title "Future Philology!", in which he concluded by demanding no less than that the author resign "from the position in which he supposedly teaches scientifically," Thales of Miletus was not the topic.[11] That within the dispute over the origin of tragedy and the

---

9 Herodotus., *The Histories*, I, 170.
10 Ibid., I, 74.
11 Wilamowitz-Moellendorff, *Zukunftsphilologie! eine Erwiderung auf Friedrich Nietzsches "Geburt der Tragödie,"* Berlin, 1872 (later edition in *Der Streit um Nietzsches "Geburt der Tragödie."* Published by Gründer, Hildesheim, 1969, 55).

context of its demise with Socrates a tragedy of philosophy itself could be discerned, would first be recognizable a quarter century later, when Nietzsche was already long silenced and Wilamowitz, having arrived at the top rank in his discipline, had to hold the speech for the Kaiser's birthday, which bore the wide-ranging title, "World Periods."

Wilamowitz's speech revealed that the beginning of philosophy on the coastal edge of Asia Minor already grasped what Wilamowitz' contemporaries believed was only first grasped during the age of Hellenism, which colonized the cosmos to replace the declining *polis*: the view of the world as a whole was attained by foregoing a political whole. Where Nietzsche saw in Thales' account of the world's origin precisely the founding act, though futile, of a state constitution ready for implementation against the polycentrism of myths, Wilamowitz takes the developing natural philosophy as consistent with that finally lacking possibility. The interest in the sky becomes the expression of earthly homelessness.

The Milesian watching the stars did not become the laughing-stock of the Thracian woman without reason (*Grund*): "The Ionian men, who first turned their gaze to the sky, not to banish the spirits or to read the future, but in order to learn the laws of the sky's phenomena, and for them the order and harmony of nature, the unity of all life emerged from that study. This founding of natural science had no fatherland, and would have hardly otherwise been able to observe the world as a whole."[12] Effortlessly, the sophistic sentence, "man is the measure of all things," is projected towards Ionia and made into the expression of an individualism only thinkable as stateless, an individualism which those Ionian men would not have dared, "if they had not been world citizens and only exerted a destructive effect on the existing states." In anticipation of the judgment of his historically oriented contemporary colleagues, Wilamowitz immediately adds: "Who could hold it against the political historian if he reviles the fatherlandlessness of these Ionians?" Here at the beginning of philosophy resides a conflict, which even "the greatest Athenian,"[cxix] to whom Wilamowitz would dedicate so much life energy and lifetime, could not negotiate.

After he showed his esteem for the preliminary philosophy of water as protomatter in the lecture from 1872 about the pre-Platonic philosophers Nietzsche says, "We must be suspicious of everything else that one wishes to know about Thales."[cxx] The philologist still does not know what the philosopher will find important about this state of affairs. Next comes the concentration on dispelling myth in one single sentence, which replaces it ironically. Nietzsche finds it problematic that the old collection of sayings, from which he construes

---

12 Wilamowitz-Moellendorff and Neumann, *Weltperioden*, 9.

the reliability of Aristotle's quotation and the anecdote by Plato, should not once have been repeated afterwards. Where Aristotle reports, Seneca actually quotes word for word, and, moreover, in both cases a plausible connection with the central doxogram is given: "the earth swims on water" allows Aristotle to extend Thales' proposition, and "earthquakes come about from the motion of these waters," as Seneca quotes word for word. For Nietzsche Seneca's version is just "a noteworthy passage." It is not yet recognizable what effect his discomfort with such extensions will have. But finally we see that it will not have been for any other motive than to deem inauthentic the *Nautical Astronomy* attributed to Thales. That book title, on the other hand, seems, in a way that is palpable for everyone, to unify both of Thales' theoretical passions, for stars and for water: in all of these cases, it is about the secondary acquisition of explanatory accomplishments from that one primal principle, which is meant to set a great image (*Anschauung*) apart from myth, without providing the detail of answers to questions.[cxxi]

We recognize with little effort that a not yet fully ripened problem of Nietzsche's comes along with the conflict between that originary proposition and its "applications:" that of the antagonism between philosophy and science. On the one hand, in the philosopher-lecture of 1872 he says explicitly that as a mathematician and as an astronomer Thales stands "at the peak of Greek science;" yet the defense against any extension of the authorized transmission shows that Nietzsche is set on having the scientist Thales step down behind what Nietzsche wants seen as the philosophical in him. His direction of orientation is not the cosmos, but the polis and its relationship to *mythos*. With that, it also becomes understandable why Nietzsche lets the anecdote fall so easily within the authorized collection of "*apomnemoneumata;*" it shows science as the wrong turn by the philosopher, who does the wrong thing at the wrong time or who prematurely quit warning the polis for the nocturnal refuge of resignation. Even if the contrast is not yet fully displayed, it is still already recognizable that Thales of Miletus should not stand at the beginning of the history of science, but at the beginning of philosophy, and that these are everything but one and the same.

When Plato manufactured the connection between the beginning of philosophy and its fulfillment, by projecting the Thales anecdote onto his Socrates, he neglected the discrepancy, which was supposed to have been so important to Socrates: the retreat from natural philosophy and his new definition of the theoretical task centered on humanity and its morality. Nietzsche has followed this line of Plato's: his Thales of Miletus is the first opponent of myth in favor of the self-assertion of the Ionian cities, and his Socrates is the perfector of destroying myth, particularly in the form of tragedy. Thales, like Socrates, supposedly stood against myth, except that Socrates no longer understood what it was about when he did it—and even if he had understood, it would have been too late. Thus the death of Socrates no longer functions within the archaic reservoir of images as epigonal delay on completing a decision, which had been pronounced by Thales under the compulsion of naked self-assertion. The decision was philosophy; the historical consequence, science. Socrates pulled philosophy down to the bourgeois sphere, privatized its public spirit and prepared it to become an assisting organ in the long run for the realization of Christianity.

Philosophy and science stand in a broken relation to one another. If Thales was "a creative master," who began to see nature in its depths, without being reliant on fantastic fables, then he stands indeed unmistakably across from nature in the attitude of science, yet only in order to leave it behind him just as soon: "If in doing so he used and then passed on the methods of science and of proof he but demonstrates a typical characteristic of the philosophic mind. If he indeed used science and the evincible, but soon surpassed them, then this is indeed a typical hallmark of the philosophical mind."[13] Thales uses all calculability, as solar eclipses and pyramid measurements are proven, advances past them just as fast in the direction of the unusual, astounding, difficult, divine, and at the same time useless, because it was not about human goods according to Aristotle's claim as quoted by Nietzsche. The drive for knowledge, which stands behind science, is as such blind: "Science rushes headlong, without selectivity, without 'taste,' at whatever is knowable, in the blind desire to know all at any cost. Philosophical thinking, on the other hand, is ever on the scent of those things which are most worth knowing, the great and important insights."[cxxii] For this differentiation, Thales simply yields no evidence. His astronomy, conducted in a sea trade city, could hardly be opposed to mastering the calculable facts nor even be worthy of reverence for surpassing mere calculation. It seems more likely that it was about assuring others that nature was calculable so that they could reliably put nature's calculability in service to economic goals for their own livelihood.

Nietzsche's proposition about the difference between science and philosophy sounds good and formulates an expectation that has remained alive under the changing name of lower and higher "critique" up until the present day and that lives on today more than ever. But the proposition exposes an ease of differentiation, which does not work: science as industriousness about everything knowable and thus about everything, insofar as it is knowable; philosophy as infinite refinement

---

13   Nietzsche, *Philosophy in the Tragic Age of the Greeks*, 42–3 (*Gesammelte Werke*, IV, 163–8).

in the choice of objects solely by the norm of their worthiness of being known. Such a formula bespeaks almost nothing about the factual relation between philosophy and science, because—as we may deeply regret—the value of a piece of knowledge first becomes evaluable once this knowledge has become known. For that reason, setting everything knowable on equal footing at the outset always precedes the act of profiling what is worth knowing. This fact can indeed bring belated "critical" evaluation to a halt and reduce it to empty complaining. For to act as if the standards for the worthiness of being known were only arbitrarily set after the fact and could just as well have been set before the fact is simply misleading a public, which has become nearly illiterate in such elementary states of affairs through its losses of history.

A few years after the exciting interpretation of Thales' only authenticated sentence, Thales becomes an example for Nietzsche of how philosophy grasps and condenses the dignity of its objects, an example targeted against the drive for knowledge as a case of lower movement and thus as the drive responsible for the nocturnal scene in Miletus and its interruption. Now philosophy begins "by legislating greatness." Here a sentence like Thales' does not so much express a theoretical explanation of origin and union as it provides a name for that greatness—a naming act that displays superiority over facts and the drive to gather them. Philosophy corrals this drive, particularly when it "considers the greatest insight, that of essence and core of things, to be attainable and attained." Nothing more happened when Thales said, "Everything is water."

In the moment when that was said, "man is stung up out of the wormlike probings and creepings-about of his separate sciences. He intuits the ultimate resolution of all things and overcomes, by means of such intuition, the vulgar restrictions of the lower levels of knowledge."[cxxiii] What justifies "standing quietly and becoming serious" after Thales' dictum is the state of affairs that the sentence, "everything is water," only masks another statement in metaphor: "everything is one," as Musaeus left it behind for the Athenians, according to legend.[cxxiv] The pertinence of the Thalean dogma to the situation of the Ionian polis is thus dispensed with; in lieu of the concentration on the singular, but futile decision against myth, Nietzsche now finds the decision for the aesthetic finality of philosophy. Water does not stand for Thales' vision (*Anschauung*), but for the lack of early philosophical capacity to come up with an expression for vision: "Thus Thales had seen the unity of all that is, but when he went to communicate it, he found himself talking about water!"[cxxv] Regarding this last sentence of the Thales chapter, we only need to go one step further: in order to look at the unity of being, Thales turned his back to the city nightly and saw the starry sky; right then, he fell into the water.

Nietzsche was too fascinated with the first proposition ever spoken in philosophy to have been able to turn a comparable attentiveness to the night scene of the well plummet.^{cxxvi} If this anecdote, to whose historical license he had testified, could not have met his taste for what should have happened in order to suit the beginning of philosophy, then one will have to raise the question of whether the modern substitution for this anecdote, derision towards the Creation story by the Castilian King Alfonso the Wise, would not have fit more exactly into Nietzsche's concept. We may wish to flesh out how he would have needed to transform this story in order to procure a creative expression for his "reoccupation" of the place of the dead God through the Übermensch. But we do not need to strain our imagination; he did that, or even more precisely: he found what suited him.

In the third treatise of *On the Genealogy of Morals*, the topic is the bad reputation, that of just letting things be, into which contemplative people easily fall—a reputation to which they react in turn by learning "to arouse a decided fear of oneself."[14] The oldest philosophers, here incarnated by the Brahmins, would have needed "to fight down every kind of suspicion and resistance" against the rise of the philosophical in themselves and did this with the training methods of brutal eras. They had to rape the gods and received ideas within themselves "so as to be able to *believe* in their own innovations." That is the point at which Nietzsche recalls the story, which he calls famous, of King Vishvamitra who—as the product of such a tradition of self-discipline—"through millennia of self-torture acquired such a feeling of power and self-confidence that he endeavored to build a *new heaven*."

The story of the king belongs within the inquiry into the meaning of ascetic ideals. It is not a theoretical head start, like the one that the Castilian king had achieved through his astronomical tables, that makes the Indian king into the prototype for the boldness that he articulates. Recklessness against himself legitimates him for another kind of theory, which approaches post-Christian modernity and its transformed asceticism as opposed to antiquity and its ideal of *theoria*. The Indian king only represents an exotic exaggeration of theory.

The Castilian king had derided the Creation story because it refused theory by withholding the precise descriptions that appeared appropriate for a god's work. After Nietzsche had stumbled upon Thales' proposition as an ersatz-myth for the Ionian unification, he saw the

---

14 Nietzsche, *On the Genealogy of Morals*, "Third Treatise: What is the meaning of ascetic ideals?" §10, 115, 1887 (*Gesammelte Werke*, XV, 392f.).

unity of the world at stake, which could not be expressed in any of the propositions about it. It remained open to intuition, which, admittedly always metaphorical, always has to be anthropomorphic, as all science had become "an attempt to humanize things" in the end for Nietzsche.[15] Renunciation of the self, which marks the ascetic ideal, means renouncing immediate access to oneself, without mediation from an anthropomorphic world, aesthetic enjoyment of which—according to the scheme invented by Romanticism and Idealism—is only the rediscovery of the I in the other. In any case, the enjoyment of the world could be understood as an elemental form of aesthetics, as opposed to Kant's disinterested agreeability, since he always referred back to the I on the detour around the world. This is how deriding the Creation story may now be understood, as a position which considers everything oppositional about the world as disparaging to the I, whose projection is nonetheless the only order in the world, and, due to the depth of this disparagement, sees no other way out than to build another heaven.

Not one among all of the Creation story's detractors noticed the eschatological trait that their gesture belies: even the Apocalypse of John had put "a new heaven and a new earth" into view for the promised end of days. The eschatology of the Bible was—what it could not articulate without becoming Gnosticism—the preformed derision towards the Creation story: with the proclamation of His Revelation, God himself repealed what he had confirmed to Himself about His Creation, that it had become good. The biblical God had nevertheless been the one who had drawn the consequence of that derision, which neither the Castilian king nor any of his protégés in modernity had dared to draw explicitly: whatever is as decrepit as the world must first be destroyed, so that it can develop anew and immutably and better.

Nietzsche's Indian king comes close to proposing as much. He is a pragmatic Gnostic or a Gnostic practitioner, as Nietzsche himself was with the Übermensch, who is also based on nothing other than the ability to withstand the death of God or even to have killed God himself. This means taking the apocalypse into one's own hands. It reminds us of Thales, who supposedly believed that changing a single sentence would be enough to set the Ionian world free from its oppressor.

What came about from the modern derision towards the Creation story according to Nietzsche's view of things? The will to violence towards the world becomes technical will, which does not accept

---

15 Nietzsche, *The Gay Science*, §112, "Cause and effect," 113 (*Gesammelte Werke*, XII, 147).

things as they are and not at all as a Creator may have made them: "Our whole attitude towards nature, the way we violate her with the aid of machines and the heedless inventiveness of our technicians and engineers, is *hybris* ..."[16] This sentiment stands in immediate vicinity with the legend of King Vishvamitra and his self-certainty created by means of asceticism.

---

16 Nietzsche, *On the Genealogy of Morals*, III, 9, 113 (*Gesammelte Werke*, XV, 390).

Thirteen How to Recognize what Matters

The world was there "when the first man raised his head."[cxxvii] A formulation as trivial as it is ambiguous, reported by Hans-Georg Gadamer from Heidegger's early Marburg years; Heidegger used it in order to find a language for the conjunction that occurs in the word *"Dasein,"* between the human's "there" (*Da*) and "Being" (*Sein*),[cxxviii] before he later came to distrust language so much more fundamentally. It is telling of the insecurity that Heidegger's indeterminacies unleashed that his entourage of students had "disputed for weeks" at the time about whether he "had meant Adam or Thales by this first man," a confusion which Gadamer explicates with the addendum: you see from that question that those who asked it were "still not very far advanced" with their insights.[1] Maybe today we will be allowed to say, on the contrary, that few questions so astute would ever be posed to Heidegger in all of the years that followed.

The old formula, that man's raised head shows him practicing his essential determination, to behold the universe,[cxxix] seemed too static once the alleged moment—which altered the old formula slightly—had been imagined, in which *Dasein* and Being emerged as a unity. The intelligence of the seemingly simple problematic does not consist in the foregrounded confrontation of the theological protagonist with the philosophical one; it seems instead that they want to know whether the understanding of Being granted to the human being is an anthropological state of affairs or a philosophical one, one arising with the history of the human or with that of philosophy.[cxxx]

It would first be revealed how justified that debate had been at the late Heidegger's turn, when he located Being's prior unconcealment in its history with the *pre*-pre-Socratics and wanted to recognize the traces of its possession, now just meagerly remaining and difficult to

---

1 Gadamer, "Being, Spirit, God," 65.

decipher, which were already disappearing into concealment when the documented history of philosophy began with Thales. By that point, Thales was already among those who wanted to pass a being (*Seiendes*) off as Being itself (*Sein*). Completely unaware of the fact that now "Being" would no longer be that of the being at hand, he consequently ushered in our fate, the forgottenness of Being (*Seinsvergessenheit*) from the beginning onward, along its course, which has since left everyone—and us most of all—nothing but the unjustifiable expectation of its retrograde return.

If one sees the early student debate in light of the late "history of being,"[cxxxi] then the answer "Adam" would be the more accurate one for sure. That said, we must spare ourselves from thinking that the raising of the head as imprinted by Michelangelo is bound up, for those who came later, with the melancholy conclusion that there were no more stars at in the Paradisiacal part of the sky; after all, only the three outer planets primarily occupy the sky at midnight after the descent of the evening star or before the rise of the morning star. As watchers of the sky, Adam and Thales must have been very dissimilar; but they were at least metaphorically comparable through the immediate consequence of their self-elevation: their fall. One does not need to overestimate such associations; yet, with Heidegger's introduction of the "history of being," the fateful dimming of a one-time clearing (*Lichtung*) for humanity has taken primacy for this event, in order to make human beings all the more permanently into the ones affected by the displacements and troubles for which they can no longer bear the responsibility—no different than if he were still the wrong-doer from the first day of his head-raising.

That the one who first lifted his head, according to the formula as debated in the Marburg seminar, did not do something which was common practice in the human world by force of human nature, but abandoned the path of the habitual and removed himself from useful traffic in the world, may be understood as phenomenology casting its dismissive verdict against anthropology: history, not nature, would have played out in that original event (*Urereignis*) of ontology. For this purpose, Thales appears to fit more precisely. It would not be accidental, therefore, that Heidegger turned vehemently back to Thales during the late changes to his treatment of Being.

In 1962, under the title *What is a Thing?*, Heidegger published the text of a lecture from the winter semester of 1935–6, at whose beginning he mentioned the Thales anecdote. He used it to illustrate the irrelevance of a question "that one can really do nothing with," as appears to be the case with the question of the thing.[cxxxii] This peculiarity does not burden the question and questioner, but rather develops into the very criterion for their philosophical relevance and propriety.

The risk involved in being a philosopher was unknown to Thales of Miletus; that much is conceivable. But it is that ignorance that always returns "since philosophy always starts from an unfavorable position."[cxxxiii] At that point, the reader implicitly hears that something like philosophy did not start once and for all. This is different from the sciences, where there is a "direct transition and entrance" from everyday notions. This difference, the lack of recourse to philosophy from within the everyday, has the effect that "philosophy is always something deranged (*verrücktes*)."[cxxxiv] If the protophilosopher had thus been targeted by the laughter of the Thracian maid, then it emerges from these premises that Heidegger must not have considered Thales the founder of science, not even of astronomy, but of philosophy. From the maid's lifeworld, there can never be any insight into the purposiveness of his activity.

Heidegger takes over the "little story" from Plato's *Theatetus*—where it is "preserved" (*aufbewahrt*) according to his careful word choice—and he appends Plato's elucidation to it: "This jest also fits all those who become involved in philosophy."[cxxxv] He continues what Nietzsche had started: playing science and philosophy off of one another.[cxxxvi] But is the Thales anecdote appropriate for showing the philosopher as someone who asks or even could ask the scientifically useless question, "what is a thing?" It is apparent that Plato does not want the story in Socrates' mouth to refer at all to the natural-philosophical sins of Socrates' youth. It refers instead to what would have him put to death: the brutal consequence of the foreignness of introducing a new theory of the human into a lifeworld that had already become somewhat accustomed to natural philosophy. If there had to be a link between the pathos of plummeting and that of death by the hemlock cup, then the Platonic Socrates would undoubtedly be relating his death to his philosophy's truth, and indeed going so far as to say that one could only die in this way if one had this philosophy. That would also be the case because only with that philosophy can someone become far enough removed from the polis' lifeworldly common sense to appear as its alien and enemy, against whom it has no other means than deadly detachment.

For Heidegger—to remain within his picture—the philosopher's plummet has become the criterion for knowing that he is on the right path. It enfeebles the point a bit that so much is said about the maid's laughter and so little about the philosopher's plummet; however, it cannot be forgotten that the Thracian woman perceived the plummet and would have nothing to laugh at without it. Would the one who plummeted only first realize after the maid had laughed that he was up to something above and beyond what could prove its utility in a statement such as the prediction of a solar eclipse? Heidegger's work with the anecdote tends towards this reversal.

How to Recognize what Matters   121

Philosophy is when somebody laughs. And when someone laughs out of obtuseness. The young physicist comes to mind, who finds an opportunity one single time to hear a lecture from Heidegger in the late thirties; the topic was "logic" and the discussion that day was about Heraclitus. He held his breath, according to his published account, and his reaction was: "That is philosophy. I do not understand a word. But that is philosophy."[2] That might not be meant to say that philosophy is when somebody does not understand; however, that cannot be very far from what was meant if it should ever be possible for something that someone has not understood to qualify as philosophy with such plain evidence.[cxxxvii] What else if not obtuseness (*Unverstand*) would be the essential kind of understanding (*Verständnisart*) in this form of thought?

We see that the Thracian woman with her exotic distance from the Milesian citizen has become superfluous. Even someone just like him would have to laugh at him. And it does not matter that he had chosen the highest and most obscure (*am fernsten gelegenen*) object there could be in the universe in order to become the laughing stock of the maid. The proof: since he could have and did become the laughing stock, his question must have been philosophical, that is, absolutely inaccessible from the perspective of the lifeworld.

Phenomenology aroused the expectation that its way of philosophizing could restore the lost connection from the positive sciences to the lifeworld, through descriptive achievements of their passageways and through intuitive foundations for conceptuality. Granted, Heidegger did not originate in phenomenology, but only passed through it; nonetheless, *Being and Time* had justified the expectation that the deficient mode of the theoretical attitude could be understood as deficient from the point of view of the unfolding constitution of Dasein. *What is a Thing?* shows the opposite tendency: philosophy eludes every passageway leading from the lifeworld to its own particular attitude, whereas the sciences have only gradually cut themselves off from the everyday through the distances they have covered in terms of history and specialization.

To explain the abyss between lifeworld and philosophy as constitutive of philosophy and to set everyone on the path who wants to arrive from the former to the latter is a dangerous proposal. It contains the danger of subverting philosophy, of attributing the distinction of philosophical transcendence to every kind of junk as long as it just achieves sufficient inaccessibility: "Philosophy, then, is that thinking with which one can start nothing and about which housemaids necessarily laugh."[cxxxviii] Anyone can see indeed that the reversal is forbidden

---

2   Weizsäcker, "Begegnungen in vier Jahrzehnten," 241.

where the philosopher shows up every time a maidservant laughs, but the statement never gets withdrawn to the extent that would be necessary if rhetorical extravagances were to be avoided. Does this not demand that philosophers seek out the question—if it is not yet known—at which laughter can be expected most surely and heard the loudest? "And genuine housemaids must have something to laugh about." An encouragement for professional hecklers to mock unintelligible propositions?

Heidegger could hardly have asserted by accident that it is "not a mere joke" to define philosophy by the laughter it provokes and in partnership with the laughing woman. To reflect on this definition requires us to deepen it, and for the kind of depth that must enter the picture—perhaps a depth without bottom[cxxxix]—the cistern from the Thales anecdote comes to mind: "We shall do well to remember that by our strolling we can fall into a well whereby we may not reach ground for quite some time."[cxl] Here an abrupt disappearance of harmlessness must be attested. The fallen Milesian astronomer must be imagined at a moderate depth of the cistern shaft if he is supposed to be reached alive and in one piece by the maid's laughter and folk wisdom. In Heidegger's scene it is no longer imaginable that anything could arrive at the still living body of the fallen man—certainly nothing from out of the lifeworld, which would neither comfort nor help him in that state. Once again, as before in the case of its ancient formulation, the "little story" has become mortally dangerous. This time, Thales does not need to be wizened with age to be seen as susceptible to the gravest danger; it suffices that he has involved himself with "depth" and "ground"—perhaps groundlessness—for the imagination to reach the limit at which laughter could become inhumane.

Consequently, the unapproachability of the one who fell down into the morass of the ground,[cxli] for anyone in the lifeworld, is the twist on the story; for it makes the Thracian woman laughable, who commentates and laughs at the drama of the question of the thing. She believes in a fall where there can only be a plummet. The external harmlessness of the question of the thing can only be interrupted by the most extreme exaggeration of the risk involved in the movement commenced on the impulse of the question.

Asking about the essence of the thing means getting to the bottom of that very thing, the return to which had been the founding call of phenomenology.[cxlii] It was not to become metaphysics at any price and could only have become that for the price of losing its reputation with the philosophy departments of the time. It did very quickly become metaphysics, whatever else it may be called. And metaphysics (of the type that Aristotle founded, perhaps even named) always oversteps a boundary; but it does this under the pressure to continue questioning—a pressure which receives its energy from the lifeworld and from those elements of a situation that remain inescapable even after leaving it.

That work, which would later indeed take on the name *Metaphysics*, assures itself this unbroken context right in its first sentence: "all men by nature desire to know."[cxliii] Not by accident, the one who claims this must speak in the same breath about Thales of Miletus—as a procedure consistent with this putatively simple state of affairs; and Aristotle does just that when he conducts the genealogy of his question.

It could be said that everyone who philosophizes must understand the first sentence of Aristotle's *Metaphysics* in his or her own way. Heidegger translates it in his own way entirely: "The care for seeing is essentially inherent in man's being."[3] Appended is the point that the nominalized infinitive *eidénai* may not be translated with "knowledge." Through "seeing," combined with "care," the reference back to the lifeworld that this sentence introduces seems even closer; the passageway becomes even shorter. But this is deceiving. Seeing gets defined as "perceiving the distance"—which suits the "little story" well, but moreover it fits the claim that the story is about the un-ready-to-hand (*Unzuhandene*). The formula "care for seeing" is thus a paradox: it makes the elusive object (*das Fernliegende*), which can "only" be perceived, into what matters to the human beings (*nahegeht*).

The parenthetical where Heidegger translates the Greek word for knowledge with the root for "seeing" distracts from a ruse, which makes up the entire argument in Heidegger's version of Aristotle, and thus covers it up; the Marburg lecture of summer 1925 introduced the definition of *Dasein* as "care" in the first sentence of Aristotles' *Metaphysics* without uncomfortably justifying that he can only have extracted that meaning from the Greek word *orgesthai*. "Care"—if one may quantify such a matter—is even less present in the text than "seeing."

The expression "care" for trivial "striving" disempowers the innate tendency towards knowledge and brings it down to something like an anthropological status. As if Aristotle had already recognized the essence of *Dasein* in *orgesthai* and let restful "seeing" come to the foreground through a kind of retarding shut-down: the theoretical attitude as minimal form of care, as depletion of *Dasein*'s care (*Entsorgung des Daseins*), as deficiency of its Being-in-the-World. Thence also the conclusion that Aristotle "actually reversed" this account at the start of his *Metaphysics*.[cxliv] Here it appears that Heidegger has

---

3 Heidegger, *History of the Concept of Time*, 275, 1925 lecture (Gesamtausgabe, XX, 380–2).

not decided what he will decide in *Being and Time*: in the theoretical attitude, *Dasein* does not rise to its constitutive totality, but is disempowered to the point of gaping indifference.

In the distinction of "seeing" lies an ambivalence about its implications. The "concern (*Besorgen*) for distance" as "a leaping over and a leaping away from the everyday world of work" leads near the reprimand of the Thracian maid: to "[tending] not to tarry in what is nearest" and to expanding the distance out towards the still completely unexperienced, into curiosity as "not tarrying (*Unverweilen*)," as "leaping off from one to another."[cxlv] Curiosity calls something to mind "solely in order to have seen it," but it holds itself back by "not having to get involved," in the form of a "merely being entertained by the world."[cxlvi] That statement unleashed a whole arsenal of possibilities for cultural criticism. It contrasts with the delirious statement about what seeing supposedly meant for the Greeks, given that their "highest form of knowing is that which is related to the being that truly and properly is," which meant nothing other than: "pure, visual relatedness to the thing itself."[4] Whenever Greeks come up, the unwitting switch from optical to tactile metaphorics helps achieve the status of higher—even of the highest—seriousness.

Merely letting-himself-be-entertained by the world may be an unjust charge against the protophilosopher, as he does risk falling, but his fall certainly portends his beginning's fallenness, when tarrying in the midst of things gave way to letting-things-be.[cxlvii] For care is the "nature" of a being (*Wesen*) that cannot maintain itself as nature and is thus "by nature" in a state of care about itself. The claim that such a being must see and wants to see rests on this premise.

Theory gains independence from its existential reliance on *Dasein*'s fundamental constitution as care, and this independence reaches its completion in the course of European history, not when theory purifies itself of its earthly remainder and ascends to the heights of its purity, but rather when it loses its ground, its root lattice, its nutrients, its justification. But this critique of the supposed terminal phase of the positive sciences, which could be construed from *Being and Time* and has been since 1927, is no longer the starting point for the consequences that Heidegger draws a decade later. The starting point's lostness is not an existential fact, out of which restitutive recollections can be deduced, but a rift in historical consistency, which—as in the case of Ariadne's thread—can augment the degree of error and loss with every attempt to repair it. In the language of the ancient anecdote, the figure of care, the Thracian woman, has disappeared from the scene; without her, there is not the faintest possibility that, through her laughter,

---

4   Heidegger, *Logic*, 102, 1925/26 lecture (Gesamtausgabe, XXI, 56).

anyone could even come to consider caring for the philosopher who plummeted into the well.

The interrogator of the thing's essence moves in a dimension in which the tumble into the depths is no longer the mishap arising from a forgetful-unidirectional glance. The title "metaphysics," at least according to Heidegger, designates "that procedure during which one especially runs the risk of falling into a well."[cxlviii] That is not just "maybe once," but "especially" (*besonders*)—a risk that is far removed from all of the assurances that were otherwise supposed to have emerged from theory's successes to the benefit of the human *Dasein*-movement. Considering that the theoretical attitude had still been characterized in *Being and Time* as care, in light of its relationship to *Dasein*'s self-preservation, deficiency no longer sufficed to vaunt the special status of that attitude and whatever is only accessible from that attitude, if the discourse is supposed to be about the "thing." Metaphysics can only be the washed-out derivative of the understanding of Being presiding in *Dasein* as care. What it takes to escape the grasp of metaphysics—that is, to slough off whatever content of metaphysics has been determined by history—is only determined purely formally by recourse to the origin scene (*Ursprungsszene*) represented in the Thales anecdote: in what relationship to the lifeworld are we put by the question "what is a thing?" The perplexity over the thing question in the lifeworld is supposedly greater and different than theory's unusualness is for the lifeworld. To the philosopher's benefit, the bizarre presumption of being right proves valid, insofar as it must be a powerful force that allows him to go on thinking against the habitual—and not just far from the habitual—when laughter, in the midst of the everyday concern with errands (*Besorgungen*), lambastes the one thinking. At the other end of philosophy, furthest off from its Milesian origin, the alternative between near and far (*Nähe und Ferne*), between obvious and obscure (*Nächstliegenden und Fernstliegenden*), is no longer resolved by the fact that the far off is determined by the nearby (*das Ferngelegene am Nahegelegenen*) and can be understood as a projection from here; quite to the contrary, the nearby (*das Naheliegende*) is precisely a form of displacement and concealment of what matters. Therefore, all paths can only lead astray from the obvious: "We ask about what is all around us and can be grasped (*Handgreiflichen*), and yet we alienate ourselves from those immediate things very much more than did Thales, who could see only as far as the stars."[cxlix]

"Only as far as the stars"—when would this leveling of the longtime highest and still outermost theoretical possibility, of penetrating what was never accessible to humanity, allow itself to be rendered with such a deprecating clause? Metaphysics, under the title of transcendence, wanted to compel theory beyond the cosmological limit, beyond the stars; but it is impermissible after Kant to speak as if that goal still needed to be avoided today: "But we want to pass beyond even these things to the unconditioned, where there are no more things that provide a basis and ground."

The maids—that is Heidegger's plural—laugh at the philosopher; they cannot grasp that he does not stick to the obvious, and thereby lets it become his downfall, because it is so obscure to him. The late Heidegger, for whom the names of "thing" and "Being" became so close to one another, no longer recalls the elementary result of his early analytic of *Dasein*, although it could be taken to signify an escalation of the philosopher's own experience with himself, which is emblematized in the Thales anecdote: indeed, the obvious, what lies at his feet, is so obscured to the Milesian that he tumbles over it; but the realism evoked in the tumble and the laughter provoked by it cover and silence the fact that there is a further beyond the obvious over which we tumble. Heidegger pronounced that succinctly as a facet of his early ontology's hermeneutic window: "The being that we ourselves always are is ontologically farthest from us."[5] Already for the fundamental ontology, not just first for the late "thing," is the Milesian well plummet only a prelude to the difficulties of philosophy, with its concern for achieving the right distance from the "worrying understanding (*besorgenden Verständigkeit*)." The distrust towards everything not yet at the farthest position becomes methodical, because the experiences of transcendence's self-exceeding gives no criterion for this limit-concept. What was thus already there in the history of contemplation can hardly be "true" in a conclusive sense because it could not be laid far enough away for that, as is indeed always first proven after the fact, when people can detach (*ent-fernen*) themselves again.

The study of Being must constantly detach itself, particularly from everything that has already been there before. That also goes for the historical distance in which Thales belongs: the pre-Socratics, to the surprise of those who considered them to represent starting points—as well attested by written transmission—prove to be a mere afterglow of what came before them. The mythology painstakingly reworked by them, perhaps more concealed than overcome, is also just such a sunset view of something withdrawing itself irrecoverably from us. And withdrawing mercifully, because we would simply not be up for its unconcealment, as has always been the case with whatever yields the highest privilege to the survivor capable of documenting what he may only perceive fading behind him. Pre-Socratics and myth become as virulent as anything that has nothing to do with the rationality of care. How could people have expected to approach *Dasein* and its

---

5   Heidegger, *Being and Time*, §63, 287.

everydayness on the way to the beyond? As if they had wanted to learn something about the maid from the starry sky. The distrust—that one has removed oneself far enough from the everyday, or even worse, that one has leapt away from the everyday without leaving any continuity to follow back—must be transformed into a method and articulated in the formula: one's own tendency to hide is to be studied *on the way out* of hiding. While the "distance" had stood far away, but in the same direction as the "nearness," from the center of its object-referent, this methodical rule is precisely for reversing the direction already being pursued by lifeworldly action at any given moment; it is for reading against the grain and hammering against it.

Heidegger performed a destruction of the history of metaphysics. The way he treated the Thales anecdote shows what the "residuum of destruction" is, as there had been a "residuum of reduction" for phenomenology's originator.[cl] The founding model, which had always appeared valid across the history of philosophy, remains apparent: at every stage, philosophy was about proving that we are captivated and determined by the foregroundedness of an appearance or a manifestation. Even the anecdote discussed in this book emerges against a wider background, multiplies its polysemy: on the one hand, the Thracian woman is acceded to, insofar as she makes a case based on the urgency of the obvious (*das Nächstliegende*) against the philosopher's passion for the farthest (*das Fernste*); but she is only right to laugh once her laughter reveals a kind of ignorance that can no longer be made fun of, because it is a symptom, which reveals that something essential is happening, something either not understandable or not yet understood. Neither does the philosopher understand her laughter nor is her laughter understanding, although it would one day be understandable as such. But it is valid to say about this beginning that they *both* do not know what they are doing—that is, they do not know what philosophy is and why it makes an exception of itself so ridiculously from the standpoint of the lifeworld. That this beginning is already an end and only introduces the ignorant wait for another beginning, which would be called "metaphysics," and which still, in the question of beings' "meaning of Being," only forms its last resistance to the question of the "essence of the thing"—all of this is supposed to become apparent for the first time through Heidegger's gaze on the Thales scenario, from this terminal point in the destruction of its history.

Despite the turn against the metaphysical tradition, this explication has an anachronistic element that builds pathos for the inaccessibility of thought still-to-come, whose arrival is still not uncertain. It lies in the way that the subject of the necessary laughter at philosophy and its definitive uselessness has long disappeared from reality. The plural, with which the one Thracian maid of Miletus has been made into an indefinite quantity, is no accident; for the philosopher's position has become once more, through a most circuitous route indeed, the center from which everyone who feels like laughing has been thrust from their own positions into eccentric positions. So simply, so unpretentiously, so originally was the question of the thing's essence supposedly asked. It is thought of as a vantage point that, from the perspective and position of the lifeworld, can only be alienating, revolting, impossible; it is no longer a matter of a large or small correction, but rather of the exception, the selection, the state of grace, from which one cannot teach and initiate others and for which no one can train with the classical tools of philosophy. You awaken and see "the thing" just like that, or you will never comprehend it.

Historically speaking, the connection to modernity and its Enlightenment is torn off at that point, judged as finished; phenomenologically, the reduction of all philosophical questioning is given up at the lifeworld's horizon, called off, cancelled. The criterion for determining who measures up to the demand is that no one else can confirm that for him. The comprehending one is recognized in that no one comprehends that person. He stands there as the *factum brutum* that detached itself from every effort at persuasion and consensus.[cli] That explains the plural maidservants: everyone has joined in the laughter. Nothing authenticates the one laughed at besides his own claim, which comes in the form of paradoxical evidence: this is philosophy, but no one understands anything. That is how the factical[clii] became the criterion for the essential.

At this point, we can formulate Heidegger's divergence from phenomenology: in the method founded by Husserl, others' reaction to the philosopher's thought (which Heidegger considered necessary, insofar as it poses the question of the thing's essence) would neither be significant nor permissible at all. The essential lies in triviality;[cliii] it precisely does not require anyone to detach from the lifeworld to eccentric positions, but rather to describe what foundational achievement within the lifeworld is concealed in any such position—that is, in the eccentric positions of the positive sciences. Phenomenologists must take paths, not make leaps.

Quite the contrary: Husserl's late *Crisis* treatise, which shows no acquaintance with Heidegger's development after *Being and Time* or could not make its acquaintance,[cliv] is oriented against something like a tendency to leap in the European history of theory and develops the program of the restoration of one path's continuity, a path still considered viable. It is not the phenomenologist that the maids laugh at; in a close brush (*Grenzfall*), he only needs to say something to them concerning what they themselves must say that they saw as well, but cannot say. Husserl's programmatic statement that phenomenology is the science of trivialities signifies nothing more. Now philosophy too has finally become what morality has been forever: that which is understood to be self-evident—but philosophy also possesses the concealment of everything self-evident precisely for that reason. From the perspective of this premise underlying phenomenology, it cannot be permitted to let philosophy's idiosyncrasy be indicated precisely through the outbreak of misunderstanding: "the question 'what is a thing?' must always be rated as one which causes housemaids to laugh."[clv] From the phenomenological outlook on the relationship between lifeworld and essentiality, this becomes a sentence of incomprehensible arrogance. It certainly does not surprise someone who had already seen the Thales anecdote as a testament to just such a haughty sentiment.

Fourteen Interdisciplinarity as Repetition of Protohistory

Does all of this anecdote's history and reception involve a specific form of presumption, which characterizes philosophy as an attitude towards reality and its professional mandataries, since their beginnings and over the course of their mounting self-consciousness? It is indicative that the question could only be posed under two conditions: at some point, the history of this anecdote's reception must have been presented, at least in its outlines; then, there had to be an unsatisfied public, which felt that the moment of arrogance expressed in the story required some further step. That public must have thirsted to make this history into an organ for disclosing a state of affairs so that the story could definitively terminate the anecdote's service to philosophers' self-consciousness—now that the story had achieved the ultimate by serving Heidegger. What is happening now is no longer the reception of the anecdote, but the reception of the reception.

Such conditions play out within the modern technics of interdisciplinarity. With the help of a model, we take the history of the reception into account, and then take a stand on it: "I can only read the story of Thales and the *schadenfroh* Thracian maid—as well as the history of this story's success among philosophers from Plato to Heidegger—with a certain discomfort, which escalates at points to a feeling of embarrassment."[1, clvi]

Interdisciplinarity means that the eccentric position receives a new label: there are spectators outside of the scene, who regard this scene as an object of discussion. They discuss the philosopher's behavior and the maid's behavior, measure the height of the fall, which gets reassessed from a cistern to a simple ditch in the various versions of the story.[clvii] All of this occurs from a distance, which, for its part,

---

1 *Poetik und Hermeneutik. Arbeitsergebnisse einer Forschungsgruppe*, VII., eds W. Preisendanz and R. Warning. München, 1976, 429–44.

is neither philosophical nor does it regard philosophy as anything other than a literary genre. In the same way that literature scholars study social history, one could conduct the psychopathology of the figures who discuss this anecdote—especially if they reveal a persistent interest in recognizing themselves or something else in this story: "I get irritated here and elsewhere by the keenness, with which this story gets retold precisely by those persons to whom the maid's laughter should actually also pertain."[clviii] Letting the laughter at the first philosopher "raise its voice" repeatedly, proving the legitimacy of the eccentric position through him, that cannot be called anything but a "peculiar masochism."

Actually one can only laugh at the philosophers or enjoy laughter at their expense if one considers oneself to be their exception. And in this discipline evidently—I cannot speak for other disciplines—everyone considers himself to be the exception to all others. But that was already the intention, with which Plato appropriated the Aesopic fable for the mouth of his Socrates. In Plato's time, the guild members were still (or first) called sophists, and the one person who wanted to be known for exempting himself from the view that made wisdom into the etiquette for what could be performed invented the distinction "philosopher" for himself. One can only be the exception, and remain so, if one is the first or the last: Thales or Socrates—or Heidegger. For as soon as the first has been, according to this scheme, one can only still want to be the last. And that is why so many people want that, again and again.

For the others, who do not make it to being first or last, this statement applies: "They only apparently enter into complicity with the maid and laugh only for a moment, rather torturedly at that, with the Thracian maid, in order to laugh immediately afterwards along heartily with their colleagues about the dumb maid. Who actually falls in the ditch here?"[clix]

In a style of observation fondly called "social critique" a generation ago, the Thales anecdote becomes exasperating, no matter how often the reception history makes concessions to the Thracian maid.[clx] What bothers the critic is that the one laughing has herself become laughable in the end—which expresses a self-consciousness that theory has so successfully accomplished its task that it is now easily bearable that, in the beginning, somebody had laughed at theory. And when I say that, I mean: somebody laughed at a behavior that theoretical goals perceptibly inscribe on the theorist. If offense is taken at how philosophers treat the anecdote, then that is also a symptom indicating that being able to tolerate the laughter has once again become unacceptable after there had been no need to take it seriously for so long. A lens—glad to portray itself as class-specific—sees the self-satisfaction with which philosophers have referred to this piece of imagery as a reason to position them within the class condemned to die out, the class which could not and still cannot handle the laughing maid from Thrace.

Given this situation, the interdisciplinary reception of the reception supports the diagnosis that the end of philosophy is announced just as it sees its own task in the treatment of its beginning.

Afterword: Reading into the Distance

One night while stargazing, a philosopher trips and falls. Someone nearby laughs. The fabled encounter is then remembered for over two millennia in the writings of philosophers who retell it and reinterpret its meanings. *The Laughter of the Thracian Woman* accounts for this history of repetition. In this little story's many retellings Hans Blumenberg finds the long story of theory's uneasy relationship with the rest of life.

Blumenberg studies a particular metaphoric effect of short anecdotes and suggestive images: they can illustrate ideas that elude definition. When we portray nature as a book, history as a march, being as a dwelling, or consciousness as a stream, metaphors make these grand abstractions thinkable. Some concepts can be expressed through reliable formulae; the triangle, for instance, is the shape created by three intersecting lines. Other concepts refer to measurable or observable objects, such as electricity and metal. Philosophy, however, works with ideas that resist definition, and thus it turns to metaphors that link indeterminate ideas to familiar images. In *Laughter*, Blumenberg shows how the images in this one anecdote (stars, a falling man, laughter) orient a wide range of theoretical claims. His other works repeat this interpretive procedure with different images—including light, lions, shipwrecks, caves, and the Crucifixion.[1]

Blumenberg died on March 28, 1996, and little has since been publicly revealed about his life.[2] He was born in Lübeck, Germany, on July 13, 1920. He attended a 500-year-old, humanistic secondary school, Katharineum zu Lübeck. Gothic script over the school organ spelled, "The fear of the Lord is the beginning of wisdom," and that sentence's ambiguity led Blumenberg to a heretical reading: not that wisdom

---

1   Blumenberg, "Light as a Metaphor for Truth: At the Preliminary Stage of Philosophical Concept Formation"; Blumenberg, *Löwen*; Blumenberg, *Shipwreck with Spectator*; Blumenberg, *Höhlenausgänge*; Blumenberg, *Matthäuspassion*.
2   A brief biography can be found in the introduction to Brient, *The Immanence of the Infinite*, 3–8.

begins when humans fear God; rather, that ever since human wisdom began in Eden, God has feared humans, "dangerous fellow knowers in the knowledge of good and evil."[3] A classmate read it as an admonishment telling students to fear their Nazi-sympathizing teachers.[4] In 1939, Blumenberg graduated as valedictorian, and the principal refused him a ceremonial handshake. Humiliations mounted in severity as his mother's Jewish ancestry made him a target of Nazi persecution. Barred from universities, he studied Catholic theology at a seminary in Paderborn and Frankfurt. When forced to quit the seminary in 1940, he returned to Lübeck and worked at the Dräger-Werk manufacturing plant. In 1944, he was interned with other prisoners of mixed Jewish descent in a labor camp in Zerbst. After his former employer got him released, he went into hiding with the family of his future wife, where he hid until the war ended.

After the war, he renounced sleep for one night every week and used the time to write—as compensation for his years in the seminary, forced labor, and hiding. As he explained to Odo Marquard, "you have lost no time in your life. I lost eight years that I need to make up."[5] At age 25, Blumenberg began studying philosophy, German literature, and Classical philology at the University of Hamburg. In nearby Kiel, he wrote a dissertation on medieval Scholastic ontology in 1947, followed by a *Habilitationsschrift* on Husserl's phenomenology in 1950. Soon after, he began his diachronic studies of European intellectual traditions and taught in Kiel, Hamburg, Gießen, Bochum, and finally Münster, where he retired as professor emeritus in 1985. He died several days before the city of Lübeck was to confer Honorary Citizenship on him as an apology for Nazi persecution. While his early work deals with major epochal shifts in intellectual history, his case studies on the indispensible function of seemingly trivial metaphors (this book included) appeared during the prolific final decade of Blumenberg's life.

Blumenberg worked across disciplines throughout his career. Of his first university appointment, he writes, "in a university as small as the Christiana Albertina in Kiel—which had to survive every winter without the amateur sailors of the summer—interdisciplinarity did not need to be expressly invented ... Almost everyone knew almost everything about almost everyone."[6] In 1960 and in 1971, he wrote entries for Erich Rothacker's series *Archiv für Begriffsgeschichte*, a set

---

3   Blumenberg, *Matthäuspassion*, 29.
4   Ulrich Thoemmes, "Kindheiserinnerungen eines Lübecker Arztes," qtd. in ibid., 28.
5   Marquard, "Entlastung vom Absoluten," 25.
6   Blumenberg, *Die Vollzähligkeit der Sterne*, 547.

of "monographic pre-writings" for a 12-volume dictionary chronicling the histories of philosophical concepts.[7] Blumenberg's entries announce the project of "metaphorology," research on the boundaries and interplays between metaphors and concepts. Between 1963 and 1974, he and Hans-Robert Jauß organized annual symposia of the *Poetics and Hermeneutics* group, whose interdisciplinary syncretism and philosophical rigor attracted leading scholars of literary criticism, sociology, philosophy, and other fields. During the group's 1974 symposium, Blumenberg contributed a long essay that he later developed into *The Laughter of the Thracian Woman*.[8]

Blumenberg's prolific writings were wide-ranging in scope, and he did not reduce the scope of his thought for the classroom. His publications span thousands of pages, and lengthy posthumous publications still emerge from his archive every few years. Blumenberg draws on the history of philosophy to construct diachronic arguments, such as this book's claim that one anecdote reveals an ongoing concern of European thought. Students often found his learnedness overwhelming. Philosopher Volker Gerhardt recalls the humbling experience of attending Blumenberg's lectures: "no one else could produce such laughter in his audience, and no one else could produce such bad conscience."[9] The bad conscience resulted from feeling that no one could have read enough to grasp Blumenberg's analyses in full. In another anecdote that Gerhardt recalls, one student after another, intimidated by Blumenberg's erudition, failed to attend a seminar on the very day he or she was scheduled to give a presentation. To prevent further absences, Blumenberg announced that he would quit teaching seminar-style courses and only deliver lectures.

In the last two decades of his life, Blumenberg quit giving extramural talks and attending symposia. During his last years, he categorically refused social or academic invitations to leave his house in Altenberge, a village near Münster. He was ambivalent when Karsten Harries invited him to speak at Yale:

> The Philosophy Department at Yale extended its invitation; [Blumenberg's] first response was positive. But as the date at which he would have had to leave Germany approached and as with

---

7   Rothacker, "Geleitwort," 8. The first volumes of the dictionary, the *Historisches Wörterbuch der Philosophie*, appeared in 1971, and it was completed in 2007. The first volume includes an apology for its exclusion of metaphor from its scope. The *Archiv*, however, still exists as a journal series today and has expanded its scope to include influential metaphors among its concerns.
8   Blumenberg "Der Sturz der Protophilosophen," in *Das Komische*, 11–64.
9   "Blumenberg's Philosophische Anthropologie," 2011.

every passing week the possibility of leaving home threatened ever more insistently to become reality, his brief communications became more discouraging. In the end he did not come at all. Were there health problems that interfered? I don't remember. But somehow this change of heart seemed to fit quite well the mental image I had already formed of him from his work: first the lure of the far away, the fascination with journeying, far away from Münster, from Westphalia, from Germany; in the end the decision to content himself with just thinking about such journeys and to stay at home. Here, too, centrifugal and centripetal forces were at odds. The centripetal forces won out. And something like that seems to me to hold also for his thinking. Expressed in hyperbolic terms: Blumenberg was always unwilling to trade astronoetics for astronautics. I share his unwillingness.[10]

Harries refers to Blumenberg's preference for stationary speculation over investigative experience. Blumenberg coined the word "astronoetics" to describe speculations and thought experiments about space travel. Rather than travel anywhere, he would spend time at home contemplating whether the conditions on other planets might make it easier to be a good person.[11]

Blumenberg's insights did, however, exert a major impact on post-war German philosophy. His metaphorological works hone a method for analyzing changes and continuities in the semantic function of diachronically pervasive metaphors.[12] This method influenced intellectual historian Reinhart Koselleck and leaders of the so-called Constance School, Hans-Robert Jauß and Wolfgang Iser, whose work on literary reception studies anticipates post-structuralist insights. After an epistolary correspondence with Carl Schmitt that began in 1971, Blumenberg expanded the second edition of *The Legitimacy of*

---

10   Harries, *Infinity and Perspective*, 318–19.
11   Blumenberg, *Die Vollzähligkeit der Sterne*, 156.
12   In 1971, when the first volume of the *Historisches Wörterbuch der Philosophie* announced that its entries would not discuss metaphors (citing lack of historical research), Blumenberg published another piece making a case for metaphorology: "Metaphorology achieves an ancillary service to conceptual history, by bringing it into proximity with a genetic structure of concept formation, in which the demand [Cartesian] for distinctness is not fulfilled, but which allows us to recognize the result's distinctness as impoverishment of imaginative background and lifeworldly continuities." Blumenberg, "Beobachtungen an Metaphern," 163. Blumenberg considered the conceptual history movement not to have taken their anti-teleological approach to philosophy far enough; the next stage for research would have to be research on which metaphors enabled concepts to become intuitive enough to be widely received.

the Modern Age to include deeper criticism of Schmitt's secularization hypothesis, which stated that "the political concepts of modernity are all secularized theological concepts" to make the second edition more polemical and more metaphorological than the first.[13] Blumenberg contends that only as old metaphors with transformed meanings did God, the king, and the end of history endure the transition to modernity. The persistence of images cherished by medieval Christendom should not mask the conflict between modern thought and theology.[14] Modern thought aims to satisfy curiosity, which Christian theology had formerly condemned as a distraction from salvation. His phenomenological writings focus around Edmund Husserl's work. Blumenberg finds utility in Husserl's turn to metaphor (such as the "stream of consciousness") to mark perplexity, and he disputes Heidegger's claim to have relinquished metaphor.[15] This book has been translated into French, Spanish, Italian, Portuguese, and English.[16]

Self-isolation sets the scope of late works, like this book. In Blumenberg's last decades, when he was amassing notecards by the thousand, drafting multiple books, and writing a *feuilleton* column

---

13 Schmitt, *Political Theology: Four Chapters on the Concept of Sovereignty*, 44. Their correspondence has also been published as Blumenberg and Schmitt, *Briefwechsel 1971–1978 und weitere Materialien*.

14 In the book section "Secularization: Critique of a Category of Historical Wrong" Blumenberg argues that Schmitt conflates the iconoclasm of secular Enlightenment thinkers with the legally sanctioned seizure of Church property after the French Revolution, a policy known as "secularization." Schmitt uses the pathos of the latter to endow every case of "secularization" with the injustice of theft: "[T]his expression's weight of meaning makes it evident that a sanction must be thought of as having been violated and that a character of forcible injustice must be included in the concept." Blumenberg, *The Legitimacy of the Modern Age*, 23.

15 His argument against Heidegger appears *in nuce* in Blumenberg, "Prospect for a Theory of Nonconceptuality," 100–101. A posthumous work takes up Husserl's and Heidegger's metaphors: "Metaphorology tries or can try to resolve or undermine false incomparabilities, to produce relatabilities, even against the will of those involved. The closer Heidegger seems to come to his goal of answering the question of the meaning of Being, the more he needs to leave descriptive partial achievements behind him and to let metaphorical orientations shine through." Blumenberg, *Quellen, Ströme, Eisberge*, 125. Blumenberg criticizes Ritter, Schmitt, and Heidegger on the same grounds: passing metaphors off as definite concepts. See the two previous notes.

16 His other works currently in English translation include: Blumenberg, *Paradigms for a Metaphorology*; *Care Crosses the River*; *Shipwreck with Spectator*; "Light as a Metaphor for Truth: At the Preliminary Stage of Philosophical Concept Formation"; *The Genesis of the Copernican World*; "An Anthropological Approach to Rhetoric"; *Work on Myth*, 1985; and *The Legitimacy of the Modern Age*.

for the *Frankfurter Allgemeiner Zeitung*, he not only spent little time in others' company but also stood at a distance from the left-liberal philosophy that occupied contemporary German thought. He rejects the "Hegelianizing verdict" that historical developments are final and that present concerns must therefore supersede past ones.[17] On grounds of "taste," Blumenberg cut a chapter on the rhetoric of Nazi heroism from *Work on Myth* before publication. It would have been the only chapter on recent history, and he claims that it cost him more work than most of the rest of the book.[18] His work is silent about the state of the world under late capitalism, the taint of Nazism in post-war German philosophy, and the demise of high culture with the rise of mass production and new media—the contemporary issues whose relevance was promoted by other leading post-war German philosophers Jürgen Habermas, Karl Jaspers, and Theodor Adorno.[19] He does not even engage with Hans-Georg Gadamer's systematic interpretive apparatus, perhaps because he does not share Gadamer's aim of putting past perspectives in dialogue with present ones.[20]

In many works, including the present book, Blumenberg turns his attention away from his living colleagues' concerns towards forgotten problems from the history of philosophy. Had he engaged

---

17   In the 1974 *Poetics and Hermeneutics* conference, Blumenberg sarcastically paraphrases Odo Marquard's views (presented at the same conference) on the history of philosophy. His point is that verdicts about the past should not define the state of culture in the present: "For a Hegelian, one thing is certain: if something died then it is dead. From this premise, the statement follows that philosophy is the 'last' refuge of un-seriousness. It is the survivor… Philosophy only survives at all because art no longer can. It no longer does—perhaps. But why can't art survive any more? Because of that Hegelianizing verdict." Preisendanz and Warning, *Das Komische*, 441.

18   Letter from Blumenberg to Götz Müller (July 20, 1981) in Blumenberg, *Präfiguration*, 62. The cited book contains the chapter suppressed from *Work on Myth*. Blumenberg accounts for his abstention from publicly condemning former Nazi colleagues in a letter to Jacob Taubes (May 24, 1977). After acknowledging an "insurmountable personal repugnance" for former Nazis, he writes: "But I am revolted by the intellectual game played with this repugnance, which brings who-still-is? and who-no-longer? among the pretensions of intellectual arbitration. I have never had personal or intellectual sympathy with Martin Heidegger, but I rail against his new censors." Blumenberg and Taubes, *Briefwechsel 1961–1981 und weitere Materialien*, 174.

19   This does not stop scholars from finding the intersections between Adorno's work and Blumenberg's. See, for instance, Zill, "'Sagen, was sich eigentlich nicht sagen lässt' – Adorno, Blumenberg, und andere Leser Wittgensteins," 53.

20   Blumenberg locates historical discontinuities where continuity was assumed whereas Gadamer pursues "fusion of horizons" between past and present interpreters. This at least shows a different aim—if not a different theory of interpretation. Gadamer, *Truth and Method*, 406.

with the topical theories of his time, he may have enjoyed even wider influence in his lifetime, but he relished independence from the philosophical fashions of the Zeitgeist. He refused "the present as a standard bearer" determining which philosophical questions matter most.[21] Blumenberg's work remains, in many regards, a reflection on reclusion: a highly documented account of a life spent apart from the world, suspicious of common understandings, and in pursuit of the lessons of solitude.

A very adaptable anecdote

The Laughter of the Thracian Woman: A Protohistory of Theory follows one anecdote's long history of adaptation without assigning it one transhistorical meaning.[22] Its meanings change as it is retold in new historical circumstances. The anecdote's oldest recorded iteration appears to be an Aesopic fable, where astronomy stands for any impractical activity that prevents people from noticing their surroundings:

> An astronomer was in the habit of going out regularly in the evening to observe the stars. Once as he was strolling through the outskirts of the town with his attention completely fixed on the heavens, he fell into a well before he knew what was happening to him. While he was howling and shouting, a passer-by who heard his pitiful tones came up and, as soon as he found out what had happened, remarked, "My good fellow, while you're trying to watch things in the heavens, you don't even see things on the earth."[23]

Aesop's fable ends as many fables once did, with a suggestion for its use in public speech: "One might use this story of men who, while they make a great show of wisdom about matters of opinion, can't even deal

---

21 Blumenberg, "Ernst Cassirers gedenkend," 172.
22 *Laughter*'s argument structure is not easy to discern. Phillip Stoellger argues that *Laughter* analyzes the anecdote's reception history abductively; it accumulates evidence for its conjecture about the cause for the anecdote's persistence. The book conjectures that the anecdote persists because the anecdote expresses an otherwise inexpressible and ineradicable tension pervading theoretical thought. Stoellger explains further that theorists reject the anecdote as a self-portrait, not because it makes theory look ridiculous, but because it shows theory as visible whereas invisibility is "understood as a completion" of theory's intentional structure which aims towards abstraction, not perceptible manifestation. Stoellger, *Metapher und Lebenswelt*, 284.
23 Aesop, *Aesop without Morals*, 110. Despite the whimsical title, this collection contains the most philologically accurate translation of the fable available in English.

with matters of common experience."[24] The moral could be used to criticize any form of excess—whether the consequences are personal, interpersonal, or political.

The fable first circulated in handbooks for orators who used them to exemplify situations indirectly. The handbooks did not present fables with morals at the end (*epimythia*), but rather began each fable with a short description of its potential use within a speech (*promythia*). *Promythia* provided an index to guide the handbook user to an apt metaphor for the point he sought to prove. A sample *promythium* runs: "To a man who is rich, and also a scoundrel, the following fable applies."[25] Once fables began being read as literature they were set to verse; the version quoted above is thus more literary than a handbook version with a *promythium*, but less literary than a verse version.[26]

With later rises in literacy, authors used the fable to criticize pagan philosophy, astrology, lack of scientific rigor, and intolerance towards visionaries ahead of their time. For over two and half millennia, it has appeared in Mediterranean and European texts by theologians, preachers, philosophers, and other thinkers, among them Tertullian, Chaucer, Montaigne, Francis Bacon, Immanuel Kant, Ludwig Feuerbach, and Martin Heidegger. But it was Plato's version that launched its career among the writers:

> Why, take the case of Thales, Theodorus. While he was studying the stars and looking upwards, he fell into a pit, and a neat, witty Thracian servant girl jeered at him, they say, because he was so eager to know the things in the sky that he could not see what was there before him at his very feet.[27]

Some versions would conjure the maid's laughter as a way of condemning the impracticality of rival theories; others would recall Thales' plummet as an example of self-sacrificial commitment to the contemplative life.

Over a century after Aesop's death, Plato uses the anecdote in the *Theaetetus* dialogue, where the anonymous astronomer has become Thales of Miletus, already legendary as the inaugurator of Greek science and philosophy, whose "renown for wisdom reached the

---

24   Ibid., 271. Deficiency in "matters of common experience" (*ta koinà*) either means being useless to others or being helpless to help oneself.
25   Quoted in Perry, *Babrius and Phaedrus*, xi–xv.
26   For further discussion of the history of the fable as a literary genre, see Hansen, *Anthology of Ancient Greek Popular Literature*, 463.
27   Plato, *Theaetetus*, 174A 121.

Afterword: Reading into the Distance 141

skies."[28] Blumenberg calls attention to Plato's departure from Aesop in labeling the figures as an astronomer and a maid: "The figures of the confrontation have gained concreteness and background" (p. 6). But Blumenberg's textual history is not universally accepted, as he himself acknowledges (p. 10). A recent classicist has argued that fables, including this one, were not necessarily the work of an "Aesop," but were often simplified stories drawn from famous lyric poems, comedies, or Platonic dialogues.[29] The fable quoted above, with anonymous astronomer and passerby, is from the tenth-century AD Augustana Collection, which supposedly reproduces a late fourth-century BC text compiled by Aristotle's student Demetrius of Phalerum. But Plato's dialogue predates Demetrius' compendium, and Thales and the maid appear in other, later-dated "Aesopic" fable compendia.[30]

The burden of proof is on Blumenberg, then, when he argues that Plato had received the fable with anonymous characters and was the first to dub the anonymous astronomer "Thales" and the passerby a "Thracian servant girl." Instead of a nondescript, affectless passerby, Plato has an enslaved Thracian woman burst out laughing at Thales "because he was so eager to know the things in the sky that he could not see what was there before him at his very feet."[31] The astronomer becomes the epoch-defining protophilosopher Thales, and the anonymous moralizer remains nameless but receives three marks of subordinate status in Greek society: barbarian, female, enslaved.[32]

---

28 Diogenes Laertius, *Lives of Eminent Philosophers*, 41. Blumenberg takes up the questionable value of Thales' philosophy outside of *Laughter*. Thales offers a fear-reducing effect: theoretical explanations for what is (everything is made of water) and predictions of what will come (solar eclipses). However, the water cosmology did not have the staying power of more abstract cosmologies. As Blumenberg says, "But the turn to water was not a lucky stroke, as we see immediately in the Ionian philosophical school. One could insert air with the same right, or, after a few false starts, retreat to saying that the indefinite (*to apeiron*) stands at the beginning." Blumenberg, *Die Verführbarkeit des Philosophen*, 127.

29 Adrados, *History of the Graeco-Latin Fable*, 394, 484 supports the study of more than 500 works considered to be fables. This translation of the original Spanish, standard work on the fable, traces the history of the Graeco-Latin fable, investigates its origins, reconstructs lost collections from the Hellenistic Age, and establishes relationships between the fablist of the Imperial Age and the study of Medieval, Greek and Latin fables. Supplements at the end of each chapter have been added, giving information on a new bibliography and some new data, together with references to subsequent studies."

30 See Kurke, *Aesopic Conversations: Popular Tradition, Cultural Dialogue, and the Invention of Greek Prose*, 269 f18.

31 *Theaetetus*, 174A 121.

32 Blumenberg considers the maid's enslavement more significant than her gender and nationality for Plato's use of the story: "Not necessarily a female slave and

Whether or not Plato named the figures, he equipped his version of the anecdote for subsequent appropriations by expressing such sore sensitivity to ridicule from philosophy's opponents. In Blumenberg's words, "a lot could be projected onto the Thracian woman as enemy of theory, as unproclaimed, prototypical antagonist to Socrates" (p. 23). Plato replaces Aesop's general criticism of doing "unusual things" with a specific one: "The same jest applies to all who pass their lives in philosophy."[33] But why does the maid laugh? All three major contemporary theories of laughter could apply: she could laugh at a perceived incongruity, out of relief, or from a confirmed sense of superiority.[34] She remarks explicitly on the *incongruity* between trying to see the stars and not even seeing the ground. As Harald Weinrich suggests, she might laugh out of *relief* at seeing a member of the slave-driving class fall temporarily from his commanding status.[35] But Blumenberg attributes something like the *superiority* theory to Plato: Plato construes the maid's laughter as a signifier of the brutality of philosophy's opponents. Her amusement becomes analogous to Athens' hatred towards philosophy, which the dialogue's readers would know had already led to Socrates' death sentence. Plato also uses laughter to prefigure Socrates' fate in the *Apology*, where Socrates claims to know the identity of only one of his accusers, Aristophanes, whose comedy *The Clouds* had ridiculed Socrates as a dangerous swindler.[36]

Plato emphasizes the grim fate of the philosopher in this little story, in order to make it a kind of *protrepticon*—a call to engage in philosophical theory at any cost. But many subsequent authors

---

by no means necessarily a Thracian one" (p. 12). Adriana Cavarero disagrees and counters that female gender, more so than status, would attune her to be critical of Thales' ambitions: "I am not sure that she was a servant or that she came from Thrace, but some woman laughed at the philosophers. A quick smile can often be seen on the faces of women as they observe the self-absorption of brainy intellectual men. Philosophers have put this down to biased ignorance, not realizing that it is the expression of a kind of detachment that locates the roots and meaning of female existence elsewhere." Cavarero, *In Spite of Plato*, 50.

33 *Theaetetus*, 174A–B 121.
34 A recent study finds that theories of laughter generally fall into one of these three types. Beard, *Laughter in Ancient Rome*, 36–42.
35 "Aesop, however, no matter whether we take him for a historical figure or a mythical one, is a person of the lowest station, a Phrygian slave, as it is told. Also of low station was the Thracian maid, a female 'guest worker' from a barbarian land. We can therefore imagine the fable's poet with his sympathies on the side of the laughing maid, as the fable's moral makes clear." Weinrich, "Thales und die thrakische Magd: allseitige Schadenfreude," in: Preisendanz and Warning, *Das Komische*, 436.
36 Plato, *The Last Days of Socrates*, 18d 41. Socrates does not say his name, but calls him "a playwright."

Afterword: Reading into the Distance 143

endorse the maid's laughter at the astronomer. In these cases, the maid usurps the protophilosopher's position as the authentic theorist. After all, while Thales observes the stars, she observes his observation; she can thus claim to have a perspective that assesses both his behavior *and* what he saw.[37] Her laughter—whether innocent, misunderstanding, or *schadenfroh*—marks her perspective as distant from the earnest stargazer's. Retellers of this story always side with one figure or the other: philosophers *either* join the maid in mocking Thales, while claiming to be exceptions to theory's absentminded excesses, *or* they lament the astronomer's humiliation, while claiming their own membership in Thales' guild, the rare and misunderstood class of philosophers.[38] No consensus emerges about whether it is better to fall or to laugh, perhaps because, as Hannah Arendt says, even the most absentminded philosopher "shares the 'common-ness' of all men, and it is his own sense of realness that makes him suspect the thinking activity."[39] Intellectuals learn quickly that time does not wait for them to think.

A few lucky theorists find time to think when research institutions sponsor their work. Pure theoretical speculation cannot reliably yield marketable results—but its practitioners can meet professional decorum: "professional theorists are most readily accepted when they approach the phenotype of the now universally familiar bureaucrat and thereby lay claim to the seriousness that comes with dealing in large amounts of money" (p. 2). Earning money lets theorists claim greater seriousness and avoid being harassed for their vocation. Funding cuts to humanities programs thus jeopardize theory's public standing. Even in antiquity theory's reputation already depended on revenue. Blumenberg cites the "counter-anecdote" Aristotle tells:

---

37 This anecdote could redefine "theory" as constituted not by *seeing* (as its Greek etymology suggests), but by *being* seen. Rodolphe Gasché interprets Blumenberg's analysis of the anecdote as revealing theory's fundamentally "theatrical" quality: "Blumenberg's archeology of theory, as a history of scenes in which theory offers itself to view, suggests a much deeper internal connection of theory and theater than is commonly assumed." Gasché, *The Honor of Thinking*, 197. Thales' spectator becomes a crucial stand-in for the divine spectator, the only one who could affirm to the theorist that he has indeed discovered the highest possible object to theorize.
38 Blumenberg himself does not valorize Thales' heroic presumption. As Robert Savage notes, the maid's laughter has important consequences for theory: it exposes theory's constitutive blind spots and removes the illusion of a "safe spectatorial distance" from its objects. Theory can only persist by acknowledging the apparent ridiculousness of its own errors and thus laughing "along with the maid without relinquishing its vision of the whole." Savage, "Laughter from the Lifeworld," 128.
39 Arendt, *The Life of the Mind*, 80.

Thales proves that theory can be profitable by using astronomy to successfully speculate on a olive harvest (p. 15). After making a huge profit, he speaks up for poor theorists by saying that "philosophers can easily be rich if they like, but that their ambition is of another sort."[40]

Despite the institutionalization of theory, alienation is still the theorist's transhistorical condition, according to Blumenberg. The fable persists because theorists desire a narrative to account for "the strangeness that something like 'theory' exists at all," this "exotic behavior" which remains uncommon because the demands of life inhibit it from within, as others' indifference does from without (p. vii, p. 1). But Blumenberg restricts such general claims about the anecdote's transhistorical function to the book's opening, and thus it is difficult for the reader to discern what comes of that claim over the course of *Laughter*. The reader is struck instead by a seemingly disconnected series of chapters analyzing the same story.[41] What emerges over the chapters is a sense that most elements of the Thales anecdote are adaptable while its appeal rests on structures that persist.[42] Besides the maid's ridicule, the most stable structure in the anecdote is the distance between the theorist and the starry sky.

The sky's meaning changes when new ideas take hold about what lies beyond the familiar world. The sky represented heaven in Christian symbolism, and heaven was there to pray for, not to study empirically, and thus Christian authors viewed Thales' tumble as "the downfall of someone who had not wanted to go high enough" (p. 30). The distance that Thales falls also takes on historically specific meanings. To promote the virtue of charity, Christian versions of the anecdote do not display cruel laughter, even at a sinner's injury. For later Christian authors, the fall must be portrayed as physically harmless, and only symbolically fatal: "the abyss turns into the pit of sin" (p. 24).

The anecdote continued to prove useful for criticizing presumptuous philosophy in the context of less orthodox religious views. In early modern France, the skeptical philosopher Michel de Montaigne makes a proactive pedagogue out of the maid:

---

40 Aristotle, *Politics*, Part A, Book XI, 1259 a9–18, 111.
41 This book's Spanish translators catalogue the range of transformations of the two characters on the inside flap of the book. Thales becomes "a hero, a buffoon, an astrologer, a politico, a terrorist, a scientist, a charlatan," while the maid becomes "young, mature, old, a shrew, a courtesan, wicked, vengeful, a demigod, lyrical, contemptuous, lewd, ingenious, sensitive, insensitive, realistic, and unrealistic." Blumenberg, *La risa de la muchacha Tracia*.
42 Paul Fleming develops a similar thesis. See Fleming, "On the Edge of Non-Contingency."

Afterword: Reading into the Distance   145

I feel grateful to the Milesian wench who, seeing the philosopher Thales continually spending his time in contemplation of the heavenly vault and always keeping his eyes raised upward, put something in his way to make him stumble, to warn him that it would be time to amuse his thoughts with things in the clouds when he had seen to those at his feet. Indeed she gave him good counsel, to look rather to himself than to the sky.[43]

Looking at the stars orients the philosopher's thought in a misleading direction, according to Montaigne, but so would watching the ground beneath his feet. Everything exterior is already too far away to yield the most valuable kind of knowledge: the self-knowledge attained through self-reflection. Montaigne only hopes to bridge the metaphorical distance between mind and object by reaching provisional truths immanent to the mind itself.[44] As Blumenberg explains, Montaigne uses the Thales anecdote to express skepticism that insight would result from any experience other than solitary self-examination.

During the nineteenth century, the laughter in the anecdote switches sides in a way that reflects science's new supremacy in European culture. In 1874, the Polish newspaper *Gazeta Narodow* publishes a fraudulent journalistic article mocking the Russians' lack of familiarity with science, by describing how a police officer in Tobolk, Russia, wanted to arrest the famous German naturalist Alexander von Humboldt when the latter "seemed suspicious and very dangerous" for setting up his telescope on a hill: "a long tube that seemed to me and to the whole society to be a cannon" (p. 100). (This article becomes even more absurd when we consider that Humboldt had died 15 years earlier.) Blumenberg explains that this new anecdote retains the old antagonism between those who understand theory and those who do not, although the sides have reversed: "For a civilization familiar with the ritual activities of the theorist, the work-related annoyance of a state officer towards the sky observer has no chance of being taken seriously" (p. 99). Blumenberg takes this excursus from the anecdote's place in intellectual history to describe its place in cultural history; it means that, in nineteenth-century Poland, and *a fortiori* everywhere west of Russia, theoretical work had become so familiar that it had

---

43 Montaigne, "The Apology of Raymond Sebond," *Essays, The Complete Works*, 488.
44 Blumenberg's *Habilitation* claims that the metaphor of distance allows both scientific and philosophical rationalists, like René Descartes, to imagine objects of inquiry as *spatially* distant from the mind: "Not that Descartes would first have to have 'created' this ontological distance through an 'act' of self-distancing; rather, he found himself in this distance." Blumenberg, "Die ontologische Distanz," 17–18.

become laughable to distrust the activities that comprise scientific theory.

Less than a full century later, sympathy with the Thales figure proves compatible with the opposite appraisal of modern science and with condemning practical pursuits in general. In Freiburg, Germany, of 1935, Martin Heidegger evokes the Thracian maid's failure to grasp the philosophical value of absentmindedness—in the context of a lecture on Kant's notion of the "thing." After reading his own translation of Plato's anecdote, Heidegger defines philosophy as "that thinking with which one can start nothing and about which housemaids necessarily laugh."[45] Plato had analogized the maid's laughter to the Athenian jury that executed Socrates. With a similar tone of alarm, Heidegger warns his students that anti-philosophical Thracian maids remain ubiquitous in today's technocracy, and that philosophers must embrace philosophy at risk to their personal safety. Engaging with the central questions of metaphysics "signifies only that procedure during which one runs the danger of falling into a well."[46] For Heidegger, Thales' absentmindedness bespeaks misunderstood goals, which, if understood, would fully legitimate neglect towards everyday concerns.

Blumenberg finds that Heidegger's use of the anecdote illustrates the moment where he departs from Husserl's phenomenology, which sought to describe the general structures of experience (p. 128). Conceptually, Heidegger differed from his teacher Husserl by claiming that philosophy's proper object was existence rather than consciousness.[47] Husserl restricts himself to describing everyday, conscious mental processes whereas Heidegger aims to describe the relationship between existing individuals and Being itself. Metaphorically, this difference reopens the question of whether nearby objects should generally matter more than distant ones. For Heidegger:

---

45 Heidegger, *What Is a Thing*, 3. Blumenberg does not focus on responding to Heidegger, but shares Heidegger's interest in the unrepresentable. Helmut Müller-Sievers notes that a "subterranean engagement with Heidegger... modulates the argumentative path" in many of Blumenberg's works published and posthumous. Müller-Sievers, "Kyklophorology: Hans Blumenberg and the Intellectual History of Technics," 159.
46 Heidegger, *What Is a Thing*, 4.
47 Blumenberg discusses this difference and its implications at length in "Dasein oder Bewußtsein," in Blumenberg, *Beschreibung des Menschen*, 9–47. While he criticizes both Husserl and Heidegger for their belief that they were describing structures that extended beyond the human condition, and he recognizes Heidegger's innovations in describing the emotional aspects of this condition, his sympathies are with Husserl's more skeptical methods and goals.

one's own tendency to hide is to be studied *on the way out* of hiding. While the "distance" had stood far away, but in the same direction as the "nearness," from the center of its object-referent, this methodical rule is precisely for reversing the direction already being pursued by lifeworldly action at any given moment; it is for reading against the grain and hammering against it. (p. 127)

By contrast, "Husserl's programmatic statement that phenomenology is the science of trivialities signifies nothing more" than that he investigates familiar objects, ones that "maids," or any non-philosophers, could say that they "saw as well" (p. 128). Replacing the "science of trivialities" with the theory of absolute Being relieves Heidegger of that accountability: he is no longer discussing objects of which others could claim knowledge.

The distance of the stars from earth can metaphorically represent theory's exoticism because distance metaphorically suggests the unfamiliar, as Blumenberg shows throughout his work. This insight into the foundational role of a distance as a metaphor had already emerged in Blumenberg's *Habilitationschrift* from 1950 about the function of distance metaphors in the "scientific" self-understanding of modern disciplines: "The idea of rigorous scientific work is bound up inextricably from its starting point at the beginning of modernity with the notion of being as possible pure objectivity [*Gegenständlichkeit*, literally "standing-across-ness"], as what can be grasped from out of the distance and across a distance 'clearly and distinctly.'"[48] Besides the procedural demands of "rigorous scientific work" (numerous observations, precise methods of quantification, control of variables), the very notion of rigor draws on a distance metaphor: we imagine a distance separating the theorist from the object under investigation, as if theory must metaphorically pursue knowledge across space. In turn, we imagine the distance collapsing if the theorist achieves understanding of the object. In a posthumous work, Blumenberg claims that human beings generally engage in action across distance (*actio per distans*): we utilize long-range weapons to make war across the greatest spatial distances possible.[49] We plan across temporal distances, which requires us to imagine objects as they will be, and we theorize across metaphorical distances, which means imagining what we can never perceive.

If the Thales anecdote's persistence over millennia indicates theorists' ongoing unease about the metaphorical distance of their objects, that unease is never explicit in the texts cited in *Laughter*.

---

48 Blumenberg, "Die ontologische Distanz," 19 (italics mine).
49 Blumenberg, *Theorie der Unbegrifflichkeit*, 10–13.

Blumenberg, however, is not primarily seeking to discover one ongoing underlying tension in the anecdote. His metaphorological project does not even promise insight into contemporary metaphor use; rather, it observes changes in the use of particular metaphors that could reveal where "implicit questioning has 'lived itself out' in metaphors."[50] His retrospective approach to latent meaning resembles the method he ascribes to Heidegger: "one's own tendency to hide is to be studied *on the way out* of hiding" (p. 127).

His indifference about the contemporary function of this anecdote is especially evident in his choice never to mention Hannah Arendt's ongoing engagement with the anecdote in *Laughter*. His unpublished notecards reveal that he did know of her work on it.[51] Arendt turns to the anecdote to promote critical theory as an alternative to philosophy's aloofness from collective human concerns. She cites Hegel's sympathy with Thales in the anecdote (another reception Blumenberg omits) as a mark of failure to continue the political work Kant had begun, so anomalously in the history of philosophy: "If we are thinking in terms of progress, [Hegel's philosophical elitism] certainly is a 'relapse' into what philosophy had been since its beginning, and Hegel repeats the story Plato told about Thales, with a great show of indignation at the laughing Thracian peasant girl."[52] A similar reading occurs in *The Life of the Mind*.[53] In a radio address for Heidegger's 80th birthday, she diagnoses philosophers' laughable tendency towards political mésalliances.[54] Plato attempted to morally improve the murderous tyrant

---

50   Blumenberg, *Paradigms for a Metaphorology*, 15. Note the difference between Blumenberg's claim that different metaphor *uses* bespeak different worldviews and Lakoff and Johnson's more obvious claim that different *metaphors* do so. Johnson and Lakoff, "Conceptual Metaphors in Everyday Life," 289.
51   "VORSOKR. THALES: 6 HANNAH ARENDT," Blumenberg, "Zettelkasten 14: T–V (Titel von Bearbeiter/in) [Nasenkarten:T, Theologie, Schöpfung, U, V]."
52   Arendt, *Lectures on Kant's Political Philosophy*, 35.
53   Arendt accuses Plato of mistaking internal tension during the thinking process for external hostility. She thinks that philosophy has still under-theorized the "*intramural warfare* between man's common sense, this sixth sense that fits our five sense into a common world, and man's faculty of thought and need of reason, which determine him to remove himself for considerable periods from [the common world]." Arendt, *The Life of the Mind*, 81–2. Instead of seeing the self as divided between common sense and individual thinking, "the philosophers have interpreted that intramural warfare as the natural hostility of the many and their opinions toward the few and their truth." She takes issue with "the entirely serious way in which [Plato] tells the story of the Thracian peasant girl" where "the traditional persecution mania of the philosopher" leads Plato to misinterpret her "innocent" laughter as akin to the sentiment behind Socrates' jury.
54   "[Plato] did not notice that this venture, seen from the peasant girl's perspective,

Dionysius by teaching him mathematics, and she compares Plato's effort to Heidegger's notorious praise of Nazism. Perhaps Blumenberg omits reference to this pertinent reception not only because Arendt is a contemporary but because he disapproves of "social critique" directed at philosophy—a tendency which he diagnosed in his own colleagues (p. 131). *Laughter* does remark briefly on the contemporary appropriation of the fable in the last chapter, which analyzes the discussion of the anecdote at the 1974 *Poetics and Hermeneutics* symposium. After the 1974 meeting alluded to at this end of *Laughter*, he no longer attended *Poetics and Hermeneutics* symposia.

From spatial to temporal distance (1974 to 1987)

Fourteen years prior to publishing *The Laughter of the Thracian Woman*, Blumenberg published an essay version with a different analysis of the anecdote's modern reception. *Laughter* presents the Thales anecdote as a site where modern thinkers project anxieties onto theory's defining first steps, but its precursor reads the anecdote as a site for expressing modern anxiety over heliocentric astronomy, which demoted human life from its presumed supremacy in the natural world. The book extends the focus from the earth's position in space to include Thales' temporal distance from the anecdote's retellers. In 1974, Blumenberg presented this first extended analysis of the Thales anecdote in the form of a long essay for the *Poetics and Hermeneutics* symposium. The essay, "The Protophilosopher's Plummet—on the Comedy of Pure Theory, with Recourse to a Reception History of the Thales Anecdote" (*Der Sturz des Protophilosophen*), appears among other pieces by Blumenberg and his colleagues (including Hans-Robert Jauß, Wolfgang Iser, Odo Marquard, and Jean Starobinski) in the symposium proceedings, *The Comic* (*Das Komische*).[55] Other essays in the volume cover topics from

---

must seem considerably more comical than Thales' mishap ... Evidently, human beings have not yet discovered what laughter is good for—perhaps because their thinkers, who have always been ill disposed toward laughing, have left them in the lurch in this respect, although some of them have racked their brains about the immediate causes of laughter." Neske and Kettering, *Martin Heidegger and National Socialism*, 216.

55 Paul Fleming compares this 1974 title with the 1987 book title and notes that the former mentions Thales; the latter, the maid. The focus thus shifts from theory's own task to the unquestioned lifeworld against which theory constitutes itself. "... [B]y titling the book version *The Laughter of the Thracian Maid*, Blumenberg draws the perspective back, placing the reader on the edge of the scene, observing the tension, the composition of elements, and the necessary laughter (which, for example, is not in Aesop) shooting through the field of philosophy and its literal pitfalls." Fleming, "On the Edge of Non-Contingency," 31.

the structures of comic literature to the social and psychological functions of humor.

The proceedings open with Blumenberg's essay, which begins by describing how "Plato compares the fate of his teacher Socrates with the figure of protophilosopher Thales of Miletus," a case he repeats verbatim in *Laughter*'s second chapter.[56] Yet the two texts differ significantly in scope. The book calls the anecdote "a protohistory of theory" because it substitutes for lacking knowledge about the historical origin of theory by depicting Thales confronting problems at the origin point. "The Protophilosopher's Plummet" does not designate the story a substitute for history—and nowhere uses the word "protohistory." The earlier essay instead focuses on the Copernican Revolution and how the tension between geocentric and heliocentric views impacts reinterpretations of Thales' stargazing in the anecdote.

Blumenberg's essay puts various modern thinkers to trial by evaluating their degree of insight into the impediment that their position on earth puts on understanding the universe. Eighteenth-century astronomer Johann Heinrich Lambert termed this evaluative approach the "Copernican comparative," which "could imply that the fundamental Copernican principle of putting in question and penetrating the illusion of the observer's being located in the center of the universe had not yet been applied sufficiently"—as Blumenberg writes one year later in *The Genesis of the Copernican World*.[57] The only philosophical text quoted in "Plummet" but not *Laughter* interprets Jacob Burckhardt's laughter at the "bustle of the industrial world" at the 1878 Parisian World Fair. Astronomy no longer represents the epitome of scientific ambition, and thus "post-Copernican laughter can no longer go after the sky observer."[58] Blumenberg then traces Burckhardt's scornful laughter to his untenable distinction between philosophy as pure theory and science as unthinking practice.

Specific inadequacies vary among modern theorists: "Francis Bacon was, in spite of his decided rejection of Copernicanism, one of those Copernicans in spite of himself, who could not let go of the principle whose consequences he dismissed."[59] Bacon is a "Copernican in spite

---

56   Blumenberg, "Der Sturz des Protophilosophen. Zur Komik der reinen Theorie-anhand einer Rezeptionsgeschichte der Thales-Anekdote," 11.
57   Blumenberg, *The Genesis of the Copernican World*, 526. Here he also evokes "the anecdote about Thales" when describing Lambert's putative lack of common sense as a display of "the disproportion ... between higher contemplation and a sense of reality." Ibid., 529.
58   Jacob Burckhardt, *Briefe*, IV, 264, in Blumenberg, "Der Sturz des Protophilosophen. Zur Komik der reinen Theorie-anhand einer Rezeptionsgeschichte der Thales-Anekdote," 60; ibid., 61.
59   Blumenberg, "Der Sturz des Protophilosophen. Zur Komik der reinen

Afterword: Reading into the Distance   151

of himself" because he rejected Copernicus' system, but adopted his principle that we should not "scrutinize the highest things" while "ignorant of those nearest to us."⁶⁰ In the essay's final sentence, Blumenberg locates a perversion of Copernican thinking in Heidegger, who believes that by rejecting the earthly vantage point he surpasses the possibilities of empirical science and grasps universal truth:

> That is the post-Copernican anachronism, that the eccentric position, which is exposed to laughter, still allows the access that was presumed to exist at the cosmic center before Copernicus, namely access to knowledge of whether thought has extended its reach beyond the graspable over to the "thing," to the "essence of reasons," to "Being."⁶¹

This passage from "Plummet," about the earth remaining the "cosmic center" after Copernicus, becomes just one claim among others in *Laughter*, which opens and concludes by discussing problems of temporality. In *Laughter*, the concern with *when* Thales fell (which theorists everywhere project into theory's undocumented past) subsumes the concern in "Plummet" with *where* he was (the earth as vantage point). The anecdote thus displays at least two functions: first, in "Plummet," as a metaphor for the synchronic—social and spatial—position of the theorist, then, in *Laughter*, as a myth about the imaginative underpinnings of theory's self-image.

In the last chapter of *Laughter*, Blumenberg reflects back on the 1974 symposium and positions the symposiasts within this anecdote's history:

> Actually one can only laugh at the philosophers or enjoy laughter at their expense if one considers oneself to be their exception. And in this discipline evidently—I cannot speak for other

---

Theorie-anhand einer Rezeptionsgeschichte der Thales-Anekdote," 41. Both "Plummet" and *Laughter* discuss Bacon's reception of the Copernican principle that "the furthest away (*Fernstliegende*) can only be recognized in what is at hand (*Nächstliegende*) ..." (Ibid.). "Plummet" focuses on Bacon's latent Copernicanism whereas *Laughter* reads "influence" into the matter: "This excursus on Copernicus' underlying principle does not amount to a history of influence (*Wirkungsgeschichte*) as normally conceived; this is clear when we observe how a decisive opponent to Copernicus such as Francis Bacon could not resist applying the principle whose consequences he rejected in order to become a kind of latent Copernican in spite of himself" (p. 62).
60   Copernicus, *On The Revolutions of Heavenly Spheres*, 12.
61   Blumenberg, "Der Sturz des Protophilosophen. Zur Komik der reinen Theorieanhand einer Rezeptionsgeschichte der Thales-Anekdote," 64.

disciplines—everyone considers himself to be the exception to all others ... One can only be the exception, and remain so, if one is the first or the last: Thales or Socrates—or Heidegger. For as soon as the first has been, according to this scheme, one can only still want to be the last. (p. 131)

Although Heidegger already occupies the position of terminal figure in the philosophical tradition, whenever theorists born after Plato cite this story, they claim to know what philosophy *had been* about and therefore still claim to be marking the end of its errant career. The book goes beyond analyzing the protophilosopher's faulty spatial vantage point—it discusses the faults within the tradition that he inaugurated. The metaphor of the philosopher who stares up and falls down is spatial, but it grounds a historical understanding.

Reading the transcribed symposium conversation about Blumenberg's essay sheds further light on the conceptual changes between the essay and the book. The interdisciplinary structure of the *Poetics and Hermeneutics* symposia suited an essay like Blumenberg's, which interprets the anecdote's aesthetic and cognitive function across the history of various theoretical discourses. The symposia featured broad, abstract topics like mimesis, modern art, identity, negativity, myth, and individuality, and the 1974 symposium, *The Comic*, exhibited the usual range: papers discussed the cultural function of fools, clowns, irony, and satire in European literature and history, as well as laughter's character as healthy, conformist, or revolutionary. Considering the diverse work under discussion, it is surprising that Blumenberg's essay prompted four scholars to submit entries on the Thales anecdote. The comedy of the situation could hardly have been lost on the symposiasts: how many scholars does it take to interpret one brief, whimsical anecdote? Apparently, it takes four.

The other symposiasts' entries respond to Blumenberg's essay with thoughts on the anecdote's narrative structure. In "Philosophy, Literature, and the 'Comedy of Pure Theory,'" French literature scholar Karlheinz Stierle claims that recent philosophers have found a way to make philosophy's failures less comic: by making philosophy self-reflexive and literary. After listing some names (Montaigne, Pascal, Lichtenberg, Nietzsche, and Valéry), he offers Baudelaire's poem "The voice" as an example where the lyric speaker "falls into holes, his eyes on the sky," but, instead of an onlooker scolding him, an inner voice consoles him, "Protect your dreams; sages have nothing more beautiful than madmen do!"[62] After Stierle thus describes the recuperated modern value of the "eccentric" and his "subjective world," German and Latin

---

62 Preisendanz and Warning, *Das Komische*, 432.

philologist Manfred Fuhrmann notes in "Height of the Fall—Taken Literally for once" that literature usually makes a tragedy of figurative or literal falls, but that the Thales anecdote sits ambiguously between comedy and tragedy because Thales is removed from view after he falls. "We cannot see how deeply he falls."[63] Fuhrmann sees the well's depth as a metaphor for the extent of Thales' personal devastation. Citing Aristotle's *Poetics*, he claims that the reader must perceive the magnitude of a figure's loss for his or her fall to be tragic.

The philosopher and French literature scholar Harald Weinrich also refers to Aristotle's *Poetics* in an erudite plea "for more understanding towards the Thracian maid," entitled "Thales and the Thracian maid: *Schadenfreude* on all sides" (translated in this book's appendix). The "rule of stations" interprets the *Poetics* as saying that common people were the stuff of comedy and noblemen the stuff of tragedy. "Our fable's ambivalence is thus grounded in its mixed, 'tragicomic' personnel."[64] These three scholars' interpretations stress the anecdote's ambiguity. Blumenberg's arguments in "Plummet" and in *Laughter* do so as well: the anecdote has staying power among authors with disparate views, he claims, because its meaning remains plastic.

Blumenberg then gives a "rejoinder" that rejects Weinrich's move to credit the maid with enlightened disdain for astrological superstition. He insists that, in Plato's version, the maid exemplifies nothing but "blindness" towards philosophy's insights. In this rejoinder, he develops the argument (like the one in Chapter 1 of *Laughter*) that theory's invisibility provokes antagonism:

> Perhaps I enter into triviality when I recall that one cannot see actions at all. They consist of the rule by which physical occurrences obtain a designation. When we believe we are seeing actions, we interpret physical appearances by reference to the identity of such a rule. Pure theory, whose intentional context does not seem to end up in a useful product, offers the observer of its manifestations no help in recognizing the rule that governs them. If Thales verifiably predicted the solar eclipse for the citizens of Miletus, if his knowledge actually made his oil mill speculation successful, then something must have happened to stop the laughter, as they say. But precisely this kind of legitimation is not vaunted as the kind that would satisfy the pure theorist. The outlandishness of an action that is not recognized as an action by a third party is the reference point for intolerance,

---

63 Ibid., 434. This particular ambiguity of the anecdote is the topic of *Laughter*'s fourth chapter.
64 Ibid., 437.

which can lie at any point on the entire scale from head shaking to murder. Laughter is just one segment on that scale.⁶⁵

As much pathos as Blumenberg musters here, *Laughter* also accounts for deviations from this view. In the rejoinder, he concedes to Weinrich that he too feels uneasy about the number of philosophers who endorse the maid's laughter. We can interpret the enigmatic last line of *Laughter* in light of this concession: "the interdisciplinary reception of the reception supports the diagnosis that the end of philosophy is announced just as it sees its own task in the treatment of its beginning" (p. 132). If the diagnosis is correct—that interpreting philosophy's history is no longer philosophy—then *Laughter* is not philosophy. But it does at least defend philosophy as an expression of the theoretical urge against whoever would define it by its history of failure or by its laughably useless appearance.

"The laughter in this story was on the wrong side" (From the archive)

In *Laughter*, Blumenberg does not explicitly divulge whether he identifies with Thales' absorption in thought or the maid's skeptical outburst at the sight of theoretical activity. His unpublished notes pertaining to the anecdote reveal ambivalence towards both positions. Since his death in 1996, hundreds of boxes, each containing several hundred index cards, have been made available for researchers to view at the German Literature Archive in Marbach. This record includes many ideas that do not directly figure in this book, in his 1974 study on the anecdote,⁶⁶ or in his sporadic mention of the anecdote in other works. Blumenberg's restraint from taking clear and decisive philosophical positions has often been noted,⁶⁷ but his unpublished notes show that he did indeed construe a message from the anecdote: the way to preempt philosophy's hecklers is to acknowledge what a ridiculous impression philosophy makes.

Among the cards beginning with the heading "THALES," Blumenberg

---

65 Blumenberg, "Wer sollte vom Lachen der Magd betroffen sein? Eine Duplik," 440.
66 Blumenberg, "Der Sturz des Protophilosophen. Zur Komik der reinen Theorie- anhand einer Rezeptionsgeschichte der Thales-Anekdote."
67 Blumenberg's restraint from making strong theoretical claims was recently thematized by Kirk Wetters. He points out that when Habermas tries to read Blumenberg's political detachment as a symptom of "the German theoretical tradition," Habermas has failed to see that Blumenberg's entire goal is to show how exaggerated the unity of that tradition is. "It is ironic that the implicit targets of Blumenberg's polemics are precisely those who are most predisposed to overlook them." Wetters, "On the Edge of Non-Contingency," 104.

justifies his affinities for each of the figures in the story. Two of the cards develop the argument that the maid not only lacks philosophical qualifications, but that she would not even qualify as a sophisticated orator because her laughter cannot measure up to the ancient rhetorical ideal of speaking the truth while laughing (*ridendo dicere verum*). For she does not claim to articulate a general truth when she criticizes Thales, but only "articulates her *Schadenfreude* ... [whereas the] truth in what she says can only be discovered if we forget her laughter for a moment."[68] However, he asserts the maid's great figurative value to philosophy on the card entitled "THE MAID RECOGNIZES THE PHILOSOPHER'S NEUROSIS." This card describes how Thales needs to stumble over the well in the maid's proximity, so that they will establish intersubjective understanding by both paying attention to the same object, the well: "It is important that intersubjectivity enters as an escalation of reality at the moment in which a witness is there; they have a common object ... The well he fell into was a common reality—what he had observed before, the stars, was only his own."

However, "the escalation of reality" through shared experience does not change the fact that the realistic attitude is inherently antagonistic to theoretical interests. In another card titled "THE RIDICULOUSNESS OF THE UNREADY-TO-HAND (*UNZUHANDENEN*) AS AN OBJECT & THE PRESUMPTION INHERENT IN THE BARBARISM OF RELEVANCE," Blumenberg explains:

> The scene's comedy is founded on the sheer distance of the mental, on the sheer unreadiness-to-hand of the stars, on the senselessness of just-wanting-to-see ... Wholehearted, undeceitful theory must demonstrate that it embodies the deceit of pragmatism in order to bring the laughter to rest. What a tableau of the European history of the attitude towards theory in this first enumeration of its possibilities in the form of an apocryphal event! Comedy demands a gaping hiatus, an abyss of incommunicability: here [in the misunderstanding of theory] is the greatest of all [gaps in

---

68 The claim that the maid's laughter does not coincide with her truth-telling occurs on the card entitled "PRESOCR. THALES: LAUGHTER AND THE RIDENDO DICERE VERUM." The maid cannot be a philosopher, according to Blumenberg, because she does not reflect on the principle behind her laugher, and philosophers' statements must promote ideals: "The Thracian maid's weakness consists of her inability to reflect on her own 'position of advantage,'" as he explains on the card "PRESOCR. THALES: THE MAID IS NOT THE OBSERVER FROM LUCRETIUS' PROEMIUM." Index card citations in this section are from Blumenberg, "Zettelkasten 14: T–V (Titel von Bearbeiter/in) [Nasenkarten:T, Theologie, Schöpfung, U, V]."

understanding]! Socrates & his judge, Archimedes & the Roman soldier, etc.[69]

Although the maid's laughter corroborates Thales' reality after he falls, this card describes how, as a comic figure, Thales cannot share her reality unless he disguises theory as something practical. The narrative structure hinges on portraying Thales' confidence—that he can close the gap between his mind and the stars—as opening up new gaps right in front of him: both in the ground and in communication, down the well and across from the maid, respectively. The "sheer distance of the mental" recalls "The Ontological Distance," Blumenberg's *Habilitationschrift*, which explains that many thinkers implicitly evoke the metaphor of distance between an object of knowledge and its knower in order to illustrate the privation of knowledge not yet known.[70] The image of ontological distance promotes hope that a mind could possess its object by metaphorically reaching for it. In keeping with this image, the notecard points out that Thales' failure to reach across the astronomical distance to the stars offers philosophy no hope; instead, it justifies the maid's amusement at the philosopher's error.

While that card judges "European history" for its repeated episodes of scornful laughter at whatever appears irrelevant to its momentary purposes, another card, entitled "PROTOTYPICAL RECKLESSNESS TOWARDS REALITY," redeems the willingness to laugh at one's own absentmindedness as a philosophical virtue:

> Can we say that conducting pure theory is fun? No. We cannot even say that we conduct it—for self-evidently theory—and perhaps theory alone—is not that kind of conduct. But we can laugh at ourselves while we conduct it. The pure theorist as comic figure, like Thales of Miletus, that is usually a self-infatuated, self-constructed, self-styled figure. For Thales is already the absentminded professor of the anecdote in pure form (*Reinkultur*), whose absentmindedness takes itself as the indicator for his recklessness towards reality—for the sake of truth.

---

69 This card's content appears in "The Protophilosopher's Plummet," followed by another example, "Galileo and Cardinal Bellarmine," and one of the only citations in "Plummet" not found in *Laughter*: "the role reversal in a report from 1971: 'Workers of the Tianjin Railway Worker University for the Humanities complained in the party newspaper *Kuang Min Jih Pao* that philosophy students at Nankai University ridiculed them when they presented their self-written philosophical treatises there at Mao's behest.'" *Der Spiegel*, 1971, Nr. 3, in Blumenberg, "Der Sturz des Protophilosophen. Zur Komik der reinen Theorie-anhand einer Rezeptionsgeschichte der Thales-Anekdote," 17.

70 See Blumenberg, "Die ontologische Distanz."

Afterword: Reading into the Distance   157

This card identifies Thales' tumble as a reminder of theorists' characteristic fault, absentmindedness, but it also redeems that weakness as amusing, rather than tragic. The Thales anecdote's purpose then is not to condemn theory, but to help theorists legitimize their own narcissism, and the maid laughs because self-importance prevents theorists from laughing at themselves. Theory retains the stigma of self-importance or narcissism because it does not submit to popular consensus about what constitutes *useful* activity. Blumenberg does not put it so sharply in his published work, where he instead presents aspects of the anecdote's historical function. His notecards interpret the anecdote's meaning whereas the book primarily draws on the fable's long reception history. While less daring than the notecards' interpretations, the book's focus on history lets Blumenberg locate the anecdote's appeal in its ability to "recall what has eluded us" and to explain why theory remains an "exotic behavior" after all of this time (p. vii, p. 1).

The published version of *Laughter* explains the book's guiding claims briefly in its short preface without giving a sense of the intervention it seeks to make, whereas an unpublished page of writing, typed on hotel stationery from the Hotel Mainzer Hof, outlines Blumenberg's purpose in writing this book in passionate detail. As with most of the documents left unpublished at Blumenberg's death in 1996, this one is undated, but its enthusiasm about what this book offers may indicate that he wrote it shortly before publishing the book. I have translated it in its entirety below:

> If it were announced today that the quite bitterly foregone protohistory of theory would soon be given over to outstretched hands, this would not be one of the high-flown ambitions that have already become habits in the theoretical scenery of the "Scientific Society" so plagued by the burden of evidence. A protohistory of theory is not, however, being promised as finally written or about to be written; more simply rather, only one protohistory of apparently unclaimed originality will be held up to view—neither one to write nor one to invent, a protohistory solely to remember and to illuminate. Everyone knows it—or almost everyone—without having experienced the excitement of all of its facets and layers, an excitement that this exposition claims to be provable and even hopes to have proven. The indefinite article is … program! It is a matter of luck, a lucky stroke, though no accident, that we find this story in the thin collection of our oldest texts and only need to accept them as ours. There is nothing to construct—for all of the pedantic passion for the constructed—for this protohistory has enough destiny to just be told. Whoever considers "storytelling" too meager may hew closely to the analytic describability of a

reception event that, after reading, should have become clearer, more penetrating, and more informative about the problem with the problems that are posed to us under the heading "theory."

That it is only *a*, and not *the*, protohistory of theory being offered should not come off as a downside, but as an advantage—instead of "reconstructing" what allows no access, only something most humble, if not contemptible, is being done: a reflection is being provoked here about what there ever was and how it first provoked such reflectiveness and then did so again and again in mutant forms—not without the threat that we will ultimately forget it when the work of the concept, of the original foundation (*Urstiftung*) of the European sciences,[71] is finally uncovered so much more precisely, as cannot be avoided, that we take it seriously enough and ever more seriously. Seriousness certainly must not be lacking, and it is the misfortune of the "protohistory" at play that it lacks some seriousness—although it is unmistakable that pains have been taken to turn it into something serious whenever retouching occurs without corroding the duty towards loyal transmission. Whoever keeps in mind that theory—as an attitude and not just as an accumulation of propositions—should have to do with human happiness to such an intensive degree that over two millennia the epitome of happiness could be seen in the eternal "theory" of the pure truth, untarnished intuition, *visio beatica*,[72] will not be surprised that its first misfortune would do more than disappoint, it would hurt. The laughter in this story was on the wrong side. And over the course of this story's history (*im Verlauf der Geschichte dieser Geschichte*) it has never ended up on the right side. Even this little book cannot achieve that. Although it does encourage wishing for that in utter secrecy behind folded hands.[73]

The ring composition of the note, beginning and ending with the image of reaching or praying hand gestures, gives a sense of Blumenberg's hopes for how people will receive his book: eagerly and reverently. This first paragraph presents the book's task as merely "to remember and to illuminate" a story. But why even remind us of this story if "everyone

---

71 The Afterword section titled "What is 'A Protohistory of Theory?'" discusses the relevance of Husserl's notion of original foundation to protohistory (p. 159).
72 *Visio beatica*. Augustine describes this quasi-visual experience as the soul's joyful anticipation of the end of times. See Ritter and Eisler, *Historisches Wörterbuch Der Philosophie*, XI, 1069.
73 Blumenberg, "Das Lachen der Thrakerin (Drucktitel) [verschiedene Fassungen: Vorstufen, Manuskript, korr. Druckfahne, Materialien zum Buch]."

Afterword: Reading into the Distance 159

knows it?" The anecdote does not even exhibit the magic associated with myth or the intricate twists associated with brilliant storytelling, but rather it only has the whimsy of a simple joke, or, as Blumenberg puts it, the anecdote "lacks some seriousness." Furthermore, he claims that the book will disappoint readers who seek realistic accounts of the past, since the history of this anecdote and its variations can only reveal "an excitement that this [book] claims to be provable." In the late 1980s, when post-structuralism's "pedantic passion for the constructed" had swept Europe, and no humanistic scholar would dare consider authorial intentions knowable, Blumenberg claims to know about "excitement" felt by long dead authors! If the eager reception he wants seems so implausible, why did he write the book at all?

Laughter presents Blumenberg's analyses of the anecdote without much theoretical scaffolding, but this unpublished note's second paragraph discloses the book's rhetorical aim: to persuade contemporary scholars in the humanities that they could learn from the anxieties implicitly expressed by their predecessors. If we imagine along with Blumenberg that a story's recurrence is evidence of an irrepressible thought, then the story could serve as a warning to all theorists: "the laughter in this story was on the wrong side." The fable implies that the theorist who seeks happiness through knowledge ends up ridiculed. Meanwhile, "on the wrong side," the pragmatic attitude, which believes it has progressed beyond theory's futile desire for "pure truth," locates our historical moment beyond theory, in a more serious epoch, where we can laugh at the pursuit of intellectual gratification. The difference between abstract theory and bodily, familial, or economic practices are reconcilable in many people's lived experience, but the moment of tension must be acknowledged, and this anecdote has provided, as Blumenberg writes in *Laughter*, "the most enduring prefiguration of all the tensions and misunderstandings between the lifeworld and theory" (p. 3).

What is "a protohistory of theory"?

In the brief author's preface to *Laughter*, Blumenberg designates two different concepts with the same word, *Urgeschichte*, which I translate "protohistory."[74] In the book's first line, the word refers to a would-be historical moment that could not be recorded because "there was no desire on the part of theory to leave a record of it" (p. vii). For the rest of the book, it refers to a story that "claimed the vacant position." The word *Geschichte* means fictional story and realistic history, depending

---

74 While already considering the translation "protohistory," I noticed that the book's Spanish translation uses the word's Spanish cognate in the subtitle: *una protohistoria de la teoría*. See Blumenberg, *La risa de la muchacha Tracia*.

on whether it follows an indefinite article (*eine*) or a definite one (*die*). The Thales anecdote has little claim to historical reality; it is only *eine Urgeschichte*, a primal story, "a story that has stood the test of history." I translate *Urgeschichte* as "protohistory" although the everyday German word is synonymous with "prehistory" in its two English senses: "events or conditions leading up to a particular occurrence or phenomenon" and "events or conditions before written or recorded history."[75] But academic discourses use *Vorgeschichte* to refer to the prehistoric past. In theology and philosophy, *Urgeschichte* refers specifically to "a supposedly divine (or ideal) origin story of humanity, as thematized in an 'original state' (*Urstand*) before the fall of man."[76] The term "protohistory" approximates this special sense of *Urgeschichte*. I do not exactly intend protohistory's special historiographical senses— "the history of the earliest times" and the history of illiterate societies written by literate foreigners—although these forms of historiography are pertinent.[77] Like *Urgeschichte*, they call for unusual measures of imaginative reconstruction.

Blumenberg neither develops the concept of protohistory further in other works nor after the preface in this book.[78] His other works do account for the related problem of speaking about our "lifeworld," those habitual, immersive activities that we only notice retrospectively after self-reflective thought has interrupted them. Like unknown protohistory, the self-evident lifeworld requires imaginative reconstruction. Agents inhabiting the lifeworld and protohistory never think to document their actions. Blumenberg finds the concept of the lifeworld in Edmund Husserl's late work, *The Crisis of European Sciences and Transcendental Phenomenology*, whose defining quality is "self-evidence."[79] It consists of working assumptions built on cultural understanding, specialized knowledge, *and* on the structure of sensory modalities. "[T]he lifeworld, for us who wakingly live in it, is always already there, existing in advance for us, the 'ground' of all praxis whether theoretical or extratheoretical."[80] The lifeworld is an unreflective mental state as opposed to the self-reflective state Husserl calls "theory." Husserl claims that phenomenology is the

---

75 "Prehistory, N."
76 Ritter and Eisler, *Historisches Wörterbuch Der Philosophie*, XI, 360.
77 "Proto-, Comb. Form"; Taylor, "Thracians, Scythians and Dacians," 373.
78 Chapters two and fourteen use the word attributively, but do not describe the concept further.
79 Husserl, *The Crisis of European Sciences and Transcendental Phenomenology: An Introduction to Phenomenological Philosophy*, 127. "The lifeworld is a realm of original self-evidences."
80 Ibid., 142.

first theoretical method to suspend the lifeworld's assumptions with adequate precision.

Mundane activities, such as driving a car, typically fail to attract enough thoughtful attention to be memorable.[81] "There are no 'stories from the lifeworld,'" Blumenberg writes, because "we have to break from it to say something about it."[82] After an unmemorable drive, we can still say with assurance that we drove somewhere, but the statement will lack an interior perspective unless something triggers reflection during the experience. Crashing a car prompts reflection and elicits an explanatory narrative of our driving behavior—but we have to invent details if we did not reflect in advance. When we do not expect to be held accountable for behaviors, we focus on performing them and experience them unreflectively, without the coherence of a narrative account. Non-reflection rarely goes uninterrupted for long, of course, as theory and lifeworld interpenetrate in real situations. The Thales anecdote is a "confrontation between theory and the lifeworld" in more ways than one; the maid might not recognize Thales' behavior as "theorizing," but the theorist crashes while performing one of the lifeworld's oldest activities: walking (p. 11).

The lifeworld goes unnoticed, but it is not "the unconscious." Unlike Freud's theory of the unconscious, Husserl's theory of the lifeworld does not attribute extrinsic motivations to lifeworldly behavior. Blumenberg joins Wittgenstein in criticizing Freud's tendency to find the same cause—repressed libido—behind every dream, joke, and compulsion. Wittgenstein states Freud's implicit formula as "this is in reality just that."[83] No evidence could suffice to justify the attribution

---

81 My car driver analogy may recall David Armstrong's analogy where the mere "perceptual consciousness" of a sleepy "long-distance truck-driver" becomes "introspective consciousness" only when he feels alert enough to begin reflecting on his driving. Armstrong, *The Nature of Mind, and Other Essays*, 60–6. Introspection, however, cannot recover what is lost during inattentiveness, as I explain here. In fact, noticing that one is driving does not even assure greater attention to the perceptual experience of driving. For this argument, see Lycan and Ryder, "The Loneliness of the Long-Distance Truck Driver."

82 Blumenberg, *Lebenszeit und Weltzeit*, 23. Blumenberg also compares the lifeworld to an amusement park in which there is "an exact equivalent between expectations aroused and fulfillments procured" (Ibid., 49). For an excellent discussion of Blumenberg's own theory of the lifeworld, German readers should consult Merker, "Bedürfnis nach Bedeutsamkeit: zwischen Lebenswelt und Absolutismus der Wirklichkeit."

83 Wittgenstein, *Lectures and Conversations on Aesthetics, Psychology, and Religious Belief*, 24 (translation modified). Blumenberg discusses the variant formula "Everything from One" in the 1974 *Poetics and Hermeneutics* conference: "But every time unity was achieved in the history of thought, it was always given up

of one source for all conscious motivations.⁸⁴ Blumenberg writes that "philosophy has argued with accomplishments of this type for the majority of its history. This sentence describes with unsurpassable precision just what phenomenology wanted to be the exact opposite of."⁸⁵ Blumenberg traces this psychological formula back to speculative cosmology: from Thales' statement "all is water," to Aristotle's hylomorphism, to monotheism's notion that everything exists because God wanted it to, to Schopenhauer's belief that will is the universal substance, to Freud's reduction of all wishes to libido. But this type of explanation proves incompatible with practical familiarity with the world: "The readiness to destroy prejudices, even at the price of the world's convenience, is what makes the long history [of such explanations] incomprehensible."⁸⁶ Husserl only studies the lifeworld's form and genesis; its content is self-evident, requiring no explanation.

Blumenberg characterizes Husserl's theory of the lifeworld as a result of a "search for a kind of 'original state' (*Urzustand*)."⁸⁷ He does not share Husserl's view that philosophy can and must purify itself of lifeworldly contamination through a strict regime of skepticism towards all working assumptions. He does follow Husserl in valuing narrative structure (over proof structure) as a means of explicating immersion in the lifeworld.⁸⁸ The Thales anecdote, however, reads nothing like Husserl's narratives. Instead of narrating the "genetic" process by which consciousness generates reality, the anecdote narrates one *contingent* moment of contact between theory and the lifeworld.⁸⁹

---

again right away because 'the One' proved to be disappointingly useless. It is the phenomenon of function loss through function fulfillment, which makes up both the world's mythical saturation with gods and the rational maximization, Everything from One." "Unernst als geschichtliche Qualität," in Preisendanz and Warning, *Das Komische*, 442.

84 Freud eventually retires the monism of libido. In his late speculations, the death drive precedes libido ontogenetically and phylogenetically. See Freud, *Beyond the Pleasure Principle*.
85 Blumenberg, *Lebenszeit und Weltzeit*, 29.
86 Blumenberg, *Die Verführbarkeit des Philosophen*, 39.
87 Blumenberg, *Lebenszeit und Weltzeit*, 31.
88 Both value the use of narrative in theoretical discourses: Blumenberg implies that narrative is a necessary substitute for answers when questions contain terms that render them unanswerable. He says explicitly of metaphor (and only implicitly of narrative) that it can "give structure to a world, representing the nonexperienceable, nonapprehensible totality of the real." Blumenberg, *Paradigms for a Metaphorology*, 14. For Husserl, narrative is part of a method that offers "an analytics of consequence-relationships, a principle of genetic order." "The Genesis of Judgment," in Husserl, *The Essential Husserl*, 303.
89 Paul Fleming keenly notes that Blumenberg's later works show increasing attention to anecdotes as if to indicate his discovery that anecdotes' complex

Universal structures are not revealed here, only the long-term attraction to narrative structures. Thales' tumble initiates an unplanned process, the reverse of the kind of methodical procedure advocated by Husserl. When Thales trips and the maid laughs, theory does not suspend the lifeworld; the lifeworld interrupts theory.

The anecdote narrates just one sequence of events, but it describes the friction around the lifeworld more memorably (if less precisely) than a phenomenologist could: "The interaction between the protophilosopher and the Thracian maidservant ... became the most enduring prefiguration of all the tensions and misunderstandings between the lifeworld and theory" (p. 3). But nowhere in *The Laughter of the Thracian Woman* does Blumenberg explain why an anecdote describes theory's place in the lifeworld better than a general explanation could.[90] Blumenberg does not theorize the anecdote as a form. He does extensively theorize myth as the source of stories that invite repetition no matter "where they came from and what they meant," like the stories children ask to hear repeated.[91] Brief and often without convincing context, mythic stories evoke "the past's past" (*Vorvergangenheit*), a time so vaguely imagined that its content has not "submitted to compromise with reality."[92] As myths evoke the past's murky past, the Thales anecdote evokes the protohistory of theory.

Husserl's *Crisis* treatise invites the misinterpretation that only in humanity's primitive past were humans ever immersed in the lifeworld. He evokes the pathos of difficult liberations to promote theory's progress, much as Plato does in the cave allegory.[93] Even today

---

configurations expressed the unpredictable nature of the lifeworld better than simple images did. Fleming, "On the Edge of Non-Contingency," 27. (Blumenberg's early methodologically oriented work names metaphor, not anecdote, as philosophy's favored solution to its ongoing aporias.) Fleming has argued that anecdotes are uniquely poised to represent historically decisive moments due to "the contingency captured in anecdotal thought." Fleming, "The Perfect Story," 82. Fleming shows that even the shortest myths, metaphors, and anecdotes that Blumenberg analyzes must portray accidents or mishaps if they are going to depict the entry point of contingency into history.

90 One scholar supports Blumenberg's argument by claiming that a description of lifeworld must be inconspicuous. The anecdote's expressive function could go unnoticed for millennia because the anecdote must pass as trivial in order to serve as an account of theory's place in the lifeworld. This claim is developed in Stoellger, *Metapher und Lebenswelt*, 284.
91 Blumenberg, *Work on Myth*, 1985, 159.
92 Ibid., 21. "The past's past" is Robert Wallace's ingenious alternative translation of the German word for "pluperfect" (*Vorvergangenheit*). The etymology could be calqued as "pre-past."
93 Blumenberg compares Husserl's lifeworld theory to Plato's depiction of mere opinion as a cave (where people compete to predict which shadows will appear

scientists cling to assumptions—blindly received from their lifeworld—about physics and subjectivity. The fact that assumptions from the lifeworld endure in an epoch so marked by theoretical innovation bespeaks the urgency and complexity of theorizing the lifeworld. Blumenberg describes Husserl's mission to theorize the lifeworld thus: "We need a theory of the lifeworld because we no longer live in a lifeworld—or at least we do not know exactly to which degree we no longer live in a lifeworld."[94] The lifeworld is fundamentally "ahistorical" as "the condition of possibility of historical worlds." And an "ahistorical" event cannot even be said to precede a historical one because it has no definite position in history: "every documentable fact given about reality—be it archaic or mythic or prehistorical—must be understood as already having exited the lifeworld, for it would be naïve to partake in a concept of history that relies on a division of disciplines between prehistory and history." In other words, when we speculate about any *real* past, even a prehistoric one, we cannot claim to theorize the lifeworldly experience, which occurs in time, but disregards time's passage.

The unfulfilled desire to know the *prehistory* of the lifeworld is expressed in a *protohistory* of theory. But the anecdote only presents "a protohistory of theory," and as Blumenberg explains in *The Laughter of the Thracian Woman*: "*A* protohistory of theory cannot replace *the* protohistory of theory. It can only recall what has eluded us" (p. vii). The event that inaugurates history cannot claim real status within history. In Blumenberg's words, "this or that historical event does not need to be brought in as an example; rather, [we need] a model to represent how it occurs that history is set in motion from out of not-yet-history."[95] "Not-yet-history" captures the ahistorical, unrealistic quality of "protohistory."

If theorists find orientation in a fictional "protohistory" (*Urgeschichte*), then Husserl may be correct to worry that theorists forgot their proper task, lost sight of theory's "original foundation" (*Urstiftung*). But Blumenberg rejects the premise of this concern by denying that the original founding is anything more than a fictional protohistory taken literally. He warns against the rhetorical allure of Husserl coinages beginning with *Ur-*: "the use of the prefix '*Ur-*' served as much to

---

next on the cave wall) and must be forcibly removed to see the daylight of knowledge. Blumenberg, *Theorie der Lebenswelt*, 177. The biggest difference between the two models is that the cave's contests go on indefinitely and knowledge acquisition is a one-time affair, whereas Husserl describes the refinement of theory as an ongoing and "infinite task."

94 Ibid., 231.
95 Ibid., 233 (emphasis added).

gives a "reoccupiable" configuration enough stability that writers from different eras may be said to turn to the same figure at all? Answering this requires a look at Blumenberg's two most original theories: his theory of reoccupation and his metaphorology. With a basic grasp of these theories, we can say what it is for the Thracian woman's laughter to be an object of metaphorology.

Reoccupation is the mechanism by which myths, dogmas, theories, and artworks incorporate other discourses' achievements. For instance, ancient theoretical claims could not "bring myth to an end" just by eliminating false beliefs.[107] Thales outdid myth by reoccupying it: "[Thales'] 'new solution' to the riddle of the world—that everything emerged from the water and is therefore still on top of it—was well attested on Homer's authority. In the *Iliad*, the river god Oceanus is the 'sire of the gods.'"[108] (p. 3) Thales implicitly replaces Homer's paternal water god with the abstraction of generative water. The great "transition from myth to philosophy" thus utilizes its predecessor; it reoccupies a mythic image that was already familiar to Thales' contemporaries.

One of Blumenberg's best known theses is that the early modern notion of scientific progress is incommensurable with the medieval notion that God is the agent of human history.[109] Against Carl Schmitt's claim that modernity preserves a Christian worldview in its *concept* of progress, Blumenberg argues that modernity only reoccupies the Christian *metaphor* of forward movement. When submitting to God's plan was no longer the greatest ethical concern, ethical thinking could address how to exercise forethought in the pursuit of newly liberated curiosity. Modern interpretations of the Thales anecdote also register this epochal shift: more modern authors than medieval authors sympathize with the Thales figure.[110]

Reoccupation not only serves what we might call more worldly forms of realism.[111] Chapter five of *Laughter*, titled "Reoccupations,"

---

107 Blumenberg, *Work on Myth*, 1985, 263.
108 Homer, *The Iliad*, XIV, li., 286; li., 232, 224, 222.
109 See "Progress Exposed as Fate," Blumenberg, *The Legitimacy of the Modern Age*, 27–52. In *The Legitimacy of the Modern Age*, it is primarily questions (such as the theological problem of evil), not images, whose reoccupation concerns Blumenberg. Questions do explicitly what images and anecdotes do implicitly: introduce disjunctions into discourse. Already in the second edition of *Legitimacy*, Blumenberg shows the metaphor is reoccupation's semantic medium, as disjunctions implicit in images make new ideas appear commensurable with the old.
110 At least three late moderns, Voltaire, Feuerbach, and Heidegger, sympathize with Thales figures (p. 60, p. 93, p. 146).
111 Blumenberg develops this term to describe the way that old images or constellations of images are used to express new ideas. Certain images were

deals with early Church interpretations of the Thales anecdote, which mock Thales' truth-seeking behavior as they promote mystical submission to divine authority. Second-century Church Father Tertullian has an Egyptian laugh at Thales' fall because the first Greek philosophers supposedly studied with Egyptians, yet failed to pick up Egyptian reverence for divine mysteries. One of the anecdote's cleverest Christian reoccupations thus modifies the maid's status so that "Tertullian could ... pit the authority of the teacher against the immaturity of the pupil" (p. 36).

Blumenberg makes a bold, perhaps unprovable, hypothesis about why theoretical writings keep returning to the same sites of meaning. A certain class of metaphoric images, "absolute metaphors," correspond neither to specific observations nor to coherent definitions, but rather "bring to light ... the historical horizons of meaning and ways of seeing within which concepts undergo their modifications."[112] For instance, "the world" is too vast to perceive visually in its entirety, and thus Kant's coinage "worldview" (*Weltanschauung*) offers the metaphor of glimpsing a world to convey what it means to have a notion of the world as a totality.[113] Absolute metaphors render totalizing abstractions thinkable; metaphorically put, they reveal "the substructure of thought, the underground, the nutrient solution of systematic crystallizations."[114] Theory relies on illustration since "theory is something that no one sees" (p. 1). Falling into a well makes it perceptible, perceptibly funny, and so memorable that "all theorists up to the present day could still recognize themselves in this story". Blumenberg does not call the anecdote an "absolute metaphor" perhaps since any story is too long, too conspicuously rhetorical to become *the* symbol for theory's essence.

Blumenberg would later posit that absolute metaphors draw material from the lifeworld. He does not, however, promise to establish which

---

preserved, for instance, when Renaissance era secular humanism replaced medieval Christian theology: "What mainly occurred in the process that is interpreted as secularization, at least (so far) in all but a few recognizable and specific instances, should be described not as the *transposition* (*Umsetzung*) of authentically theological contents into secularized alienation from their origin but rather as the *reoccupation* (*Umbesetzung*) of answer positions that had become vacant and whose corresponding questions could not be eliminated." *Legitimacy of the Modern Age*, 65. In *this* chapter, it is theology that does the reoccupying: the Church Fathers reoccupy questions about the nature and movement of the stars that arose in the context of Greek theoretical curiosity.

112 Blumenberg, *Paradigms for a Metaphorology*, 3.
113 Blumenberg, *Lebenszeit und Weltzeit*, 10.
114 Blumenberg, *Paradigms for a Metaphorology*, 5. While this shares some features with George Lakoff and Mark Johnson's cognitive theory of metaphor, Blumenberg's is more nuanced in discussing metaphor's historical emergence and functional specificity.

metaphoric images derive from which episodes in the lifeworld since absolute metaphors lack definite objects.[115] Metaphorology thus discerns historical controversies in the changing status of metaphors without condoning metaphoric obfuscation in theoretical writing. It partakes in Husserl's "critique of the untested use of all received philosophical concepts," as Husserl's student and Blumenberg's teacher Ludwig Landgrebe described the task of "transcendental phenomenology."[116] Fictional and figurative language—invented characters, omniscient narrators, and digressions that build pathos, the normal features of literature—interrupt theory's pursuit of abstract truths.[117] In theoretical texts, a few familiar metaphors recur (light as truth, truth as agent), and they tend to rely on the unquestioned authority of familiar experiences (noticing objects in our environment, recognizing a fellow person). The tension phenomenology discovers between theory and the lifeworld invites metaphorology to learn how this tension plays out in theoretical writing.

Metaphorology takes as its premise Kant's claim that "symbols" mediate our thoughts about unknowable totalities. Spurred on by Kant's claim that this function of symbols "deserves a deeper investigation," Blumenberg searches for them in philosophy texts.[118] He hopes neither to develop skill in metaphor use nor to decipher the unknown, but only to find a secret history of perplexity:

> We must bear in mind here that a metaphorology cannot result in any method for *using* metaphors, or for addressing the questions that announce themselves in them. On the contrary: as students of metaphorology, we have already deprived ourselves of the possibility of finding "answers" in metaphors to those unanswerable questions. Metaphor, as the theme of a metaphorology in the sense that will concern us here, is an essentially *historical* object whose testimonial value presupposes that the witnesses did

---

115 Blumenberg, "Beobachtungen an Metaphern," 164.
116 Landgrebe, "Die Phänomenologie als transzendentale Theorie der Geschichte," 20.
117 In early essays, Blumenberg discussed imagery in Faulkner and Eliot. T. S. Eliot's "Four Quartets" suggests to Blumenberg "the melancholy of missed possibilities, about which one does not learn whether they were ever really present." Blumenberg, "Rose und Feuer: Lyrik, Kritik und Drama T. S. Eliots," 115. As in the present work, a philosophical idea is suggested through an image: Eliot portrays the past as an aggressive man who forecloses possibilities. Blumenberg compares this to Heidegger's notion of the past as "thrownness" and claims that both express the already passé constricted mood of modernity.
118 Kant, *Critique of Judgement*, §59, quoted in Blumenberg, *Paradigms for a Metaphorology*, 5.

not possess, and could not have possessed, a metaphorology of their own.[119]

Absolute metaphors bespeak questions that philosophers put aside out of "perplexity" (*Verlegenheit*).[120] When Blumenberg finds that authors reoccupy the same absolute metaphor, it suggests to him that they were stymied by the same question, one whose indefinite *terms* make it unanswerable (e.g. Is *God* just? Does *history* have a purpose?). The Thales anecdote's capacity for reoccupation thus indicates its function as an absolute metaphor. It can express perplexity about theory's place in the world, but it does not resolve its underlying questions: must *theory* and *practice* clash? And, if so, then why?

Absolute metaphors recur without becoming clichés. "Seeing the light," for instance, refers too unambiguously to sudden persuasion to be an absolute metaphor whereas "enlightenment" is a good candidate: its various uses signify specific, incompatible ways of "seeing the light:" religious, theoretical, and everyday.[121] But polysemy alone is not a reliable criterion by which to judge their "testimonial value" to historical contests over ideas.[122] The claim that metaphorology deals with a transhistorical object may only persuade readers who read philosophy as literature and see philosophy texts as constructed worlds whose rigor conceals an unquestioned metaphoric background. While such claims to latent meaning must remain hypothetical, Blumenberg's metaphorological work has long inspired German-speaking intellectuals and has gained increasing attention in the United States. In the last few years, English translations were published of Blumenberg's

---

119 Blumenberg, *Paradigms for a Metaphorology*, 14. Just as Blumenberg asserts that metaphorology cannot teach us skillful metaphor use, a theory of the lifeworld "does not serve our understanding of the lifeworld. Its definition excludes that: the lifeworld is what is understood by itself." Blumenberg, *Lebenszeit und Weltzeit*, 22. Blumenberg calls the "diagnostic-therapeutic" application of lifeworld theory "a misunderstanding."
120 Blumenberg, *Paradigms for a Metaphorology*, 3.
121 Three years before *Paradigms*, Blumenberg wrote an essay about light metaphors. See Blumenberg, "Light as a Metaphor for Truth: At the Preliminary Stage of Philosophical Concept Formation."
122 The difficulty of naming the continuity that Blumenberg sees is the point of Robert Pippin's criticisms of Blumenberg's work in general. See Pippin, "Modern Mythic Meaning." See also Robert Savage's remarks on the inapplicability of metaphorology in his translator's afterword "Metaphorology: A Beginner's Guide," in Blumenberg, *Paradigms for a Metaphorology*, 133–46. For criticisms of manipulative reading in other metaphorological works of Blumenberg's, see Nauta, "A Weak Chapter in the Book of Nature: Hans Blumenberg on Medieval Thought"; Niehues-Pröbsting, "Platonvorlesungen: Eigenschatten--Lächerlichkeiten."

1960 manifesto, *Paradigms for a Metaphorology*, and *Care Crosses the River*, a late metaphorological book about an ancient myth that Heidegger calls an early testament to his existentialism. And the critical theory journals *Thesis Eleven* and *Telos* devoted recent issues to Blumenberg's work.[123]

Like the present book, three other metaphorological books from around the 1980s pertain to theory's place in the world. Each exposes a different site of resistance to definite expression. *Shipwreck with Spectator*, published in 1979, discusses the image of watching a shipwreck unperturbed from the shore as an illustration of the philosopher's mastery over fear.[124] *Die Lesbarkeit der Welt* (*The Legibility of the World*—not available in English), from 1981, discusses variants on the medieval metaphor of the natural world as a book written by God for human readers. Medieval herbologist Paracelsus read God's "signatures" in the shapes of plants and in their medicinal effects. At the threshold of modernity, Galileo claimed that God wrote in the language of mathematics. The book of nature even finds favor among later thinkers, from Leibniz to Novalis: this image promotes hope that the world is meant to be understood. Blumenberg's last major work, the 820-page *Höhlenausgänge* (*Exits from the Cave*—also not in English yet), from 1989, discusses caves as metaphors for thresholds that leave behind inaccessible forms of consciousness. From a teleological perspective, the condition of cave dwelling suggests primitive life—ignorance itself, in Plato's famous cave allegory.

These three metaphors implicitly endorse philosophy as a way of life. Philosophers bravely withstand shipwreck, flee the cave of ignorance, and learn to read the book of nature. Among Blumenberg's metaphor studies, only *The Laughter of the Thracian Woman* foregrounds philosophy's failure to achieve meaningful results. Thales' name of course evokes "theory's very first 'success,'" in predicting a solar eclipse (p. viii). But when he tumbles down a well because he failed

---

123 Blumenberg, *Care Crosses the River*; Blumenberg, *Paradigms for a Metaphorology*; *Thesis Eleven* 102:1 (February 2011); *Telos* 158 (2012).

124 "Sweet it is, when the wind whips the water on the great sea, / to gaze from the land upon the great struggle of another, / not because it is a delightful pleasure to be distressed, / but because it is sweet to observe those evils which you lack yourself." Lucretius, *On the Nature of Things*, II1–4 31. Like *Laughter*, *Shipwreck with Spectator* presents the philosopher in an attitude that later readers, Voltaire and Goethe, would interpret as *Schadenfreude*. Blumenberg, *Shipwreck with Spectator*, 51. *Care Crosses the River* deals with myth about the creation of humans out of mud, a soul, and "Care," so that Care would have a form with which to cross the river. The myth enters the history of philosophy when Heidegger calls it a "preontological testimony" to his existential analysis of human beings' essence as "care." Heidegger, *Being and Time*, §42.

to watch his path, it evokes the unsettling, unavoidable discrepancy between theorizing the world and living in it. The anecdote promises little hope for thinkers; it begins with Thales' stargazing and ends neither with honor nor bliss, but with stumbling and mockery.

This book elaborately demonstrates the plasticity of absolute metaphor. From Plato to Heidegger, theorists who cite the anecdote of Thales and the Thracian maid never fail to salvage their own theoretical positions—often by joining the maid in laughing at absentmindedness. They either exempt themselves from theory's excesses or accept practical oversights as a price for theoretical insights; either way, they deflect her ridicule. We unconsciously position ourselves on the right side of laughter: either laughing or laughed at, depending on which we deem more justified. The ambiguity of the Thales anecdote will always allow us an interpretation that preserves our good conscience—whether we prefer to theorize the world or just to live in it.

Spencer Hawkins
Ann Arbor, July 26, 2014

Note on Translation and Annotations

For the reader's convenience, I quote English translations of works that Blumenberg quotes. In the rare cases that I do not cite an English translation, I translate the quotes from Greek, Latin, Italian, German, or French and cite the editions he cites. Following Blumenberg, Greek words appear transliterated into Latin letters, and the edition is not specified for most ancient texts. Annotations give original language quotations for verse and for some short passages. Citations include the following as applicable: author, work, standard pagination (Roman numeral—chapter, Arabic number—section, letter—page), "in" compilation or volume title, volume number (Roman numeral), page (Arabic number). Quotations without citations are from the previous page cited.

There are four main occasions for endnote annotations: 1) to give citations that do not appear in the original text, 2) to gloss words that Blumenberg uses in special senses—literal, figurative, transitive, or "in every sense," 3) to give attributions for words that appear in quotation marks without attribution, and 4) to discuss allusions and references, such as Blumenberg's phenomenological language. Especially in the Preface, Chapter 1, and Chapter 13, some of the language reflects specialized terminology, such as "historicity," "ready to hand," and "lifeworld," but I also annotate when he uses everyday words in phenomenological senses, such as "evidence," "achievement," "event," and "theory" itself. He draws heavily on Husserl's senses of these words, which may elude English-speaking readers.[1]

German words appear in parentheses where Blumenberg suggestively repeats German morphemes, such as calling Socrates a "being

---

1 Texts in English that illuminate the intersection between Husserl and Blumenberg include an essay on Husserl's use of ground-metaphors by Blumenberg's former colleague and two recent essays on phenomenological themes in *Laughter*. See Sommer, "Husserl on 'Ground' and 'Underground'"; Fleming, "On the Edge of Non-Contingency"; Savage, "Laughter from the Lifeworld."

captivated by the 'essences'" (*von den Wesen erfaßten "Wesen"*), and where German philosophical terms exhibit meanings whose range calls for differential translation, such as *Anschauung*, which I translate alternately as perception, intuition, vision, image, and sight. I specifically marked German etymologies relating to distance (obvious—*naheliegend*, and obscure—*fernliegend*) since Blumenberg links astronomy's perceived irrelevance to human affairs with the stars' distance from earth. I put German compounds containing the morpheme *grund* in parentheses since *Grund* means "ground," "cause," and "explanation," and losing contact with the ground becomes a metaphor for pursuing theoretical explanations.

Acknowledgments

I have been extremely fortunate to prepare this translation for publication under the guidance of Imke Meyer, Series Editor for New Directions in German Studies, who shared insightful and encouraging feedback throughout the process of revising the manuscript, and of Haaris Naqvi, Senior Commissioning Editor for Bloomsbury, who showed great care for this project as we worked together on the many decisions about its scope. My doctoral advisors, Andreas Gailus, Vassilios Lambropoulos, Benjamin Paloff, Yopie Prins, and Silke-Maria Weineck, gave formative feedback on the manuscript from its earliest stages onward. I thank Suhrkamp Verlag for granting me the rights to translate this text, and I express my deep gratitude to Bettina Blumenberg who offered me permission not only to translate the book, but to include archival material in the Afterword.

I am indebted to my brilliant and generous friends and colleagues Benjamin Beckett, Sarah Buss, Raymond McDaniel, William Roby, and Michael Tondre; each read different iterations of this Afterword and commented with extraordinary acumen. Clara Bosak-Schroeder advised me on translating many difficult Latin quotations. Tomasz Kurianowicz helped me think through and translate some the most perplexing passages in the German. Manfred Sommer repeatedly helped me through translation conundra by offering potential solutions along with philosophically and philologically brilliant rationales in writing. An anonymous reviewer offered prompt, orienting, encouraging feedback on the manuscript. Paul Fleming first filled an early translation sample with marginal comments, which guided my approach to the rest of the translation. When he reviewed the completed manuscript, I worked closely with his careful instructions, especially with his guidelines for reducing the annotations. I also benefited from collegial support from Blumenberg's other translators—David Adams, Paul Fleming, Steven Rendall, Robert Savage and Robert Wallace—and from my friends' and family members' supportive attitudes. Finally, Ann Marie Thornburg offered sustained support and perceptive feedback on countless aspects of this project at every stage of my work. Any errors or infelicities in the translation are of course my own.

Notes

i   *Urgeschichte.* See Afterword section, "What is 'a protohistory of theory'?" (p. 159).

ii   *das bloße Nochvorhandensein.* Heidegger characterizes useless objects with a composite word similar to Blumenberg's: "The more urgently we need what is missing ... all the more obtrusive does what is at hand become ... [T]he helpless way in which we stand before it [exposes our deficient mode of engagement with] the mere objective presence (*das Nur-noch-vorhandensein*) of what is at hand." Heidegger, *Being and Time*, §16, 68. For Heidegger, an object's obtrusiveness, conspicuousness, and obstinacy (*Aufsässigkeit*, connoting impudence) render it "mere objective presence" (also translated "presence at hand"). An object's presence at hand strips it of its utility for human activity, but it can also serve to reveal that the object exists independently from its witness. Heidegger, *Being and Time*, §43, 195. As Blumenberg explains in this passage, this anecdote's very obstinacy (*Hartnäckigkeit*, connoting insistence) prevents it from becoming mere presence at hand: it obstinately retains its function within the human activity of theorizing. It inconspicuously but effectively depicts theory's confrontation with other activities.

iii   *Qualität.* In the preface and first chapter, several of the words in quotation marks call attention to Blumenberg's ongoing dialogue with Edmund Husserl. Husserl uses "quality" to indicate both the emotional attitude and the degree of certainty with which we receive mental "material." For a detailed discussion of this concept, see "The Intentional Act (Noesis)" in Bernet, *Introduction to Husserlian Phenomenology*, 92–5.

iv   *Einstellung.* Husserl attributes theory's prevalence to a particular "attitude:" "But in addition to the higher-level practical attitude (which we shall soon meet [again] in the religious-mythical attitude) there exists yet another essential possibility for altering the general natural attitude, namely, the theoretical attitude. To be sure, it is so named only by anticipation because out of it, according to a necessary development, philosophical *theoria* grows and becomes an end in itself or a field of interest. The theoretical attitude, though it is again a vocational attitude, is totally unpractical." Husserl, "Vienna Lecture," 282.

v   *realistisch.* The words "realistic" and "realism" occur in quotation marks at several points in this book. For Blumenberg, a notion qualifies as "realistic" when it goes unquestioned during routine activities. Realistic claims thus do not derive their quality from rational justifications, but they prompt subsequent rationalizations. "Realistic status does not mean empirical demonstrability; the place of the latter can be filled by taken-for-grantedness, familiarity, having been part of the world from the beginning." Blumenberg, *Work on Myth*, 68.

vi "You must build more wells!" Blumenberg's German readers would know of former West German President Heinrich Lübke's reputation for being clumsy with words. The quote suggests that Lübke wants to build wells for eccentric theorists to fall down them. Blumenberg had previously considered a less subtle epigraph, quoting Ernst Jünger: "Here we basically have a rediscovery of laughter as the marker of horrible and primitive enmity." Jünger, *Der Arbeiter*, VIII, 66, quoted in Blumenberg, "Das Lachen der Thrakerin (Drucktitel) [verschiedene Fassungen: Vorstufen, Manuskript, korr. Druckfahne, Materialien zum Buch]." Jünger is discussing slapstick film as an invitation for antagonistic laughter at eccentricity, where society laughs "at the expense of the individual."

vii The invisibility of the act of "theorizing" interested Blumenberg. Theory does not correspond to a particular physical manifestation. The bodily movements performed while theorizing (such as pacing or staring) may appear purposeless to onlookers, and the appearance of purposelessness can provoke laughter or hostility. At the 1974 *Poetics and Hermeneutics* conference, Blumenberg develops the claim that theory's illegibility leads to intolerance. See Afterword section "From Spatial to Temporal Distance (1974 to 1987)" (p. 149).

viii *gebannt*. Its meanings here include "bound" and "spellbound," that is, physically and psychologically stuck at work.

ix *theoria*. This Greek deverbal noun, meaning "seeing," usually carries the transitive sense of observing or being a spectator of particular things, rather than just having one's eyes open. When theory is "transitive," attention affects how we see visual objects—and affects the theorist in turn. Husserl indicates that engaging in phenomenological theory transforms a person's total experience, not just of sensing, but of existing. It effects "a complete personal transformation, comparable in the beginning to a religious conversion, which then, however, over and above this, bears within itself the significance of the greatest existential transformation which is assigned as a task to mankind as such." Husserl, *The Crisis of European Sciences and Transcendental Phenomenology: An Introduction to Phenomenological Philosophy*, 137. For Blumenberg's thoughts on the religious connotations of theory, see Afterword section "The Laughter in this Story was on the Wrong Side (From the archive)" (p. 154).

x Blumenberg recalls Heidegger's apocalyptic view that the prevalence of scientific thinking has obscured a proper understanding of Being: "Should there still be science for us in the future, or should we let it drift it toward a rapid end?" Heidegger, "The Self-Assertion of the German University," 6. (See next note.)

xi Heidegger delivered his infamous speech "The Self-Assertion of the German University" at the 1933 ceremony for his promotion to rector of Freiburg University. "The beginning" he glorifies is that of German nationalism. The speech marks "his unhappiest hour" if we take Heidegger's word in 1966 that he only reluctantly became rector and dismissed Freiburg's Jewish faculty under threat of the university's closure. Heidegger, "Spiegel Interview with Martin Heidegger," 41–43. *in seiner unglücksten Stunde* could just mean "in his unluckiest hour" since his Nazi involvements hampered his post-war career.

xii *Lebenswelt*. For a discussion of Husserl's concept of the "lifeworld" and the encumbrances that it places on "theory," please see the Afterword section titled "What is 'A Protohistory of Theory'?" (p. 159)

xiii Aristotle, *On the Soul*, 411a7 61."number-of-pages": "544","edition": "Revised edition","source":"Amazon.com","event-place":"Cambridge Mass. At the 1974 *Poetics and Hermeneutics* conference, Blumenberg gives a reason to suspect that Thales' ambiguous statement was not an expression of piety:

> In the text *On the Soul*, Aristotle reports Thales' saying, "Everything is full of gods." The polysemy of this declaration is insurmountable. It can pronounce the most extreme consequence of myth or the ultimate contempt for myth. But Tertullian preserved another saying of Thales', a response to Croesus, who wanted to know what Thales thinks of the gods; after multiple deadline extensions for the sake of contemplation, Thales answered "nothing" (Tertullian, *Ad nationes* II, 2,11 in Roberts and Donaldson, *Ante-Nicene Fathers*, III 130). Blumenberg, "Wer sollte vom Lachen der Magd betroffen sein? Eine Duplik," 440.

xiv *erfüllt*. Blumenberg notes at the 1968 *Poetics und Hermeneutics* conference that Thales' statement "everything is full (*voll*) of gods" does not distinguish between "the sentimental 'fulfilled' (*erfüllt*) and the indifferent 'filled' (*gefüllt*)." Blumenberg, "Wirklichkeitsbegriff und Wirkungspotential des Mythos," 22. Thales posits a quantitative saturation point, but the statement may also signify a qualitative change in Greek culture; the world's fullness with gods could mark the moment when non-mythological language becomes culturally necessary. In Husserl's *Ideas I*, our notions about external objects (our "intentions") are "empty" until "fulfilled." Fulfillment results when a series of sense impressions confirms an object's reality. But no series of impressions can fulfill an intention about "everything." As Blumenberg implies, Thales' statement, "everything is full of gods," universalizes what can empirically be said of only *one* street.

xv Homer, *The Iliad*, XIV, li. 286, li., 232, 224, 222.

xvi *epimythium*. See Afterward for a discussion of why *epimythia* were historically late additions to the fable genre (p. 140).

xvii *Wirklichkeitsbegriffe.* Blumenberg discusses historical confrontations between the mythic, theoretical, and dogmatic "concepts of reality" in Blumenberg, "Wirklichkeitsbegriff und Wirkungspotential des Mythos," 42.
xviii Plato, *Protagoras*, 65.
xix Plato, *Theaetetus*, 174B, 121.
xx *Zisterne.* The scene of Thales' tumble in *Theaetetus* may be less consequential than the repeated reference to a "well" makes it sound. The Greek word for "well," *phrear*, can also refer to a shallow "cistern" that feeds a fountain. See Cavarero, *In Spite of Plato*, 123.
xxi Plato, *Theaetetus*, 173C–D, 119.
xxii *Theaetetus*, 172C, 115.
xxiii In 1986, Blumenberg writes about "the bitterest of all discoveries:" that the world that will survive without us after we die. Blumenberg, *Lebenszeit und Weltzeit*, 76. He attributes the popularity of apocalyptic religious sermons to a desire for a world with finite time. As implied here, some acknowledge infinite "worldtime" but resist its bitterness with strategies for living beyond a lifetime: they seek eternal truths, learn history, or leave behind ambitious creations.
xxiv Plato, *Theaetetus*, 173E, 119–20.
xxv Ibid., 173E–174A, 121.
xxvi This claim is developed in the philology article that Blumenberg cites in Chapter 4 (p. 23). Thales may have voluntarily descended down a well during the day in order to block out ambient light and better observe star positions before nightfall. See Landmann and Fleckenstein, "Tagesbeobachtungen Von Sternen Im Altertum. Eine Philosophisch-astronomiegeschichtliche Rekonstruktion Der Thalesanekdote. Plato Theatet. 174 A."
xxvii Plato, *Theaetetus*, 174C, 123.
xxviii Ibid., 175D–E, 127.
xxix *Himmelskenntnis und Erdentüchtigkeit.* The *-kenntnis* in the word, *Himmelskenntnis*, means "knowledge," but in the sense of experiential knowledge, not factual knowledge (*Wissen*). This word choice recalls that mystics lay claim to non-rational knowledge about the sky. *Himmel*, the German word for "heaven," is even more polysemous than the English one: besides meaning the residence of God, the blessed, and other numina, it is also *the* word for "the sky." My translation oscillates between "heaven" and "sky," since Blumenberg uses the word both for a physical and an imaginary place in this chapter, for example, Plato's "heaven of forms" (23) and "Newton's physics of the sky" (30).
xxx Quote not found, but presumably from Brucker, *The History of Philosophy, from the Earliest Times to the Beginning of the Present Century*. Blumenberg deals with Brucker's work at length in Chapter 8.
xxxi *Rettung der Phänomene.* From the Greek: *sōzein ta phainomena*. This research paradigm (attributed to Plato, but likely conceived by Eudoxus of Cnidus) consisted of finding physical explanations for the apparently irregular movements of the stars and planets. Between reverence for

the stars as divine objects and the difficulty of accounting for the star patterns under the assumptions of geocentricism and perfectly circular planetary orbits, Ptolemy declared saving the phenomena a presumptuous endeavor. See Blumenberg, *The Genesis of the Copernican World*, 214.

xxxii Plato, *The Republic*, 527d, 236.

xxxiii Hegel ranks sensation as the least truth-revealing type of mental content: "The concrete content, which sensuous certainty furnishes, makes this appear *prima facie* to be the richest kind of knowledge … This bare fact of certainty, however, is really and admittedly the abstractest and the poorest kind of *truth*." Hegel, *The Phenomenology of Mind*, 149.

xxxiv Plato, *The Republic*, 529c, 238.

xxxv Ibid., 529c, 239. Blumenberg translates Plato's words as "astronomy in the authentic sense" (*Astronomie im eigentlichen Sinne*). Socrates describes a type of astronomy based not on star movement patterns, but on learning the "true motions"—which the stars and musical ratios exemplify—but which can only be grasped mathematically, and not through observation.

xxxvi *Theätet* in Plato, *Platons Werke*, I:2, 172.

xxxvii Blumenberg resumes comparing the Aesopian fable with Plato's anecdote as he did in Chapter Two.

xxxviii In Plato's *Republic*, Er is a soldier who dies and is restored to life by the judges in the afterlife "to act as a messenger to mankind, to tell them what was going on there" so that he may report on how virtue is rewarded with rebirth into fortune, and vice is punished with a future life of slavery or squalor. Er perhaps qualifies as an "idiota" because Plato endows him with no philosophical qualities: "a hero from Pamphylia … killed in battle." Renaissance thinker Nicolas of Cusa claims that it takes "learned ignorance" to return to the wise position of the "idiota" who does not attempt the impossible: to fathom infinity. Cusa, *On Learned Ignorance*; Plato, *The Republic*, 614b, 337.

xxxix *Philosophie in der Hanswurstjacke*. In notes published posthumously from between March 1868 and May 1869, Nietzsche expresses perplexity at the seemingly unphilosophical way that Bion "translated Socratic irony crudely into his life" and into a humorous literary style. "Ueber die Cyniker und ihre Bedeutung für die Literatur" in Nietzsche, *Gesammelte Werke*, V, 471.

xl *Isostheneia*. Often translated "equipollence," this term refers to the ancient Skeptics' method of refuting dogmatic arguments by making equally strong counterarguments.

xli Epicurus' thought on astronomy is less dismissive than this paraphrase may suggest. He condemns empirical inquiry into celestial phenomena: "But when we come to subjects for special inquiry, there is nothing in the knowledge of risings and settings and solstices and eclipses and all kindred subjects that contributes to our happiness." Diogenes Laertius, *Lives of Eminent Philosophers*, Vol. 2, X, 79, 609. But he advocates studying the ultimate causes of celestial phenomena: "… happiness depends …

	upon knowing what the heavenly bodies really are, and any kindred facts contributing to exact knowledge in this respect." Ibid., X, 78, 607. For Epicurus as for Plato, understanding "astronomy in the authentic sense" yields liberating wisdom. See note, p. xxxv, p. 180.
xlii	Parenthetical content by the translator. Bion of Borysthenes supposedly associated with Plato's Academy, then briefly followed Crates, before he finally became a cantankerous Cynic. Ibid., Vol. 1, IV, 51–52, 429–31.
xliii	*Zynismus*. This German spelling of "cynicism" here implies the contemporary understanding of the term: sarcastic, dismissive language or behavior. Since German capitalizes all nouns, it uses spelling rather than capitalization to differentiate the Greek philosophical school, "Cynicism" (*Kynismus*) from dismissive sarcasm, "cynicism" (*Zynismus*).
xliv	Diogenes Laertius., *Lives of Eminent Philosophers*, Vol. 1, I, 34, 35.
xlv	Ibid., Vol. 2, II, 5, 135.
xlvi	The second part of Johann Wolfgang von Goethe's drama *Faust* ends with Faust blind, decrepit, and confused at his surroundings. However, it is not a tragic end; rather, he fulfills his driving purpose, namely, to feel so moved by "the passing moment" that he addresses it with the sincere wish: "Linger awhile, you are so fair!" Goethe, *Faust*, 227. He feels this in a sudden moment of belief that humanity will create a harmonious utopia in the future.
xlvii	The literal sense of the Greek *"theoria"* (seeing), in this case, would be blissfully observing God's image. Its figurative sense would be something like understanding His divine nature.
xlviii	*epoché*. Ancient Skeptics use this term for the moment at which the philosopher withdraws from judgment about the external world. Like the Stoics, their goal in doing so was to achieve tranquility (*ataraxia*): "… we come first to suspension on judgment and afterwards to tranquility (*ataraxia*)." Sextus Empiricus, *Outlines of Scepticism*, 4. Edmund Husserl uses *epoché* as well, but as a means to learn the structure of consciousness, not to experience *ataraxia*.
xlix	*Umbesetzungen*. See the Afterword section titled "Laughter as an Object of Metaphorology" for a discussion of Blumenberg's use of the concept "reoccupation" and its relation to the interpretation of the Thales anecdote (p. 165).
l	Ovid's *Metamorphoses* opens by describing the genesis of earthly life before describing various life forms transforming into others. The first tale is about the creation of an orderly, living universe out of total chaos with human life at the apex of this orderly living cosmos:

>And even though all other animals
>lean forward and look down toward the ground,
>he gave to man a face that is uplifted
>and ordered him to stand erect and look
>directly up into the vaulted heavens
>and turn his countenance to meet the stars;
>the earth, that was so lately rude and formless,
>was changed by taking on the shapes of men.
>
>Ovid, *Metamorphoses*, 18

182 Notes

The Christian view, that human knowledge should be oriented towards pursuing salvation, could not afford a literal reading of Ovid's suggestion that merely contemplating the sky satisfied the humans' role in the universal order.

li Voltaire, *Traité de Métaphysique*, Introduction: "comme si j'étais dans le soleil."

lii *Apologete*. "Apologists" refer to Church Fathers who defended the Christian doctrine of salvation against pagan, heretical, and philosophical views before the First Council of Nicaea (AD 325). Apologetic writings paraphrase many non-Christian thinkers, such as Thales, Heraclitus, and Pythagoras. Most extant information about these thinkers comes from Apologist sources.

liii "satis est pro pedibus aspicere ..." Roberts and Donaldson, *Ante-Nicene Fathers*, IV, 179.

liv Tertullian, *Ad nationes*, II, 6 in Roberts and Donaldson, *Ante-Nicene Fathers*, III, 134.

lv Blumenberg is citing a somewhat dated work by Greek philologist Johannes Geffcken: Geffcken, Aristides, and Athenagoras, *Zwei griechische Apologeten*, 105–13.

lvi Bonaventura, *Sententiae*, I, conclusion: "*intimior animae quam ipsa sibi.*"

lvii *Ternar*. Theosophist Franz Xavier Baader (1765–1841) coined the term "Ternar" to describe the three aspects of humanity; the divine Trinity inspires the consciousness of the human condition as tripartite (body, mind, and soul), wherein the existence of the finite, mortal body signals to the mind that the soul is meant for a different plane than the world.

lviii Blumenberg often cites Husserl's characterization of theory as "endless work" (see, for instance: Blumenberg, *Ein mögliches Selbstverständnis*, 88, 106). Blumenberg criticizes this characterization because it underplays the possibility of false starts and dead ends in the history of theory. He sees it as a consequence of Husserl's fixation on establishing one perfect method: "'Method' entails bracketing thought's historicity and thus winning a 'pure' dimension of independence; it allows the human to understand and take on the task of building certainty as an endless one." Blumenberg, "Die ontologische Distanz," 185.

lix *Confessiones*, X, 16, in Augustine, *Fathers of the Church, Volume 21*, 285.

lx Blumenberg's early monograph, *The Legitimacy of the Modern Age*, includes a chapter on Augustine entitled "Curiosity is enrolled in the catalogue of vices." What makes curiosity such a pernicious source of "impious pride"—and the only vice to receive a whole chapter (Chapter XXXV) in Augustine's *Confessions*—is that curiosity takes pleasure in the mind's connection with appearances, while the Christian mind should sever its connection with earthly things. Blumenberg, *The Legitimacy of the Modern Age*, 310. "Such self-enjoyment on the part of the cognitive drive [the pleasure that curiosity pursues] is always facilitated by the degree of difficulty and remoteness of its objects ..." Ibid., 312. Therefore, astronomy especially tempts sinners to commit the vice of curiosity. Although Augustine claims to have broken with Gnostic derision towards the world of appearances and instead claims that

Notes   183

the beauty of God's Creation should guide us towards faith, he seems entirely Gnostic when he cannot recommend contemplating even the most remote stars, instead claiming that curiosity's counterpart, *memoria*, should have no object, but be like God's thoughts, "thought thinking itself." Ibid., 315.

lxi   Damian, *The Letters of Peter Damian (Letters 91–120)*, Letter 119, an eleventh-century monk and man of letters. Written during the years 1062-1066, these letters deal with a wide variety of subjects. Some letters are of historical interest, others approach the size and scope of philosophical or theological treatise. Damian's correspondents range from simple hermits in his community to abbots, bishops, cardinals, and even to Pope Alexander II. Among these letters are to be found one addressed to the patriarch of Constantinople, two to Damian's sisters, one to the Empress Agnes, and even a few to such distant personages as the young King Henry IV and the Archbishop Anno of Cologne. Like its companions, this volume uses Damian's thought to understand an important and gripping period in the history of church and state. Clearly, the most significant letter in this collection is Letter 119, written in 1063 to Abbot Desiderius of Monte Cassino and his monks, on the omnipotence of God. Translated here for the first time into English, Damian's treatise on Divine Omnipotence demonstrates his control of both theological and philosophical methodology. His opponents are contemporary rhetoricians whose denials of God's total potency in dealing with his creatures' contingencies in time past, present, and future opens them to the charge of heresy.Though Damian's vocabulary frequently challenges the combined dictionary resources of classical, patristic, and mediaeval Latin, Owen J. Blum's careful translation will guarantee the transmission of Damian's thought to all levels of readers throughout the world."

lxii   *idiota*. Tertullian's term for the uneducated, but insightful Christian—which Renaissance thinker Nicholas of Cusa revives. See pp. 23, 51.

lxiii   Burley, *Walter Burleys "Liber de vita et moribus philosophorum poetarumque veterum" in zwei deutschen Bearbeitungen des Spätmittelalters*. Recent scholars believe that Burleigh was not the author of the *Vita*. See Conti, *A Companion to Walter Burley*, 41.

lxiv   Chaucer, *Canterbury Tales*, 65. In the original:
    An housbond shal not be inquisityf,
    of Goddes pryveté, ne of his wyf.
    So he may syndé Goddés forsouyn there.
    Óf the remenant nedeth nat enquere. Chaucer, *The Canterbury Tales of Geoffrey Chaucer*, 126
Blumenberg quotes a German translation that could be rendered: "A man should not stick his nose too deep in God's secrets, and also not in his wife's secrets. For whoever asks a lot, receives many answers." *Canterbury Tales*, German translation by Detlef Droese, Zürich, 1971.

lxv   Descartes discusses "provisional" morality in the third part of his *Discourse on the Method of Rightly Conducted Reason*. It comprises three principles that Descartes applies and advocates for use when

184 Notes

suspending all beliefs for the sake of testing their veracity. Briefly, his rules were: abide by social, legal, and religious conventions when non-restrictive; maintain choices even if arbitrary; and avoid worldly ambition. The rules were meant as temporary, but they exceeded his expectations: "Since I had begun using this method, I experienced such great happiness that I did not believe any more charming or innocent one could be found in this life ..." Descartes, *Discourse on Method, Optics, Geometry, and Meteorology*, 23.

lxvi Agrippa of Nettesheim, *The Vanity of Arts and Sciences*, 86.
lxvii Ibid., 86–7.
lxviii Ibid., 87. The seventeenth-century English translator of Agrippa's work presumably mistook the maid's nationality for her proper name (as Hippolytus and Jakob Gronovius had also done) (pp. 38, 76).
lxix *Moralisten*. These seventeenth- and eighteenth-century French philosophers, the so-called "moralists," did not moralize, but criticized social mores in aphoristic work focused on humans' limited capacities for knowledge, goodness, and happiness.
lxx Montaigne, *The Essays of Michel de Montaigne*, 602. "... la philosophie n'est qu'une poësie sophistique."
lxxi Ibid., 604.
lxxii *dogmatischer Skeptiker*. A "dogmatic skeptic" is a provocative oxymoron. At least in the Phyrronic tradition, skepticism is defined by an abstention from taking *any* position, while dogmatism is defined by refusal to consider any *other* position than the one taken. However, taking a complete skeptical position requires a defense of one's choice to abstain from all dogmatic positions, which may conceal a less explicit dogma.
lxxiii Nicolas Foucquet (1615–80) was Superintendent of Finances for Louis XIV. His extravagant spending on personal luxuries led to his arrest. His three-year trial was a public spectacle due the king's involvement with the prosecution.
lxxiv Latin: Bacon, *Collected Works of Francis Bacon*, 517. English: Bacon, *The Works of Francis Bacon, Lord Chancellor of England*, 192.
lxxv Bacon, *The Works of Francis Bacon, Lord Chancellor of England*, Vol. I, 192. Bacon exploits the image of transcending the ancient boundary of the world, the Straits of Gibraltar, where columnar cliffs, called Pillars of Hercules, supposedly marked the end of the world. He quasi-allegorically interprets Europeans' expeditions around the globe as evidence that the modern age was ready for a new relationship to the world: "But to circle the earth, as the heavenly bodies do, was not done nor enterprised till these latter times; and therefore these times may justly bear in their word, not only 'further beyond,' (*'plus ultra'*) in precedence of the ancient 'nothing beyond' (*'non ultra'*) ... but likewise 'imitation of heaven' (*'imitabile cœlum'*)."
lxxvi Probably Bacon, *The Works of Francis Bacon, Lord Chancellor of England*, Vol. III, 370. *New Organon I*, §129. "Now, the empire of man over things is founded on the arts and sciences alone, for nature is only to be commanded by obeying her."
lxxvii Ibid., Vol. I, 175. *Of the Proficience and Advancement of Learning II*. This is

the only passage that Blumenberg quotes in English. Blumenberg cites Bacon's original Latin for all other quotations.

lxxviii See Chapter 5 (p. 29).
lxxix   Bayle, *An Historical and Critical Dictionary*, Vol. IV, 2864.
lxxx   Ibid. (translation modified).
lxxxi   Sa'di's version: "An astrologer came home to find a stranger in his house. He did not ask who the stranger was or what he was doing there. Instead, the astrologer became angry and began to insult the man. In response, the stranger attacked the astrologer and the two men fought, throwing the entire household into turmoil. A pious man who witnessed the entire scene said: 'How can you know the meaning of the stars if you don't even know who is in your house?'" Saadi, *Selections from Saadi's Gulistan*, 92.
lxxxii   Bayle, *An Historical and Critical Dictionary*, Vol. IV, 2864. "Hinc factum, Astrologe, est, tua cum capit uxor amantes, / Sidera significant ut nihil inde tibi."
lxxxiii *non prius*. "Not first." This is an abbreviated version of the so-called Peripatetic Axiom, which states that "Nothing is in the intellect that was not previously in sense (*quod non prius in sensu*)." *Disputed Questions on Truth*, in Aquinas, *The Collected Works of St. Thomas Aquinas*, I, 69. Thomas Aquinas construes this from Aristotle's *Metaphysics*. The language of Alsted's version of the Thales anecdote is unusual for implying that sense experience must occur as a necessary first step in an intellectual pursuit. See footnote 77.
lxxxiv   "Democritus says that the truth lies sunk in a well so deep that it has no bottom." Lactantius, *Divine Institutions*, III, 28, in Roberts and Donaldson, *Ante-Nicene Fathers*, VII, 98. Lactantius attacks this image as "foolish" since truth would be "on the highest top of a lofty mountain." Lactantius has no problem with metaphors, but only with choosing a lowly metaphor for truth instead of a lofty one. Blumenberg discusses the Patristic reception of Democritus' aphorism elsewhere. See Blumenberg, *Paradigms for a Metaphorology*, 34.
lxxxv   Abraham a Sancta Clara, *Judas der Erzschelm für ehrliche Leut', oder eigentlicher Entwurf und Lebensbeschreibung des Iscariotischen Böswicht*, 355 (my translation). The text cited in this note gives the anecdote under the following heading: "Here is answered in brief the Welsch *perche*, the Latin *quare*, and the German why (*Warum*)." Blumenberg cites a different text, which appears not to contain the quoted passage.
lxxxvi   *fast schon wieder harmlos*. We may recall Blumenberg's claim from Chapter 6 that in Middle Ages, "there was greater tolerance towards astrology than towards the purely theoretical urge" (p. XX). Abraham a Sancta Clara's whimsy in telling the anecdote suggests a return to the pre-Enlightenment view of astrology as a relatively harmless folly.
lxxxvii *definitiven Moral*. Definitive morality is the anticipated outcome of the method Descartes introduces in *Discourse on Method*. Before that outcome, Descartes relies on "provisional morality." See note lxv, p. 183.
lxxxviii In Gnostic writings, the Demiurge (Greek for "craftsman") is the

186 Notes

malicious god who created the material world and imprisoned souls within bodies so that they would be fooled into the misery-inducing belief that they exist as individuals in separate bodies. Blumenberg sees Gnostic thought as having indirectly provoked the modern overthrow of the theological worldview. See "The Failure of the First Attempt at Warding Off Gnosticism Ensures Its Return," Blumenberg, *The Legitimacy of the Modern Age*, 127–36.

lxxxix Blumenberg is quoting Leibniz's letter to Sophia Charlotte of Hanover, the first queen of Prussia.

xc Bayle, *An Historical and Critical Dictionary*, Vol. II, 901. "litteris potius quam civilibus actibus instructus, dumque caelum considerat observatque astra, terram amisit." This quote, like most references in Bayle's entry on Alfonso X, draws on the work of the prolific and controversial Jesuit historian Juan de Mariana. Bayle disputes many of Mariana's views and claims about Alfonso.

xci Ibid. After doubting the quality of Mariana's quotation, "that if God had asked his Advice when he made the World, he would have given him good Counsel," Bayle presents the conciliatory revision of Alfonso's statement cited in this paragraph. By adjusting this statement, writes Bayle, "you will diminish the scandalous Boldness of Alphonsus very much."

xcii Fontenelle himself changes the title of the heretical astronomer from "King of Aragon" to "King of Castile" in the second edition the *Conversations*. Fontenelle, *Conversations on the Plurality of Worlds*, 76 f6.

xciii Kaestner, *Gesammelte poetische und prosaische schönwissenschaftliche Werke*, II, 133.

xciv Tycho Brahe consulted astrological writings (*Astrologorum Diariis*) when arriving at his career choice, according to the seventeenth-century biography: Gassendi, *Tychonis Brahei, equitis Dani, astronomorum coryphaei, vita*, I, 5.

xcv *die Qualität der Welt*. "Quality" and "world" have specific meanings in Kant's *Critique of Pure Reason*. "Quality" is the type of cognitive category that establishes an object's reality (or lack thereof). "The world," Kant's shorthand for the universe, has neither quality of the real nor of the unreal, but is simply "divisible." Kant, *Critique of Pure Reason*, 460–4. (It cannot be unreal since our perceptions presume a source. But we cannot confirm that it is real as a whole since we cannot experience it in its totality.) Elsewhere Blumenberg refers to Husserl's notion of quality. See note iii, p. 176.

xcvi *anwendet*. Kant "applies" admonition to those seeking non-physical causes for physical events. Blumenberg recalls that Kant's *Critique of Pure Reason* makes a similar case: knowledge is attained by "applying" cognitive categories to sensory perceptions. Besides mathematical and epistemological truths, which logical deduction can achieve, understanding requires perception (*Anschauung*). Thus, when Plato "abandoned the world of the senses," he left himself nothing "to which he could apply his powers in order to get his understanding off the ground." Kant, *Critique of Pure Reason*, 129. Speculation is seductive:

	"if one is beyond the circle of experience, then one is sure not to be contradicted through experience." Kant sees this in early writings Blumenberg quotes.
xcvii	Kant, "Continued Observations on the Earthquakes That Have Been Experienced for Some Time (1756)," 371.
xcviii	Ibid., 373. In trying to lend plausibility to his conjecture, Blumenberg misquotes "a certain correct taste in natural science (*Naturwissenschaft*)" as "a certain good taste in philosophy" (*Philosophie*). The fact that Kant does not refer to philosophy in the quoted passage does slightly weaken Blumenberg's claim that this passage prefigures Kant's later transcendentalism.
xcix	Ibid., 121.
c	Blumenberg makes use of Gotthold Ephraim Lessing's German translation, which occasionally deviates wildly from the English. The deviations do not affect Blumenberg's analysis; thus, I only mark one with German in parentheses.
ci	From *Canterbury Tales*. See Chapter 6 of the present book (p. 48).
cii	"Der Schriftsteller und der Mensch," 1834, in Feuerbach, *Sämmtliche Werke*, I, 263–366. In this piece, "The Writer and the Human," Feuerbach abandons the abstract language of *Thoughts on Death and Immortality*, which presented atheism as something refined, "a thought held at a distance from the rabble." See "On my 'Thoughts on Death and Immortality,'" in Ibid., I, 213. Here stereotyped "writer" and "human" figures communicate in letters: "Thus, in a real author, the human corresponds (*korrespondiert*) with the writer." Ibid., I, 360. While the writer's "life is nothing other than the state of absentmindedness," the "human" too becomes absentminded when he falls in love with a woman. Ibid., I, 341, 362. Love distracts the human from letter writing, the writer envies his love, and the correspondence breaks down. The narrative chastises intellectual pettiness although Blumenberg cites the passages where Feuerbach advocates for theory.
ciii	Blumenberg is quoting the well-known saying that Feuerbach develops in "Das Geheimniss des Opfers," 1850, in Feuerbach, *Sämmtliche Werke*, X, 59. Feuerbach accounts for cultural identity and difference by recourse to forms of figurative and actual consumption. Love and religious devotion are expressed through figurative consumption: kissing and the Eucharist. But hatred may result from the sentiment that "whoever does not eat what I eat is not what I am."
civ	*Gattung*. In the following paragraphs, Blumenberg relies on Feuerbach's notion of *Gattung* as species, as collective humanity, which is central to Feuerbach's atheist value system: "the species is the ultimate measure of truth." Feuerbach, *The Essence of Christianity*, 131. Feuerbach derives altruism from love of the species, where any "other [human] is the representative of the species." In Christianity, God metaphorically replaces human representatives of the species, and thus dissipates our commitment to love members of our species.
cv	*Absolutismus der Metapher*. The absolutism of metaphor is a "danger" to theory insofar as it indicates theory's failure to dispense with

indeterminate images. According to Blumenberg, however, metaphors only become absolute metaphors when the image is taken as the *only* expression of an idea. An influential metaphor can endure as a "background metaphor" and not be an "absolute metaphor" as long as it is still the case that "the vehicle can become dispensable." Blumenberg, *Paradigms for a Metaphorology*, 45.

cvi   The word translated as "spring" (*Quelle*) also means "source" in the sense of historical record. The word "ground" (*Grund*) also means "explanation." Hegel's phenomenology works with the notion that history precedes and informs logical explanation, and it is thus not surprising that the Hegelian Eduard Gans allegorically links *Quelle* and *Grund*. See Taylor, *Hegel*, 131.

cvii "Science and Wisdom in Conflict," in Nietzsche, *Philosophy and Truth*, 145. The quoted text is one of seven "pre-writings" (*Vorarbeiten*) for a book Nietzsche never wrote about philosophers' impact on culture. The most complete and best known of these unpublished pre-writings from 1872–5 is "On Truth and Lie in the Non-moral Sense." Throughout this chapter, Blumenberg cites the 1920 *Musarionausgabe* edition of Nietzsche's works, although a more complete and accurate *Kritische Gesamtausgabe* edition of Nietzsche's works had been underway since 1967.

cviii Blumenberg paraphrases from Nietzsche's unpublished notes from 1872, collected under the heading, "The Last Philosopher:" "Tragic resignation. The end of philosophy. Only art has the capacity to save us ... Culture as the antidote ... God knows what kind of culture this will be! It is beginning at the end." Ibid., 153, 154. The notes urge philosophers to sacrifice accuracy for cultural impact. Nietzsche finds an exemplary case of irrational philosophy in Thales' "everything is water:" "Here we have a transference: ... The whole world is moist; *therefore, being moist is the whole world*. Metonymy. A false inference." Ibid., 48.

cix   Nietzsche, *The Pre-Platonic Philosophers*, 24.
cx   Ibid. (translation modified).
cxi   Ibid., 25.
cxii Ibid., 27.
cxiii Ibid., 28.
cxiv Nietzsche explains that Thales successfully inaugurated philosophy because his statement that "everything is water" straddled myth, science, and philosophy. It is mythical "because the sentence pronounces something about the origin of things, [scientific] because it does this without image or mythical fabelry, and finally [philosophical] because it contains the thought 'everything is one'—even if only in larval form." Nietzsche, *Philosophy and Truth*, 145.
cxv   Nietzsche, *The Pre-Platonic Philosophers*, 30.
cxvi *nur über sich selbst… schreiben*. Blumenberg gives special attention to private journal writings (by Jünger, Fontane, and Hebbel) as well as to published self-observations (by Goethe, Nietzsche, Montaigne, and Husserl).

cxvii Nietzsche, "De Laertii Diogenis fontibus," in *Gesammelte Werke*, I, 299. This contest entry by the 23-year-old Nietzsche is 92 pages long and written entirely in Latin (except for the frequent quotations in Greek). While he enjoyed the thought and research that went into this project, he was unhappy to see it published because of its "stammering" and "foolish" language. Nietzsche, letters to Deussen and Rohde, quoted in *Gesammelte Werke*, I, 452–3.

cxviii Diogenes Laertius cites Musaeus as evidence to claim the autochthony of Greek philosophy in Athens (against claims that it originated in Egypt or in the East): "It is said that [Musaeus], the son of Eumolpus, was the first to compose a genealogy of the gods and to construct a sphere, and that he maintained that all things proceed from unity and are resolved again into unity." Diogenes Laertius, *Lives of Eminent Philosophers*, Vol. 1, I, 3, 5. Musaeus' life is more mythologized and his output more mythic than Thales'. Ancient authors wrote that Musaeus was either a relative or a teacher of the legendary musician Orpheus, and that Musaeus composed the first poems about the origin of the gods.

cxix *der größter Athener*. Wilamowitz rates Herodotus "the greatest Athenian" for inventing the genre of historiography. Herodotus was born in Halicarnassus, but was later naturalized as a citizen of Athens. Herodotus writes about Thales' political influence over Miletus in *Histories* I, 74, 75, 170.

cxx Nietzsche, *The Pre-Platonic Philosophers*, 28.

cxxi "Myths do not answer questions; they make things unquestionable." Blumenberg, *Work on Myth*, 1985, 118. That rationality achieves its persuasiveness not by denying myths but by providing answers to questions left by myth is a central thesis of Blumenberg's *Work on Myth*. Here Blumenberg is reiterating his point from the beginning of this book: "Annexing the world that comes from water and rests on it to the world of the gods hardly constituted the first bold move of reason. If we knew more about how Thales had done it, we would perhaps be reminded more of the exegesis of a canonical text than of the founding of a philosophical system" (p. 3).

cxxii Nietzsche, *Philosophy in the Tragic Age of the Greeks*, 43. Blumenberg expands his criticism of Nietzsche's claim—that philosophy is more discriminate than science in its pursuit of knowledge—in the next chapter. See note cxxxvi, p. 190.

cxxiii Ibid., 44.

cxxiv See note cxiii, p. 189. It undercuts the supposed novelty of philosophical monism to ascribe the same thought to Musaeus, a legendary poet of hymns, who reputedly lived long before Thales.

cxxv Ibid., 45.

cxxvi Nietzsche alludes to the Thales anecdote in "On Truth and Lie in the Non-moral Sense," the most polished of Nietzsche's "pre-writings" for the book about philosophers, which Blumenberg cites throughout this chapter. Without mentioning Thales by name, Nietzsche portrays "the intuitive man," who orients his life by metaphors rather than concepts, "as was perhaps the case in ancient Greece ... [and who] suffers more intensely, when he suffers; he even suffers more frequently, since he does not understand how to learn from experience and keeps falling over and over again into the same ditch. He is then just as irrational in sorrow as he is in happiness: he cries aloud and will not be consoled." Nietzsche, *Philosophy and Truth*, 90–1 (*Gesammelte Werke*, VI, 91). This "intuitive man" foregoes general concepts, and is thus less adaptive to circumstances than scientific man, but he is more original and achieves greater cultural impact. In Chapter 13, Heidegger claims for philosophers what Nietzsche implies about "the intuitive man:" failure to accomplish ordinary things is a necessary sacrifice for success in attaining rare and unforeseeable goals.

cxxvii Gadamer, "Being, Spirit, God," 65.

cxxviii *Dasein*. Heidegger's term for humanity's existential status, bracketing biological and anthropological features. In *Being and Time*, Dasein's hallmarks include possessing awareness that one exists and being concerned about one's existence. Blumenberg generally rejects Heidegger's terminology. See Blumenberg, *Ein mögliches Selbstverständnis*, 91.

cxxix   Blumenberg discusses Ovid's iteration of this "old formula" in Chapter 5. See note l, p. 181.

cxxx   Husserl and Heidegger both denied the relevance of the anthropological question ("What is human?") to their philosophical goals. Blumenberg insists that they both work with an implicit theory of human nature since both consider humans *capable* of studying their interface with reality. See Blumenberg, "Ist Intersubjektivität ein anthropologisches Thema?" in *Beschreibung des Menschen*.

cxxxi   *Seinsgeschichte*. Heidegger's "history of Being," wherein Being occurs (*ereignet*), by revealing and concealing itself within human history, is part of Heidegger's later ontology. Blumenberg, like Heidegger, wrote his dissertation on medieval ontology, and he claims that Heidegger's "history of Being" gives Being the character of an "objectum voluntarium," which meant, in medieval theology, "an object that only depends on its own will to be recognizable, to hold itself from concealment." Blumenberg, *Lebenszeit und Weltzeit*, 94.

cxxxii Heidegger, *What Is a Thing*, 2.
cxxxiii Ibid., 1.
cxxxiv Ibid., 1–2.
cxxxv   Ibid., 2. 3.
cxxxvi As Nietzsche opposes science's value neutrality to philosophy's creation of values in Chapter 12, Heidegger opposes science's utility to philosophy's pure truth-seeking (pp. 113–14). Heidegger claims that modern natural science restricts our relationship with things so we fail to undergo "a change of questioning and evaluation, of seeing and deciding; in short, of the being-there in the midst of what is." Heidegger, *What Is a Thing*, 51. Statements like these lead Blumenberg to find cryptotheology in Heidegger: "Understanding has entered in place of faith as the condition for a specific promise of salvation

Notes 191

after the end of the current circumstance." Blumenberg, *Ein mögliches Selbstverständnis*, 35.

cxxxvii *Evidenz*. Phenomenology finds its evidence in experiential events (rather than logical results). Husserl applies the word *Evidenz* to trivial experiences of being conscious, insofar as they reveal the basic structure of subjectivity. See Husserl, *Logical Investigations*, §6; Moran and Cohen, *The Husserl Dictionary*, 113. Husserl does not, however, want to rank incomprehension as a kind of experiential evidence that can inform us about objects not yet comprehended.

cxxxviii Heidegger, *What Is a Thing*, 3.

cxxxix *vielleicht eine grundlose Tiefe*. This phrase could also be translated as "perhaps a profundity for no reason," which would evoke Heidegger's insistence that he has neither everyday familiar motivations nor scientific ones for asking about the essence of the thing. In this paragraph and the next, Blumenberg plays on the polysemous German morpheme *-grund-*, which can mean either the grounds for an argument or the physical ground, the earth. He discusses the metaphoric potential of "grounds" further in "Foundation and Soil, Bottom and Ground: Hitting Bottom, Getting to the Bottom of Things, Standing on the Ground," in Blumenberg, *Care Crosses the River*, 67–9.

cxl Heidegger, *What Is a Thing*, 3.

cxli *Unwesen des Grundes*. Due to the double meaning of *Grund* for both the physical "ground" and for logical "grounding," this phrase could also mean "the morass of reason." *Unwesen* is also the negative of *Wesen*, "essence" or "being," so that the phrase could be translated as "the lacking essence of reason." The phrase evokes the title of Heidegger's 1929 essay, *The Essence of Reasons* (*Vom Wesen des Grundes*). Heidegger figuratively expresses his anti-rational views by reading Thales' fall as an initiation into the irrational groundlessness of true philosophy.

cxlii *jener Sache auf den Grund zu gehen*. Blumenberg often quotes the words, "To the things themselves!" (*Zu den Sachen!*) as Husserl's motto for phenomenology. See Blumenberg, "Die sprachliche Wirklichkeit der Philosophie," 430; Blumenberg, *Quellen, Ströme, Eisberge*, 9. Blumenberg remarks that Husserl's motto stood opposed to the Viennese positivist motto, which called for "sentences about sentences, instead of sentences about things." Blumenberg, *Zu den Sachen und zurück*, 339. Both philosophies, however, shared skepticism towards causal claims, sought philosophical foundations for scientific knowledge, and worked primarily on epistemology, not ontology.

cxliii Aristotle, *The Complete Works of Aristotle*, 1552.
cxliv Heidegger, *History of the Concept of Time*, 275.
cxlv Ibid., 276.
cxlvi Ibid., 277. A similar discussion of curiosity occurs in §68(c) of *Being and Time*.
cxlvii *Verfall seines Anfangs ... Auf-sich-beruhen-Lassen*. The phrase "his beginning's fallenness" ambiguously links Thales' "tumble" to his "decadence." Here *Verfall* evokes theological "fallenness," much as *Verfallenheit* indicates failure to acknowledge death as one's most

authentic concern in *Being and Time*. "Letting-things-be" (*Auf-sich-beruhen-Lassen der Dinge*) is also ambiguous in its valence here, since release seems to result from Thales' inauthentic fallenness, but late Heidegger also advocates "releasement" (*Gelassenheit*) towards things when he recommends that humanity should make use of modern technology without letting it dictate our purpose on earth (*auf sich beruhen lassen als etwas, was uns nicht im Innersten und Eigentlichen angeht*). Heidegger, *Gelassenheit*, 24.

cxlviii Heidegger, *What Is a Thing*, 4 (translation modified).
cxlix Ibid., 9.
cl *beim Urheber der Phänomenologie*. "Phenomenology's originator" Husserl spoke of subjective consciousness as that which survives all skeptical doubts. Its indestructibility makes it a "phenomenological residuum"—after all else is questioned by "phenomenological reduction." Thus, this residuum is "a region of Being which is in principle unique and can become in fact the field for a new science—the science of Phenomenology." Husserl, *Ideas*, 63.
cli *factum brutum*. A foundational concept both in positivism and in phenomenology. Like "evidence," discussed above, *facta bruta* are irreducible experiences—specifically, experiences of sensory information. On *Evidenz*, see note cxxxvii, p. 192, and on *das Faktische*, see the note below.
clii *Das Faktische*. In everyday German, the word means "factual" in the sense of corresponding to facts (as opposed to mere opinions or fantasies). In Heidegger's lexicon, it refers to circumstances that cannot be experienced first-hand, in particular, the circumstances that precede us and "throw" us into existence. Hence, the unusual translation: "Facticity (*Faktizität*) is not the factuality (*Tatsächlichkeit*) of the *factum brutum* of something objectively present (*eines Vorhandenen*), but is a characteristic of the being of Dasein, taken on in existence, although initially thrust aside." Heidegger, *Being and Time*, 132.
cliii Blumenberg often reminds us that Husserl conceived phenomenology as a "science of trivialities," which explains how the self-evident became so, rather than undertaking to explain unfamiliar phenomena. See, for instance, Blumenberg, *Zu den Sachen und zurück*, 349.
cliv *nicht ... konnte*. Husserl might not have had access to Heidegger's late work as a result of the 1933 Civil Service Law, which barred Husserl—as an ethnic Jew—from all academic privileges in Germany, including library use.
clv Heidegger, *What Is a Thing*, 3.
clvi Preisendanz and Warning, *Das Komische*, 435. Blumenberg cites a swath of pages from the 1974 *Poetics and Hermeneutics* conference proceedings, in which four scholars including himself discuss the Thales anecdote. All quotations in this chapter are from Harald Weinrich's piece, "Thales and the Thracian maid: Schadenfreude on all sides." For more on the symposium, see the Afterword section "From Spatial to Temporal Distance (1974 to 1987)" (p. 149).
clvii Manfred Fuhrmann's three-page contribution to this piece of the

symposium publication is called "The Height of the Fall, Taken Literally for Once." Ibid., 432–5.

clviii Ibid., 435.
clix   Ibid., 436.
clx   *gesellschaftskritisch*. This may allude to Frankfurt School-style "social critique," which (like the *Poetics und Hermeneutics* group) Blumenberg does not mention here by name. Blumenberg may be thinking specifically of Hannah Arendt's reading of the Thales anecdote, which he knew about but omits from the book. See Afterword (p. 148).

Bibliography

Abraham a Sancta Clara. *Judas der Erzschelm für ehrliche Leut', oder eigentlicher Entwurf und Lebensbeschreibung des Iscariotischen Böswicht*. Winkler, 1835.
Adrados, Francisco Rodríguez. *History of the Graeco-Latin Fable*. Leiden: Brill, 1999.
Aesop. *Aesop without Morals: The Famous Fables and a Life of Aesop*. Translated by Lloyd W. Daly. New York: T. Yoseloff, 1961. http://hdl.handle.net/2027/[u]: mdp.39015056960548
—*Fabulae aesopicae collectae*. Lipsiae: B. G. Teubneri, 1911.
—*Three Hundred Æsop's Fables*. Translated by George Fyler Townsend. George Routledge and Sons, 1871.
Aesop and Samuel Richardson. *Aesop's Fables: With Instructive Morals and Reflections Abstracted from All Party Considerations, Adapted to All Capacities, and Design'd to Promote Religion, Morality and Universal Benevolence ... and The Life of Aesop*. York: T. Wilson and R. Spence, 179ff. http://hdl.handle.net/2027/[u]: dul1.ark:/13960/t2m62br2q
Agrippa of Nettesheim, Heinrich Cornelius. *The Vanity of Arts and Sciences*. J. C., 1676.
Alsted, Johann Heinrich. *Cursus philosophici encyclopaediae*. Herborn, 1620.
Aquinas, Thomas. *The Collected Works of St. Thomas Aquinas*. Electronic Edition. Charlottesville: InteLex Corporation, 1993.
—*The "Summa Theologica" of St. Thomas Aquinas*. London: Burns Oates & Washbourne, 1912. http://hdl.handle.net/2027/njp.32101075375178
Arendt, Hannah. *Lectures on Kant's Political Philosophy*. Chicago: University of Chicago Press, 1989.
—*The Life of the Mind*. New York: Harcourt Brace Jovanovich, 1977. http://hdl.handle.net/2027/[u]: mdp.39015008031786
Aristotle. *Aristotle's Nicomachean Ethics*. Translated by Robert C. Bartlett and Susan D. Collins. Chicago: University of Chicago Press, 2012.
—*On the Soul. Parva Naturalia. On Breath*. Translated by W. S. Hett. Revised edition. Cambridge, MA and London: Harvard University Press, 2000.
—*Politics*. Mineola, NY: Courier Dover Publications, 2000.
—*The Complete Works of Aristotle: The Revised Oxford Translation*. Bollingen series, 71:2. Princeton, NJ: Princeton University Press, 1984.
Armstrong, David Malet. *The Nature of Mind, and Other Essays*. Ithaca, NY: Cornell University Press, 1981.
Augustine. *Sermons on the Liturgical Seasons*. Translated by Mary Sarah. Washington, DC: Catholic University of America Press, 1984. http://libproxy.

umflint.edu:2048/login?url=http://site.ebrary.com/lib/umich/
Doc?id=10383927
—*Confessions*. Baltimore, MD: Catholic University of America Press, 1953. http://
site.ebrary.com/lib/alltitles/docDetail.action?docID=10383925
Bacon, Francis. *Collected Works of Francis Bacon*. Abingdon: Psychology Press, 1996.
—*The Works of Francis Bacon, Lord Chancellor of England*. Carey and Hart, 1842.
Bayle, Pierre. *An Historical and Critical Dictionary. By Monsieur Bayle. Translated into English, with Many Additions and Corrections, Made by the Author Himself, That Are Not in the French Editions*. 4 vols. London, 1710. http://find.galegroup.com/ecco/infomark.do?&source=gale&prodId=ECCO&userGroupName=umuser&tabID=T001&docId=CW3314129617&type=multipage&contentSet=ECCOArticles&version=1.0&docLevel=FASCIMILE
Beard, Mary. *Laughter in Ancient Rome*. Oakland: University of California Press, 2014. http://www.ucpress.edu/book.php?isbn=9780520277168
Beck, Hanno. *Alexander von Humboldt: Life and Work*. Ingelheim am Rhein: C. H. Boehringer Sohn, 1987.
—*Alexander von Humboldt*. v. Wiesbaden: F. Steiner Verlag, 1959. http://hdl.handle.net/2027/[u]: uc1.b3313373
Bernet, Rudolf. *Introduction to Husserlian Phenomenology*. Evanston, IL: Northwestern University Press, 1993.
Blumenberg, Hans. *Präfiguration: Arbeit am politischen Mythos*. Frankfurt: Suhrkamp Verlag GmbH, 2014.
—*Quellen, Ströme, Eisberge*. Edited by Ulrich v. Bülow and Dorit Krusche. Bibliothek Suhrkamp; Bd. 1469. Berlin: Suhrkamp, 2012.
—*Care Crosses the River*. Translated by Paul Fleming. Stanford, CA: Stanford University Press, 2010.
—*Löwen*. Frankfurt: Suhrkamp Verlag GmbH, 2010.
—*Paradigms for a Metaphorology*. Ithaca, NY: Cornell University Press; Cornell University Library, 2010.
—*Theorie der Lebenswelt*. 1. Aufl. Berlin: Suhrkamp, 2010.
—*Theorie der Unbegrifflichkeit*. Edited by Anselm. Haverkamp. 1. Aufl. Frankfurt am Main: Suhrkamp, 2007.
—"Ist Intersubjektivität ein anthropologisches Phänomen?" In *Beschreibung des Menschen*, 1. Aufl. Frankfurt am Main: Suhrkamp, 2006.
—*Beschreibung des Menschen*. 1. Aufl. Frankfurt am Main: Suhrkamp, 2006.
—*Die Verführbarkeit des Philosophen*. 1st edition. Frankfurt: Suhrkamp Verlag, 2005.
—*Zu den Sachen und zurück*. 1. Aufl. Frankfurt am Main: Suhrkamp, 2002.
—*La risa de la muchacha Tracia : una protohistoria de la teoría*. Translated by Teresa Rocha and Isidoro Reguera. Valencia: Pre-Textos, 2000.
—*Ein mögliches Selbstverständnis: aus dem Nachlass*. Universal-Bibliothek; Nr. 9650. Stuttgart: Philipp Reclam jun., 1997. http://hdl.handle.net/2027/[u]: mdp.39015039884963
—"Prospect for a Theory of Nonconceptuality." In *Shipwreck with Spectator: Paradigm of a Metaphor for Existence*. Studies in Contemporary German Social Thought. Cambridge, MA: MIT Press, 1997, pp. 81–102.
—*Shipwreck with Spectator: Paradigm of a Metaphor for Existence*. Studies in Contemporary German Social Thought. Cambridge, MA: MIT Press, 1997.
—*Die Vollzähligkeit der Sterne*. 2. Aufl. Frankfurt am Main: Suhrkamp, 1997.
—"Light as a Metaphor for Truth: At the Preliminary Stage of Philosophical Concept Formation." In *Modernity and the Hegemony of Vision*. Edited by David

Michael Levin. Berkeley and Los Angeles: University of California Press, 1993, pp. 30–86.
—*Höhlenausgänge*. Frankfurt am Main: Suhrkamp, 1989.
—*Matthäuspassion*. 1. Aufl. Frankfurt am Main: Suhrkamp, 1988.
—"An Anthropological Approach to Rhetoric." In *After Philosophy: End or Transformation*. Edited by Kenneth Baynes, James. Bohman, and Thomas A. McCarthy. Translated by Robert M. Wallace. Cambridge, MA: MIT Press, 1987.
—*The Genesis of the Copernican World*. Cambridge, MA: MIT Press, 1987.
—"Das Lachen der Thrakerin (Drucktitel) [verschiedene Fassungen: Vorstufen, Manuskript, korr. Druckfahne, Materialien zum Buch]." Deutsches Literaturarchiv, Marbach, etwa 1986. HS.2003.0001. Handschriften.
—*Lebenszeit und Weltzeit*. Frankfurt am Main: Suhrkamp, 1986. http://hdl.handle.net/2027/[u]: mdp.39015011704940
—*Work on Myth*. Cambridge, MA: MIT Press, 1985.
—*The Legitimacy of the Modern Age*. Studies in Contemporary German Social Thought. Cambridge, MA: MIT Press, 1983.
—*Die Lesbarkeit der Welt*. 1. Aufl. Frankfurt am Main: Suhrkamp, 1981.
—"Der Sturz des Protophilosophen. Zur Komik der reinen Theorie-anhand einer Rezeptionsgeschichte der Thales-Anekdote." In *Das Komische*. Edited by Wolfgang Preisendanz and Rainer Warning. Poetik und Hermeneutik; 7. München: Fink, 1976. http://hdl.handle.net/2027/[u]: mdp.39015004308063
—"Wer sollte vom Lachen der Magd betroffen sein? Eine Duplik." In *Das Komische*. Edited by Wolfgang Preisendanz and Rainer Warning. Poetik und Hermeneutik; 7. München: Fink, 1976. http://hdl.handle.net/2027/[u]: mdp.39015004308063
—"Ernst Cassirers gedenkend." *Revue Internationale de Philosophie* 28 (1974): 456–63.
—"Beobachtungen an Metaphern." *Archiv für Begriffsgeschichte* 15 (1971): 161–214.
—"Wirklichkeitsbegriff und Wirkungspotential des Mythos." In *Terror und Spiel. Probleme der Mythenrezeption: Poetik und Hermeneutik, Bd.4, Terror und Spiel*. Edited by Manfred Fuhrmann. München: Fink (Wilhelm), 1971, pp. 11–66.
—*Die Legitimität der Neuzeit*. Frankfurt am Main: Suhrkamp, 1966. http://hdl.handle.net/2027/[u]: mdp.39015000686223
—"Rose und Feuer: Lyrik, Kritik und Drama T.S. Eliots." In *Hochland*. 49th edition. Munich: Im Kösel Verlag, 1956, II, pp. 108–26.
—"Die ontologische Distanz : eine Untersuchung über die Krisis der Phänomenologie Husserls." Kiel: Habilitationsschrift, 1950.
—"Die sprachliche Wirklichkeit der Philosophie." *Hamburger Akademische Rundschau* 1:10 (47 1946): 428–31.
—"Zettelkasten 14: T-V (Titel von Bearbeiter/in) [Nasenkarten:T, Theologie, Schöpfung, U, V]." Deutsches Literaturarchiv, Marbach, n.d. HS.2003.0001. Handschriften.
Blumenberg, Hans and Carl Schmitt. *Briefwechsel 1971–1978 und weitere Materialien*. Edited by Alexander Schmitz and Marcel Lepper. Frankfurt am Main: Suhrkamp, 2007. http://hdl.handle.net/2027/[u]: mdp.39015074077366
Blumenberg, Hans and Jacob Taubes. *Briefwechsel 1961–1981 und weitere Materialien*. Edited by Herbert Kopp-Oberstebrink and Martin Treml. Berlin: Suhrkamp, 2013.
Böckh, August. *Philolaos des Pythagoreers Lehren nebst den Bruchstücken seines Werkes*. Edited by Philolaus Crotoniensis. Berlin: Vossische Buchhandlung, 1819.

Börne, Ludwig. *Gesammelte Schriften von Ludwig Börne*. Hoffmann und Campe, 1829.
Brient, Elizabeth. *The Immanence of the Infinite: Hans Blumenberg and the Threshold to Modernity*. Washington, DC: Catholic University of America Press, 2002.
Brucker, Jakob. *The History of Philosophy, from the Earliest Times to the Beginning of the Present Century*. Translated by William Enfield. Vol. 1. 2 vols. Dublin, 1792. http://find.galegroup.com/ecco/infomark.do?&source=gale&prodId=ECCO&userGroupName=umuser&tabID=T001&docId=CW3320995830&type=multipage&contentSet=ECCOArticles&version=1.0
—*Jacob Bruckers Kurze Fragen aus der philosophischen Historie von Anfang der Welt, biss auf die Geburt Christi, mit Ausführlichen Anmerckungen Erlaütert. [With Engravings, Including a Portrait.]*. Ulm, 1731.
Burley, Walter. *Walter Burleys "Liber de vita et moribus philosophorum poetarumque veterum" in zwei deutschen Bearbeitungen des Spätmittelalters*. Bamberg: Rodenbusch, 1969.
Cavarero, Adriana. *In Spite of Plato: A Feminist Rewriting of Ancient Philosophy*. Translated by Rosi Braidotti. Nonostante Plato. Cambridge: Polity Press, 1995.
Chaucer, Geoffrey. *Canterbury Tales*. Translated by R. M. Lumiansky. New York: Simon and Schuster, 2013.
—*The Canterbury Tales of Geoffrey Chaucer: A New Text with Illustrative Notes*. Edited by Thomas Wright. Percy Society, 1847.
Cicero, Marcus Tullius. *The Republic and The Laws*. Translated by C. D. Yonge. New York: Digireads.com Publishing, 2009.
—*Tusculan Disputations: On the Nature of the Gods, And on the Commonwealth*. Translated by C. D. Yonge. New York: Cosimo, 2005.
Conti, Alessandro. *A Companion to Walter Burley: Late Medieval Logician and Metaphysician*. Leiden: Brill, 2013.
Copernicus, Nicolaus. *On The Revolutions of Heavenly Spheres*. Edited by Stephen Hawking. Philadelphia, PA: Running Press, 2004.
Cusa, Nicholas of. *On Learned Ignorance: A Translation and Appraisal of De Docta Ignorantia*. Translated by Jasper Hopkins. De Docta ignorantia. English. Minneapolis, MN: A.J. Benning Press, 1981.
Damian, Peter. *The Letters of Peter Damian (Letters 91–120)*. Translated by Owen J. Blum. The Fathers of the Church: Medieval Continuation. Washington, DC: Catholic University of America Press, 1998.
Descartes, René. *Discourse on Method, Optics, Geometry, and Meteorology*. Indianapolis, IN: Hackett Publishing, 2001.
Diogenes Laertius. *Lives of Eminent Philosophers*. Translated by Robert Drew Hicks. Lives, Teachings, and Sayings of Famous philosophers. Cambridge, MA: Harvard University Press, 1972. http://hdl.handle.net/2027/[u]:inu.30000057468583
Dodd, James. *Crisis and Reflection: An Essay on Husserl's Crisis of the European Sciences*. New York: Springer Science & Business Media, 2006.
Feuerbach, Ludwig. *The Essence of Christianity*. Mineola, NY: Courier Dover Publications, 2008.
—*Gesammelte Werke: Kleinere Schriften I–IV (1835–1866)*. Berlin: Akademie Verlag, 1970.
—*Sämmtliche Werke*. Stuttgart: Wigand, 1903.
Fleming, Paul. "On the Edge of Non-Contingency: Anecdotes and the Lifeworld." *Telos* 158 (March 26, 2012): 21–35. doi:10.3817/0312158021.

—"The Perfect Story: Anecdote and Exemplarity in Linnaeus and Blumenberg." *Thesis Eleven* 104:1 (February 1, 2011): 72–86. doi:10.1177/0725513610394736.

Fontenelle, Bernard le Bovier de. *Conversations on the Plurality of Worlds*. Entretiens Sur La Pluralité Des mondes. Berkeley: University of California Press, 1990.

Freud, Sigmund. *Beyond the Pleasure Principle*. Translated by Gregory C. Richter. Jenseits Des Lustprinzips. Peterborough, ONT and Buffalo, NY: Broadview Editions, 2011.

Gadamer, Hans-Georg. *Truth and Method*. London: Bloomsbury Academic, 2013.

—"Being, Spirit, God." In *Heidegger Memorial Lectures*. Edited by Werner Marx. Translated by Steven W. Davis. Heidegger, Freiburger Universitätsvorträge Zu Seinem Gedenken. Pittsburgh, PA: Duquesne University Press, 1982, pp. 55–74. http://hdl.handle.net/2027/[u]: mdp.39015020766351

Gans, Eduard. *Philosophische Schriften*. Edited by Horst. Schröder. Glashütten im Taunus: D. Auvermann, 1971. http://hdl.handle.net/2027/[u]: mdp.39015030537115

Gasché, Rodolphe. *The Honor of Thinking: Critique, Theory, Philosophy*. Cultural Memory in the Present. Stanford, CA: Stanford University Press, 2007.

Gassendi, Pierre. *Tychonis Brahei, equitis Dani, astronomorum coryphaei, vita*. Apud viduam M. Dupuis, 1654.

Geffcken, Johannes, Marcianus Aristides, and Athenagoras. *Zwei griechische Apologeten*. Sammlung wissenschaftlicher Kommentare zu griechischen und römischen Schriftstellern. Leipzig: B.G. Teubner, 1907. http://hdl.handle.net/2027/[u]: uc1.b4513173

Goethe, Johann Wolfgang von. *Faust: Part Two*. Translated by Martin Greenberg. New Haven, CT: Yale University Press, 1998.

Hansen, William F. *Anthology of Ancient Greek Popular Literature*. Bloomington: Indiana University Press, 1998. http://hdl.handle.net/2027/[u]: mdp.39015058018857

Harries, Karsten. *Infinity and Perspective*. Cambridge, MA: MIT Press, 2002.

Hegel, Georg W. F. *The Phenomenology of Mind*. New York: Cosimo, Inc., 2011.

Heidegger, Martin. *Logic: The Question of Truth*. Studies in Continental Thought. Bloomington: Indiana University Press, 2010.

—*Being and Time: A Translation of Sein Und Zeit*. Translated by Joan Stambaugh. SUNY Series in Contemporary Continental Philosophy. Albany, NY: State University of New York Press, 1996.

—"The Self-Assertion of the German University." In *Martin Heidegger and National Socialism: Questions and Answers*. Edited by Günther Neske and Emil Kettering. New York: Paragon House, 1990.

—"Spiegel Interview with Martin Heidegger." In *Martin Heidegger and National Socialism: Questions and Answers*. Edited by Günther Neske and Emil Kettering. New York: Paragon House, 1990.

—*History of the Concept of Time: Prolegomena*. Studies in Phenomenology and Existential Philosophy. Bloomington: Indiana University Press, 1985. http://hdl.handle.net/2027/[u]: mdp.39015009288260

—*The Essence of Reasons*. Northwestern University Studies in Phenomenology & Existential Philosophy. Evanston, IL: Northwestern University Press, 1969. http://hdl.handle.net/2027/[u]: mdp.39015004078393

—*What Is a Thing*. Chicago: H. Regnery, 1967. http://hdl.handle.net/2027/[u]: mdp.39015004184399

—*Gelassenheit*. Pfullingen: Neske, 1959. http://hdl.handle.net/2027/[u]: mdp.39015008251004

Herodotus. *The Histories*. Translated by Robin Waterfield. Oxford and New York: Oxford University Press, 2008.

Heumann, Christoph August. *Acta philosophorum, das ist gründl. Nachrichten aus der historia philosophica: nebst beygefügten Urtheilen von denen dahin gehörigen alten und neuen Büchern*. Halle: Renger, 1716.

—*Parerga Critica Sive Hebdomadum Criticarum Hebdomas et Glossematum Decas*. Jena: Johann Felix Bielck, 1712.

Homer. *The Iliad (The Stephen Mitchell Translation)*. New York: Simon and Schuster, 2011.

Humboldt, Alexander von. *Gespräche*. Berlin: Akademie-Verlag, 1959.

Husserl, Edmund. *Ideas: General Introduction to Pure Phenomenology*. Abingdon: Routledge, 2012.

—*Logical Investigations*. Translated by Dermot Moran. Abingdon: Psychology Press, 2001.

—*The Essential Husserl: Basic Writings in Transcendental Phenomenology*. Bloomington: Indiana University Press, 1999.

—*The Crisis of European Sciences and Transcendental Phenomenology: An Introduction to Phenomenological Philosophy*. Northwestern University Studies in Phenomenology & Existential Philosophy. Evanston, IL: Northwestern University Press, 1970.

—"The Vienna Lecture: Philosophy and the Crisis of European Humanity. Appendix A." In *The Crisis of European Sciences and Transcendental Phenomenology; an Introduction to Phenomenological Philosophy*. Northwestern University Studies in Phenomenology & Existential Philosophy. Evanston, IL: Northwestern University Press, 1970.

Jasinski, René. *La Fontaine et Le Premier Recueil Des "Fables."* Paris: A.-G. Nizet, 1966. http://hdl.handle.net/2027/[u]: mdp.39015001527905

Johnson, Mark and George Lakoff. "Conceptual Metaphors in Everyday Life." In *Philosophical Perspectives on Metaphor*. Minneapolis: University of Minnesota Press, 1981.

Jünger, Ernst. *Der Arbeiter*. Sämtliche Werke, II. Klett-Cotta. http://www.calameo.com/read/000127172c54964dfdd16 (accessed July 19, 2014).

Kaestner, Abraham Gotthelf. *Gesammelte poetische und prosaische schönwissenschaftliche Werke*. Berlin: T. C. F. Enslin, 1841.

Kant, Immanuel. "Continued Observations on the Earthquakes That Have Been Experienced for Some Time (1756)." In *Kant: A Natural Science*. Translated by Eric Watkins. The Cambridge Edition of the Works of Immanuel Kant. Cambridge: Cambridge University Press, 2012, pp. 365–73. http://dx.doi.org/10.1017/CBO9781139014380.011

—"History and Natural Description of the Most Noteworthy Occurrences of the Earthquake That Struck a Large Part of the Earth at the End of the Year 1755 (1756)." In *Kant: A Natural Science*. Translated by Eric Watkins. The Cambridge Edition of the Works of Immanuel Kant. Cambridge: Cambridge University Press, 2012, pp. 337–64. http://dx.doi.org/10.1017/CBO9781139014380.010

—"On the Causes of Earthquakes on the Occasion of the Calamity That Befell the Western Countries of Europe towards the End of Last Year (1756)." In *Kant: Natural Science*. Translated by Eric Watkins. The Cambridge Edition of

the Works of Immanuel Kant. Cambridge: Cambridge University Press, 2012, pp. 327–336. http://dx.doi.org/10.1017/CBO9781139014380.009
—*Critique of Judgement*. Translated by Nicholas Walker. Oxford World's Classics. Oxford and New York: Oxford University Press, 2007.
—*Critique of Pure Reason*. Translated by Paul Guyer and Allen W. Wood. Cambridge: Cambridge University Press, 1998.
—*Kant on Swedenborg Dreams of a Spirit-Seer and Other Writings*. Translated by Gregory R. Johnson and Glenn Alexander Magee. West Chester, PA: Swedenborg Foundation, 2002. http://libproxy.umflint.edu:2048/login?url=http://site.ebrary.com/lib/umich/Doc?id=10742106
Kierkegaard, Søren. *The Concept of Irony, with Continual Reference to Socrates/Notes of Schelling's Berlin Lectures*. Translated by Howard Vincent Hong and Edna Hatlestad Hong. Princeton, NJ: Princeton University Press, 1992.
Kurke, Leslie. *Aesopic Conversations: Popular Tradition, Cultural Dialogue, and the Invention of Greek Prose*. Martin Classical Lectures. Princeton, NJ: Princeton University Press, 2011. http://site.ebrary.com/lib/umich/Doc?id=10467759
Lactantius. *Divine Institutes*. Translated by Anthony Bowen and Peter Garnsey. Liverpool: Liverpool University Press, 2004.
Landgrebe, Ludwig. "Die Phänomenologie als transzendentale Theorie der Geschichte." *Phänomenologie und Praxis*, Phänomenologische Forschungen 3 (1976): 17–73.
Landmann, Michael and J. O. Fleckenstein. "Tagesbeobachtungen von Sternen im Altertum. Eine philosophisch-astronomiegeschichtliche Rekonstruktion der Thalesanekdote. Plato Theatet. 174 A." *Vierteljahrsschrift der Naturforschenden Gesellschaft in Zürich* 88 (1943): 98–112.
Leibniz, Gottfried Wilhelm Freiherr von. *Die Werke von Leibniz gemäss seinem hanschriftlichen Nachlasse in der Königlichen Bibliothek zu Hannover*. Hannover: Klindworth Verlag, 1877.
Liddell, Henry George and Robert Scott. *An Intermediate Greek–English Lexicon, Founded upon the Seventh Edition of Liddell and Scott's Greek–English Lexicon*. New York et al.: American Book Co., n.d.
Longchamp, Sebastian G., Jean-Louis Wagnière, Jacques Joseph Marie Decroix, and A. J. Q. Beuchot. *Mémoires sur Voltaire, et sur ses ouvrages*. Paris: Aimé André, 1826. http://hdl.handle.net/2027/[u]: hvd.hnt472
Lübbe, Hermann. *Endstation Terror: Rückblick auf lange Märsche*. Stuttgart: Seewald Verlag, 1978.
Lucretius. *On the Nature of Things*. Translated by Walter Englert. Newburyport, MA: Focus Publishing/R. Pullins, 2003.
Lycan, William G. and Zena Ryder. "The Loneliness of the Long-Distance Truck Driver." *Analysis* 63:2 (April 1, 2003): 132–6.
Marquard, Odo. "Entlastung vom Absoluten." In *Die Kunst des Überlebens : Nachdenken über Hans Blumenberg*. Edited by Franz Wetz. Frankfurt am Main: Suhrkamp, 1999.
Mensch, James R. *After Modernity: Husserlian Reflections on a Philosophical Tradition*. Albany, NY: SUNY Press, 1996.
Merker, Barbara. "Bedürfnis nach Bedeutsamkeit: zwischen Lebenswelt und Absolutismus der Wirklichkeit." In *Die Kunst des Überlebens : Nachdenken über Hans Blumenberg*. Edited by Franz Joseph Wetz. Orig.-Ausg., 1. Aufl. Frankfurt am Main: Suhrkamp, 1999, pp. 68–98.
Mommsen, Theodor and Ulrich von Wilamowitz-Moellendorff. *Mommsen und*

Wilamowitz: Briefwechsel, 1872–1903. Edited by Friedrich Hiller von Gaertringen, Dorothea (von Wilamowitz-Moellendorff) Hiller von Gaertringen, and Eduard Schwartz. Berlin: Weidmann, 1935.

Montaigne, Michel de. *The Complete Works: Essays, Travel Journal, Letters*. Translated by Donald Murdoch Frame. New York: A.A. Knopf, 2003. http://hdl.handle.net/2027/[u]: mdp.39015056903753

—*The Essays of Michel de Montaigne*. Translated by M.A. Screech. London: Penguin Books, 1991. http://hdl.handle.net/2027/mdp.39015053526433

Moran, Dermot and Joseph Cohen. *The Husserl Dictionary*. 1st edn. London: Continuum, 2012.

Müller-Sievers, Helmut. "Kyklophorology: Hans Blumenberg and the Intellectual History of Technics." *Telos* 158 (March 26, 2012): 155–170. doi:10.3817/0312158021.

Nauta, Lodi. "A Weak Chapter in the Book of Nature: Hans Blumenberg on Medieval Thought." In *The Book of Nature in Antiquity and the Middle Ages*. Leuven and Dudley, MA: Peeters, 2005.

Neske, Günther and Emil Kettering. *Martin Heidegger and National Socialism: Questions and Answers*. New York: Paragon House, 1990.

Niehues-Pröbsting, Heinrich. "Platonverlesungen: Eigenschatten-- Lächerlichkeiten." In *Die Kunst des Überlebens : Nachdenken über Hans Blumenberg*. Edited by Franz Wetz, Frankfurt am Main: Suhrkamp, 1999, pp. 341–68.

—"Der Kynismus des Diogenes und der Begriff des Zynismus." *Archiv für Begriffsgeschichte* 25:1 (1981): 128–9.

Nietzsche, Friedrich. *The Gay Science: With a Prelude in German Rhymes and an Appendix of Songs*. Edited by Bernard Williams. Translated by Josefine Nauckhoff. Cambridge: Cambridge University Press, 2001.

—*The Pre-Platonic Philosophers*. Translated by Greg Whitlock. International Nietzsche Studies. Urbana: University of Illinois Press, 2001.

—*Philosophy in the Tragic Age of the Greeks*. Translated by Marianne Cowan. Washington, DC: Gateway Editions, 1996.

—*Philosophy and Truth: Selections from Nietzsche's Notebooks of the Early 1870's*. Translated by Daniel. Breazeale. Washington, DC: Humanities Press International, 1990.

—*On the Genealogy of Morals and Ecce Homo*. Translated by Walter Kaufmann. London: Random House, Inc., 1989.

—*Gesammelte Werke*. Musarionausgabe. München: Musarion Verlag, 1920. http://hdl.handle.net/2027/njp.32101075376077

Ovid. *Metamorphoses*. Edited and translated by Charles Martin. New York: W. W. Norton & Company, 2009.

Pippin, Robert B. "Modern Mythic Meaning: Blumenberg Contra Nietzsche." *History of the Human Sciences* 6:4 (November 1, 1993): 37–56. doi:10.1177/095269519300600403.

Plato. *Protagoras and Meno*. Translated by Robert C. Bartlett. Cornell University Press, 2004.

—*The Last Days of Socrates: Euthyphro, Apology, Crito, Phaedo*. Translated by Hugh. Tredennick and Harold. Tarrant. London: Penguin Books, 2003. http://hdl.handle.net/2027/[u]: mdp.39015050748774

—*The Republic*. Edited by G. R. F. Ferrari. Translated by Tom. Griffith. Cambridge and New York: Cambridge University Press, 2000.

—*Theaetetus, Sophist*. Cambridge, MA: Harvard University Press, 1977.
—*Platons Werke*. Translated by Friedrich Schleiermacher. Berlin: G. Reimer, 1856.
Plessner, Helmuth. *Lachen und Weinen: eine Untersuchung nach de Grenzen menschlichen Verhaltens*. Sammlung Dalp, Bd. 54. Bern: Francke, 1961.
"Prehistory, N." *OED Online*. Oxford University Press. http://www.oed.com.proxy.lib.umich.edu/view/Entry/150122 (accessed June 8, 2014).
Preisendanz, Wolfgang. and Rainer. Warning (eds.). *Das Komische*. Poetik und Hermeneutik 7. München: Fink, 1976. http://hdl.handle.net/2027/[u]: mdp.39015004308063.
"Proto-, Comb. Form." *OED Online*. Oxford University Press. 2014. http://www.oed.com.proxy.lib.umich.edu/view/Entry/153235 (accessed June 8, 2014).
Ritter, Joachim and Rudolf Eisler. *Historisches Wörterbuch Der Philosophie*. Basel: Schwabe, 1971. http://hdl.handle.net/2027/[u]: mdp.39015014314499
Roberts, Alexander and James Donaldson (eds.). *Ante-Nicene Fathers: The Writings of the Fathers down to A.D. 325*. New York: C. Scribner's Sons, 1899. http://catalog.hathitrust.org/Record/010248796
Rothacker, Erich. "Geleitwort." *Archiv für Begriffsgeschichte* 1 (1955): 5–10.
Saadi. *Selections from Saadi's Gulistan*. New York: Global Scholarly Publications, 2004.
Savage, Robert. "Review Essay: Laughter From the Lifeworld: Hans Blumenberg's Theory of Nonconceptuality." *Thesis Eleven* 94:1 (August 1, 2008): 119–31.
Schmitt, Carl. *Political Theology: Four Chapters on the Concept of Sovereignty*. Translated by George Schwab. Chicago: University of Chicago Press, 2005. http://site.ebrary.com/lib/umich/Doc?id=10412034
Schumacher, Hermann Albert. *Südamerikanische Studien: Drei Lebens- und Culturbilder. Mútis. Cáldas. Codazzi. 1760–1860*. Berlin: E. S. Mittler & Sohn., 1884.
Sextus Empiricus. *Outlines of Scepticism*. Cambridge: Cambridge University Press, 2000.
Sommer, Manfred. "Husserl on 'Ground' and 'Underground.'" In *Phenomenology of Interculturality and Life-World*. Edited by Rulun Zhang, Ernst Wolfgang Orth, and Chan-Fai Cheung. Freiburg im Breisgau: Verlag Karl Alber, 1998.
Stanley, Thomas. *The History of Philosophy, in Eight Parts*. London: Humphrey Moseley, and Thomas Dring, 1656.
Stobaeus. *Ioannis Stobaei Florilegium*. Leipzig: Sumptibus et typis B. G. Teubneri, 1855.
Stoellger, Philipp. *Metapher und Lebenswelt: Hans Blumenbergs Metaphorologie als Lebenswelthermeneutik und ihr religionsphänomenologischer Horizont*. Tuebingen: Mohr Siebeck, 2000.
Strauss, David Friedrich. *Voltaire: Sechs Vorträge*. Bonn: Emil Strauss, 1895. http://hdl.handle.net/2027/[u]: wu.89104021084
Taylor, Charles. *Hegel*. Cambridge and New York: Cambridge University Press, 1977.
Taylor, Timothy. "Thracians, Scythians and Dacians." In *The Oxford Illustrated History of Prehistoric Europe*. Edited by Barry Cunliffe. New edition. Oxford and New York: Oxford University Press, 2001, pp. 373–410.
Tiedemann, Dietrich. *Griechenlands erste Philosophen: oder, Leben und Systeme des Orpheus, Pherecydes, Thales und Pythagoras*. Leipzig: Weidmann, 1780.
Varnhagen von Ense, Carl August Ludwig. *Tagebücher*. Hamburg: Hoffmann und Campe, 1868.
Voltaire. *A Philosophical Dictionary*. Boston: J. P. Mendum, 1852. http://hdl.handle.net/2027/ucl.b4506123

Weizsäcker, Carl Friedrich. "Begegnungen in vier Jahrzehnten." In *Erinnerung an Martin Heidegger*. Edited by Günther. Neske. Pfullingen: Neske, 1977. http://hdl.handle.net/2027/[u]: mdp.39015019804866

Wetters, Kirk. "Work on Philosophy: Hans Blumenberg's Reformulations of the Absolute." *Telos* 158 (March 26, 2012): 100–118. doi:10.3817/0312158021.

Wilamowitz-Moellendorff, Ulrich von. *Zukunftsphilologie! eine Erwiderung auf Friedrich Nietzsches "Geburt der Tragödie*. Berlin: Gebrüder Borntraeger, 1872.

Wilamowitz-Moellendorff, Ulrich von and Karl Johannes Neumann. *Weltperioden*. Göttingen: Dieterich'sche Univ.-Buchdruckerei, 1897. http://hdl.handle. net/2027/[u]: njp.32101076539822

Wittgenstein, Ludwig. *Lectures and Conversations on Aesthetics, Psychology, and Religious Belief*. Oakland: University of California Press, 2007.

Wolff, Emil J. H. *Francis Bacon und seine Quellen*. Vol. 52. Literarhistorische Forschungen 40. Berlin: E. Felber, 1910.

Zedler, Johann Heinrich, Johann Peter von Ludewig, and Carl Günther Ludovici. *Grosses vollständiges Universal-Lexicon Aller Wissenschafften und Künste, Welche bißhero durch menschlichen Verstand und Witz erfunden und verbessert worden: Darinnen so wohl die Geographisch-Politische Beschreibung des Erd-Kreyses, nach allen Monarchien, Kayserthümern, Königreichen, Fürstenthümern, Republiquen, freyen Herrschafften, Ländern, Städten, See-Häfen, Vestungen, Schlössern, Flecken, Aemtern, Klöstern, Gebürgen, Pässen, Wäldern, Meeren, Seen, Inseln, Flüssen, und Canälen; samt der natürlichen Abhandlung von dem Reich der Natur... Als auch eine ausführliche Historisch-Genealogische Nachricht von den Durchlauchten und berühmtesten Geschlechtern in der Welt, Dem Leben und Thaten der Kayser, Könige, Churfürsten und Fürsten, grosser Helden, Staats-Minister, Kriegs-Obersten... Ingleichen von allen Staats-Kriegs-Rechts-Policey und Haußhaltungs-Geschäfften des Adelichen und bürgerlichen Standes... Wie nicht weniger die völlige Vorstellung aller in der Kirchen-Geschichten berühmten Alt-Väter, Propheten, Apostel, Päbste, Cardinäle, Bischöffe, Prälaten und Gottes-Gelehrten... Endlich auch ein vollkommener Inbegriff der allergelehrtesten Männer, berühmter Universitäten, Academien, Societäten.... Ver – Vers*. Leipzig and Halle: Zedler, 1746.

Zill, Rüdiger. "'Sagen, was sich eigentlich nicht sagen lässt' – Adorno, Blumenberg, und andere Leser Wittgensteins." In *Nicht(s) sagen: Strategien der Sprachabwendung im 20. Jahrhundert*. Edited by Emmanuel Alloa. Berlin: Transcript Verlag, 2008, pp. 41–60.

Index

Abraham a Sancta Clara 78–9, 185n. lxxxv *see also* theology
absolute 43, 96, 147, 157, 187–8n. cv *see also* metaphor, absolutism of metaphor and absolute metaphor
action: (il)legibility of theory as an 1, 31, 81, 99, 127, 147, 153, 160
Aesop 5, 10–11, 21–3, 25, 42, 46–7, 50, 58, 66, 90, 131, 139–42, 149n. 55, 180n. xxxvii
Agrippa of Nettesheim, Heinrich Cornelius 51–3, 184n. lxvii
Alciato, Andre 49–50, 68
Alfonso X of Castile 79–84, 115, 186n. xc *see also* astronomy
Alsted, Johann Heinrich 70, 185n. lxxxiii
Anschauung (perception, intuition, vision, intuition, image) 18, 58, 86, 99, 168, 174, 186n. xcvi
Arendt, Hannah 143, 148–9, 193n. clx
Aristophanes 7, 15, 19–20, 142 *see also* comedy
Aristotle 12, 15–18, 39, 64, 75, 103, 107, 112–13, 122–3, 143–4, 153, 162, 178n. xiii, 185n. lxxxiii *see also* Thales of Miletus, olive oil-press speculation counter-anecdote
astrology 33–4, 46–53, 58–61, 68–9, 73–8, 90–1, 140, 153, 185n. lxxxi, 186n. xcv
astronomy
  Alexander von Humboldt's 99–102
  Alfonso of Castile sponsors 80–1, 84
  Copernicus' influence on later culture 61–2, 149–51
  distinguished from astrology 46, 52–3
  as metaphor *passim*
  optics at the bottom of the well 10
  Plato's mathematical 18–20, 180n. xxxv
  public perception of 2
  Voltaire's 60
Augustine 30–1, 40–1, 158n. 72, 182n. lx *see also* theology

Baader, Franz Xavier 122n. lvii *see also* theology
Bacon, Francis 62–7, 150–1, 184n. lxxv
Bayle, Pierre 67–9, 80–2, 107, 186nn. xc, xci
Beard, Mary 142, 165–6 *see also* comedy

Being, Heideggerian modes of
  Dasein 119, 123–6, 190n. cxxvii
  Seiende 119
  Sein 118, 190n. cxxxi
Blumenberg, Hans
  "Beobachtungen an Metaphern" 136, 169
  Care Crosses the River 171, 191n. cxxxix
  Die Lesbarkeit der Welt 65, 171
  Die Vollzähligkeit der Sterne 134, 136
  Genesis of the Copernican World, The 80n. 2, 150, 179–80n. xxxi
  Lebenszeit und Weltzeit 161, 162, 165, 168, 170, 179n. xxiii, 190n. cxxxi
  Legitimacy of the Modern Age, The 95n. 6, 136–7, 167–8, 182–3n. lx, 185–6n. lxxxviii
  Matthäuspassion 133–4
  Paradigms for a Metaphorology 148, 162, 165, 168–71, 185n. lxxxiv, 187–8n. cv
  Shipwreck with Spectator 28, 92n. 1, 133n. 1, 171
  Theorie der Lebenswelt 163–4n. 93
  Work on Myth 138, 163, 167, 176–7n. v, 189n. cxxi
Böckh, August 23n. 1
Bonaventura 40 *see also* theology
Börne, Ludwig 17–18
Brahe, Tycho 20, 86, 186n. xciv *see also* astronomy
Brucker, Jakob 16, 71–4, 190n. xxx
Burley, Walter 47, 107, 183n. lxiii

Cavarero, Adriana 142n. 32, 166, 179n. xx
Châtelet, Émilie du 60 *see also* astronomy
Chaucer, Geoffrey 49, 68, 166n. 106, 183n. lxiv
Cicero 15, 17n. 6, 29, 47, 53

comedy viii, 6, 7, 13, 15, 22, 25, 152–3, 155
concept
  history of 107, 158
  limit-concept 126
  metaphorological theory of 133, 135–6n. 12, 167–8
  the nature of conceptuality 8, 12
  of reality 6, 13, 27, 96, 103, 179n. xvii
Copernicus, Nicolaus 20, 21, 52, 53, 59–62, 80, 96, 150, 151 *see also* astronomy
counter-anecdote *see* Thales of Miletus, olive oil-press speculation counter-anecdote; variant anecdotes
curiosity (*curiositas*) 35, 41, 48, 70
  see also eroticism; memory

Damian, Peter 42–4, 65, 183n. lxi
  see also theology
Descartes, René 63, 74–5, 136n. 12, 145n. 44, 183n. lxv, 185n. lxxxviii
Diogenes the Cynic 24–5, 74
  Cynicism 181nn. xlii, xliii
Diogenes Laertius 17, 24–6, 53, 56, 67, 69, 72–4, 76, 104, 107, 108n. xli, 140, 189n. cxviii
distance symbolism
  distant yet (*Noch-Entferntsein*) 94
  to dis-tance oneself (*sich ent-fernen*) 126
  farthest (*entferntesten/Fernste*) 80, 89, 125, 127, 151n. 59
  in Francis Bacon 61
  general discussion 145–53, 156
  in the Latin Patristic 30, 40–1, 185n. lxxxiv
  mattering (most) to someone/coming close(st) (*am nächsten gehen*) 68, 123
  near or far (*nah oder fern*) 40

(most) obscure/lying far off (*fernliegend/am fernsten gelegenen*) 55, 61, 64, 68, 121, 123, 125, 174
the (most) obvious/lying near(est) (*Naheliegende/ Nächstliegende/naheliegend/ nahegelegen*) 8, 30, 55, 61, 64, 69, 79, 87, 98, 125, 151n. 59, 174
in Plato 9
surrounding/neighboring (*das Nächste*) 20, 89
temporal distance, temporal proximity (*Zeitenferne, Zeitennähe*) 70

Ense, Carl August Ludwig Varnhagen von 100
Epicurus 24, 28–9, 37, 180–1n. xli
eroticism 48, 68, 166
Eusebius 31 *see also* theology

Fénélon, François 7n. 4
Feuerbach, Ludwig 92–8, 167n. 110, 187 *see also* Hegel
Fleming, Paul 144, 149, 163, 173, 175
Fontenelle, Bernard le Bovier de 82, 186n. xcii
Franck, Sebastian 53
Frankfurt School 193n. clx
Adorno, Theodor 138 *see also* Arendt, Hannah
Freud, Sigmund 26n. 6, 161–2

Gadamer, Hans-Georg 118, 138
Galilei, Galileo 60, 61, 63, 84, 156n. 69, 165, 171 *see also* astronomy
Gans, Eduard 97–8 *see also* Hegel
Gasché, Rodolphe 143n. 37
Geffcken, Johannes 182n. lv
Gerhardt, Volker 135

Gnosticism 34n. 9, 36n. 13, 38, 39, 116, 182–3n. lx, 185–6n. lxxxviii
gods *see* Thales of Miletus, theology
Goethe, Johann Wolfgang von 70, 171n. 124, 181n. lxvi
ground (*Grund*) *see* metaphor, of the ground
Guicciardini, Francesco 50

Hegel, G. W. F. 19, 97, 138, 148, 180n. xxxiii, 188n. cvi
Heidegger, Martin 2, 6n. 2, 118–31, 137, 138n. 18, 146–9, 151, 152, 167n. 110, 169n. 117, 171–2, 176n. ii, 177–8nn. x, xi, 190–2
Herodotus 109–10, 189n. cxcix
Heumann, Christoph August 74–7
Hippolytus 38, 43, 76n. 12, 184n. lxviii *see also* theology
Homer 4, 108, 167 *see also* mythology
Humboldt, Alexander von 99–102, 145 *see also* astronomy
Husserl, Edmund 41, 128, 134, 137, 146, 147, 160–5, 167, 173, 176nn. iii, iv, 177n. ix, 178n. xii, 181n. xlviii, 182n. lviii, 190n. cxxx, 191n. cxxxvii, 192

Iambe 42–4, 65–6 *see also* mythology
idea
eternal 36
expressed in metaphor 133, 167n. 109, 187–8n. cv *see also* concept
Platonic 21
Idealism 2, 11, 19, 20, 92, 97, 116 *see also* Hegel; idea
idiota (wise fool) 23, 43, 49, 51, 180n. xxxviii, 182n. lxii

intention
intentionality (being conscious of something) 1–2, 22, 41, 139n. 22, 153, 176n. iii, 178n. xiv
motivation, purpose, purposiveness vii, 16, 22, 30, 35n. 12, 39, 51, 55, 57, 74, 88, 95, 102, 104, 107, 112, 131, 159, 161–2, 170, 181n. xlvi, 177n. vii, 191n. cxxxix
rhetorical or authorial 10, 36, 39, 62, 69, 99n. 13, 119, 157
intuition see *Anschauung*
Irenaeus of Lyons 40 *see also* theology

Judaism 134, 178n. xi, 192n. cliv
Jünger, Ernst 177n. vi

Kaestner, Abraham Gotthelf 82–5
Kant, Immanuel 38, 86–9, 105, 116, 126, 140, 146, 148, 168–9, 186–7 *see also* natural science
Kepler, Johannes 20 *see also* astronomy
Kierkegaard, Søren 7
Kurke, Leslie 141n. 30 *see also* Aesop

Lactantius 14n. 2, 185n. lxxxiv *see also* theology
Lakoff, George and Johnson, Mark 148n. 50, 168n. 114 *see also* metaphor
Landmann, Michael 23–4n. 2
Fleckenstein, L and J. O. 179n. xxvi
Leibniz, Gottfried Wilhelm von 79–81, 171, 186n. lxxxix
lifeworld
Europe's lifeworld 101
opposed to theory 3, 11, 68, 89, 108
theory of the 92, 120–9, 136n. 12, 147, 159–65, 168–70, 178n. xii
Thracian maid as representative of the lifeworld and opponent to theory 18, 20, 27, 87, 149n. 55, 173
translation note on 173
see also phenomenology
Longchamp, Sebastian G. 60–1
Lübbe, Hermann 16n. 4
Lucretius 28, 155n. 58, 172n. 124 *see also* Epicurus

Marqurd, Odo 134, 138, 149
memory (*memoria*) 40, 41, 182–3n. lx
Merker, Barbara 161n. 82
metaphor
absolutism of metaphor and absolute metaphor 96, 168–70, 172, 187–8n. cv
astronomer as metaphor for impiety 42–3
distance metaphor *see* distance symbolism
fables as 140
falling as 119
of the ground 45, 87, 92, 98, 111, 173–4, 188n. cvi, 191
Husserl on 162n. 88
metaphorology 133, 135–7, 148, 162–3n. 89, 165–71
monism as 114–16
Nietzsche's psychology of 189–90n. cxxxvi
optical and tactile 65, 96, 124
sweat as 41
of the telescope 86
metaphysics 42, 57, 87, 122–7, 146
Minucius Felix, Octavius 32–3 *see also* theology
Montaigne, Michel de 54–8, 74, 91, 140, 144–5

motivation *see* intention
Müller-Sievers, Helmut 146n. 45
mythology 3, 23, 38, 42–3, 65–6, 71,
    103–15, 163, 167, 171, 188n.
    cxiv

natural science 16, 79, 83–9, 97,
    104, 111, 112, 120, 145, 187n.
    xcviii, 190n. cxxxvi *see also*
    astronomy
Nauta, Lodi 170n. 122
near *see* distance symbolism
Newton, Sir Isaac 20, 179n. xxxix
Nicholas of Cusa 23, 51, 180n.
    xxxviii, 183n. lxii
Niehues-Pröbsting, Heinrich 25n.
    5, 74n. 8, 170n. 122
Nietzsche, Friedrich Wilhelm
    24, 103–17, 120, 152, 180n.
    xxxix, 188–90

olive oil *see* Thales of Miletus,
    olive oil-press speculation
    counter-anecdote
Origen 36 *see also* theology
Ovid 30, 181–2n. l

perception see *Anschauung*
phenomenology 119, 121–2, 127–9,
    134, 146–7, 160–5, 169, 173,
    177n. ix, 180n. xxxiii, 188n.
    cvi, 190n. cxxxvi, 191n.
    cxlii, 192nn. cl, cliii *see also*
    Hegel; Heidegger; Husserl;
    lifeworld
Philo Alexandrinus 30 *see also*
    theology
Pippin, Robert 170n. 122
Plato 5–24, 28–9, 38, 47, 53–4,
    66, 69, 74, 90, 96, 103, 106,
    108, 112, 120, 131, 146, 149,
    150, 152, 153, 163, 166, 171,
    179–81, 186n. xcvi
    Apology 142

Meno 23
Phaedo 7, 10
Protagoras 6–7
Republic 12, 17, 19–20, 23, 28, 64,
    180
Theaetetus 5–6, 9, 16, 31, 103n. 2,
    140–2
Plessner, Helmut 166
Pliny 16, 73
Poetics and Hermeneutics: The
    Comical (Das Komische,
    1974) 135, 138n. 17, 142n. 35,
    149–54, 161–2n. 83, 177n. vii,
    192–3nn. clvi–clx
    Terror and Play (Terror und Spiel,
    1968) 178nn. xiii, xiv, 179n.
    xvii
positivism 191n. cxlii, 192n. cli
protohistory vii–viii, 16, 150,
    157–8, 159–64
protophilosopher *see* Thales of
    Miletus, protophilosopher

realism and the realistic vii, 6, 15,
    18, 36, 37, 49, 55, 59, 60, 63,
    68, 73, 83, 84, 89, 99, 103,
    126, 144n. 41, 167, 176–1n. v
    history as 90, 94, 96, 159, 164
    as opposed to morality 50
    as opposed to myth 105, 106,
    108
    as opposed to theory 9, 17, 20,
    56, 57, 80, 86, 87, 93, 155
    see also concept, of reality;
    lifeworld
reoccupation (*Umbesetzung*) 68, 85,
    86, 99, 115, 166–8, 170, 181n.
    xlix

Sa'di Shirazi 68, 185n. lxxxi *see also*
    variant anecdotes
saving the phenomena (*sozein ta
    phainomena*) 18, 179–80n.
    xxxi

Schadenfreude 4, 23, 55, 70, 130, 143, 153, 155, 142n. 35, 171n. 124, 192n. clvi
Schmitt, Carl 136–7, 167
science *see* astronomy; natural science
skepticism
 ancient Skeptics 28, 32–3, 51, 69, 180n. lx, 181n. xlvii
 Husserl's skeptical *epoché* 145, 162, 191n. cxlii, 192n. cl
 Montaigne's skepticism 54–8, 144, 184n. lxxii
Sommer, Manfred 173, 175
sophism 11, 42, 54, 72, 73, 76, 90, 111, 131
soteriology (Christian doctrine of salvation) 24, 30–1, 37–8, 50, 137, 181n. l, 182n. lii, 190n. cxxxvi *see also* theology
Stanley, Thomas 74–6
Stoellger, Phillip 139n. 22, 163n. 90
Stoicism 24, 28, 37, 181n. lxvii
Strauss, David Friedrich 61n. 11

Tatian 39–40 *see also* theology
Taubes, Jacob 138n. 18
Taylor, Charles 188n. cvi *see also* Hegel
Tertullian 23, 32–8, 42, 166n. 106, 168, 178n. xiii, 183n. lxii *see also* theology
Thales of Miletus
 anecdote of Thales and the Thracian maid *passim*
 "Everything is water" vii–viii, 3, 32, 62–3, 98, 103, 111, 112, 114, 141n. 28, 105, 109, 110, 162, 167, 188n. cvii, 189n. cxxi
 olive oil-press speculation counter-anecdote 17, 48, 76, 90, 93, 105, 109, 153

protophilosopher 3, 5, 11, 12, 15, 16, 26n. 6, 32, 62, 71, 73, 93, 94, 95, 103, 107, 108, 109, 120, 124, 141, 143, 150, 152
"world is full of gods, The" vii–viii, 3, 66, 105, 106, 108, 109, 161–2n. 83, 167, 178n. xiii, 189n. cxxi
theodicy 79, 80, 89
theology 29–53, 96, 118, 134, 137, 160, 168n. 112, 183n. lxi, 190nn. cxxxi, cxxxiv, 191n. cxlvii
 see also myth/mythology; soteriology; Thales of Miletus, "Everything is full of gods"
Thomas Aquinas 31n. 3, 185n. lxxxiii *see also* theology
Thracians 12, 23, 101, 108, 142n. 32, 160n. 77
Tiedemann, Dietrich 90

understanding (*Verstand*) 23, 87, 88, 121, 126 *see also* Kant, Immanuel
unity
 indefinite article (*eine*) vii, 158, 160
 monism 162n. 84, 189n. cxxiv
 political unity 104

variant anecdotes
 Alexander von Humboldt and the Russian policeman 100
 Alfonso the Wise's blasphemy as variant 79–81
 Anaximenes and Thressa (Cornelius Agrippa) 52–3
 extended moral (Samuel Richardson) 90
 grotesquely embellished variant 78
 Iambe and the philosopher 42–3

Thales and the Egyptian
   (Tertullian) 35–6
Thales and the Milesian maid
   (Michel de Montaigne) 54
Thales should have looked
   inside the well (Francis
   Bacon) 62
Thales and Thratta 38
Tycho Brahe and his coachman
   (Immanuel Kant) 86
vision see *Anschauung*
Voltaire 31, 60–1, 79, 167n. 110,
   171n. 124

Wallace, Robert 163n. 92
water *see* Thales of Miletus,
   "Everything is water"
Weinrich, Harald 142, 153–4, 192n.
   clvi
Weizsäcker, Carl Friedrich 121n. 2
Wetters, Kirk 154n. 67
Wilamowitz-Moellendorff, Ulrich
   von 12, 110–11
Wittgenstein, Ludwig 161

Zedler, Johann Heinrich 73
Zill, Rüdiger 138n. 19

www.ingramcontent.com/pod-product-compliance
Lightning Source LLC
Chambersburg PA
CBHW062224300426
44115CB00012BA/2212